Jasmin's Witch

Emmanuel Le Roy Ladurie

Jasmin's Witch

translated by Brian Pearce

George Braziller

NEW YORK

Published in the United States in 1987 by
George Braziller, Inc.

Originally published in France in 1983 as
La sorcière de Jasmin by Editions du Seuil

First published in England by Scolar Press

For information, address the publisher:

George Braziller, Inc.
60 Madison Avenue
New York, New York 10010

Library of Congress Cataloging-in-Publication Data

Le Roy Ladurie, Emmanuel.
Jasmin's witch.

Translation of: La sorcière de Jasmin.
Bibliography: p.
Includes index.
1. Jasmin, 1798-1864. Françouneto. 2. Witchcraft in literature. 3. Huguenots in literature. 4. Gascony (France) in literature. 5. Huguenots—France—Gascony—History. 6. Witchcraft—France—Gascony—History.
I. Title.
PC3402.J27F73413 1987 849'.14 87-9393
ISBN 0-8076-1181-6

Printed in the United States
First printing, August 1987

Contents

List of Plates

following page 86

MAPS

Author's acknowledgements

I must, first of all, express my thanks to Alfred Soman, Georges Dumézil, Robert Muchembled and Christian Guyonvarc'h, who helped me to find my way through the conceptual landscape of *Françouneto* and to avoid some traps.

In preparing this work I also received invaluable help from M. Jean Burias, director of services at the record office of Lot-et-Garonne, and his dedicated colleagues, as also from Mme Esquirol, curator of the Agen museum, and M. Alain Mousseigne, curator of the museum of the Augustinians in Toulouse. MM Daniel Fabre, Esquieu, Yves Castan, Hanlon, Jean-Robert Masson, Mlle Bouissy, Mme M.-J. Tits and M. l'Abbé Mateu were generous with advice and help. I should like them to find here the proof of my gratitude.

At Grenoble people say: *J'ai été au Cour-ce,* or *J'ai lu des ver-ce sur Anver-ce et Calai-ce.* If such speech is heard at Grenoble, an intelligent town still having some bonds with the Northern districts which have got the better of the South as regards language, what can you expect at Toulouse, Bazas, Pézenas, Digne? In such places they ought to stick up posters at the church doors, to teach French pronunciation.

'A Minister of the Interior who wanted to do his job thoroughly, instead of intriguing with the King and in the Chambers like M. Guizot, ought to ask for a loan of two million a year to bring up to the educational level of the rest of France the inhabitants of that *unlucky triangle* that lies between Bordeaux, Bayonne and Valence. In those parts *they believe in witches,* they cannot read and they don't speak French. Such regions may by a fluke produce an outstanding man like Lannes or Soult, but the bulk of the population is unbelievably ignorant. *I imagine that by reason of its climate and the passion and energy this imparts to the body, this triangle of country ought to produce the finest men in France.* Corsica suggests this idea to me.

'That little island, with its 180,000 inhabitants, gave eight or ten remarkable men to the Revolution, whereas the Département du Nord, with 900,000 inhabitants, produced hardly one. And who that *one* might be I don't know. Needless to say, priests are all-powerful in this unlucky triangle. Civilisation extends from Lille to Rennes and stops near Orleans and Tours. To the South-East, Grenoble is its brilliant boundary.'

– Errors, half-truths and prejudices, yet sometimes superb, taken from Stendhal's *Life of Henri Brulard* (English translation by Jean Stewart and B. C. J. G. Knight, Merlin Press, 1958, pp. 167–8).

Jasmin's Witch

Jasmin, Hairdresser-Poet

Jacques Boé, known as 'Jasmin', was born in 1798 into a poor family in the town of Agen, where he worked from his youth as a hairdresser. He published long poems in his mother-tongue, which the people of Agen did not yet call *occitan*. These poems were inspired by local and popular traditions, some from the town or its suburbs, others of purely rural origin. Jasmin had a deep knowledge of all these traditions, thanks to the everyday contacts he automatically enjoyed as a writer who was also a shopkeeper. A Catholic, he flirted (no more than that) with a moderate Orleanism. His biographers repeat the story of how, when he had become famous and was invited to court, Jasmin unceremoniously sat himself down on the throne of Louis-Philippe, who awarded him a pension. Furthermore, as time passed, Jasmin acquired the face, if not the corpulence, of a minister of the July Monarchy, or (anachronistically) of a pillar of the Third Republic in the 1880s. All he lacked was the umbrella. During his lifetime, this warm-hearted man enjoyed a regional fame, a fame which in some ways can be called prodigious. Without bringing him in money, it spread all over the south of France and even to Paris. After his death, in 1864, his renown slowly faded through more than a century. But it remains lively still, even today, in Agen and among the many lovers of Occitanian literature. The town of Agen continues to honour Jasmin, and that is to its credit; but does it really take him seriously as a writer and even a thinker?

Jasmin's 'Gascon' language is admirable in almost every respect, but his style is in many ways outmoded. Assimilating one of the works of this poet, in the way that George Sand did,[1] therefore means cracking the bone of an out-of-date sentimentality so as the better to savour the substantial marrow of a plebeian and very lively Gascony. Jasmin's *Françouneto*, dated 1840, preceded by more than a score of years Michelet's *The Sorceress* (1862): comparing the work of the Agen poet with that of the great historian of the French people, we observe less genius but, on the other hand, a rather greater degree of accuracy.[2] *Françouneto* was taken from a narrative that was oral and rural. In 1835–9 this had been circulating for five or six generations in the village of Roquefort, near Agen. The use made of it by Jasmin, a genuine collector of peasant lore, shows a considerable amount of reflexion and understanding of the essence of witchcraft in the south of France. The following pages are therefore devoted to three tasks:

1. An examination of the place of the Gascon witch in traditional society, based on Jasmin's poem;
2. Publishing a prose translation of *Françouneto*;
3. Dating, through archival evidence, the real origins of Françouneto. In my view, the story belongs to the age of Louis XIV (about 1660–1700) and not at all to that of Charles IX, or to the 1560s, as was supposed by Jasmin, who was misled on this point.[3]

PART ONE

Three Gascon Witches: Françouneto, Gérarde Mimalé, Marie de Sansarric

Françouneto is the heroine of an oral tradition which was collected and then interpreted by Jacques Jasmin in 1840. She was a witch, or an alleged witch, in a hamlet in the Condomois* under the *ancien régime*. In order to place this girl in a wider context, we will briefly mention some of the geographical, historical and statistical facts assembled by Robert Muchembled in a recent work on the subject of witchcraft. Witchcraft, it seems, has always existed as an instrument, either benign or maleficent, for the purpose of manipulating the world of the peasantry – or by which that world imagined it was being manipulated. Historians certainly find traces of it as far back as the fourteenth and fifteenth centuries,[1] and they also find a clearly-defined period when witches were persecuted, in the strict sense of the word. This period was inaugurated (it had other beginnings, too) in the ecstatic atmosphere of Rhineland mysticism, when Sprenger and Institoris published their *Malleus Maleficarum* (1486), a book destined to become the approved manual for witch-hunters. The agonising crises of the fourteenth and fifteenth centuries also made their contribution. Repression reached its height between 1560 and 1630, and then decreased at rates which varied from country to country, during the second half of the seventeenth century and the first third of the eighteenth. The area affected by these phenomena

* The commune of Roquefort, where Françouneto lived, is today included in the *département* of Lot-et-Garonne, alias the diocese of Agen. Before the Revolution, this commune was in the northern part of the diocese of Condom (see the various terriers of the diocese of Condom referred to under Sources and Bibliography, p. 183). Roquefort can therefore be seen as belonging either to the former Condomois or to the Agenais of both former and present times.

extended from Poland through Germany, Switzerland, France and other countries in western Europe, to the English colonies in North America. Subsequently, legal repression of witches continued for a time and then ceased. There was a new mildness, resulting mainly from a change of outlook among the authorities. It is also possible that the eighteenth century, while retaining a respectable contingent of witches (though now less persecuted), was a time that engendered less tension and popular frustration, such as could give rise to witchcraft, than had been the case in the seventeenth century, with its great waves of impoverishment, economic stagnation and general crisis.

Robert Muchembled's statistics are unpretentious, and aim to provide only a partial view of the problem. They relate to a number of territories in Germany, England, present-day Belgium, France, Switzerland, Finland and Spain. They deal with more than ten thousand cases of persons who, under the *ancien régime*, were judicially prosecuted for witchcraft.[2] Of these persons, nearly half appear to have been executed. (Muchembled's figures are all the more exact for being imprecise: the best solution, from this standpoint, is to do as I have done, and give them in round terms.) It can be seen that we are far from the 'million witches slain or burnt,' the fantastic figure sometimes put forward by well-meaning writers with a view to supplying additional support for the (incontestable) thesis that women have often been oppressed during the course of history. Of what use is an incorrect million for proving a correct idea? In any case, these small numbers – a few thousand killed, about ten thousand accused – doubtless fall short of the reality. They serve to provide relative magnitude. They emphasise the in any case marginal character of witchcraft in a Europe of one hundred million people. Here we see a big difference (of degree more than of nature) between Europe and the Africa of the Azande, studied by Evans-Pritchard, in which everybody, or nearly everybody, either practised witchcraft or suffered its effects.

Certain commonplaces need to be mentioned. Women, young

but particularly middle-aged or elderly, made up 77.7 per cent of the persons accused of witchcraft.[3] There is nothing surprising about that fact; women constituted the weakest and most vulnerable half of mankind in those days. Their criminal activity as 'witches', whether genuine or completely invented, was complementary to that of men. Men devoted themselves not so much to the magical arts as to the good old masculine specialities: murder, robbery. As mistresses of language, of loquacity and gossip, women were marked out to be practitioners of symbolical crime (harmful spells) rather than real delinquency (homicide). The association between the second sex and herbal medicine, always suspected of having a supernatural side to it, is well known. Finally, in Western and Judaeo-Christian culture, woman has not enjoyed a good press. More precisely, she has had a twofold image, being at once seductive and dangerous – Eve, Judith or Herodias, even Pandora.

Interpretations of witchcraft have varied since the sixteenth century. The demonologists Lancre and Boguet, at the beginning of this period, denounced it as the Devil's own doing. The rationalists of the eighteenth century saw it as a vestige of ancestral superstition. For Michelet[4] the witch was at one and the same time satanic and consolatory, dangerous yet expert in herbal medicine. Margaret Murray, in a book[5] wherein sound inspiration and near-nonsense are mingled, saw in the arts of sorcery the survival of an ancient pagan religion. The practitioners of devil-worship in the America of the 1960s were to draw upon their reading of Murray. They organised witches' sabbaths (*sabbats*) and even revels (*esbats*) that passed for the resurgence of an old-time paganism. Actually, the word *esbat* reproduces a term of old French (*esbat des sorcières*) which we find in sixteenth-century demonological writings. But not everything in the heritage of Margaret Murray is to be rejected. Carlo Ginzburg[6] has discovered, among the peasants and semi-witches of sixteenth-century Friuli, the vestiges of an old fertility cult which had nothing Christian about it and which extended from the Baltic countries to the Latin and even the partly Slavonic regions of north-eastern Italy.

What he found in Friuli was the strange rural sect of the *Benandanti*, friendly sorcerers who were contemporary with France's Wars of Religion. Each of them armed with a stalk of fennel, they made their way in dreams, or in a half-dreaming ecstasy, to the valley of the magicians. There, fennel in hand, they gave battle to the bad sorcerers, who brandished stalks of sorghum to defend themselves. These strange conflicts went on for a long time without result. Were the good magicians getting the better of their opponents? Then the harvests of grain or of wine would be excellent in the coming year. On the other hand, if the wicked sorcerers were winning, there would be famine. These rites were focused, typically, on the fecundity of the soil. In many respects the magic of the *Benandanti* was like that of the classical shamanism described by ethnologists. In order to reach the (mythical) locations of the struggle they waged against the baneful bearers of sorghum, the *Benandanti* abandoned, in spirit, their own bodies and set off on a long journey. Their bodies lay paralysed on couches, victims of what used to be called a cataleptic or lethargic fit. The body of a *Benandante*, fallen into unconsciousness, re-awoke only upon the return of the spirit of its proprietor, once the magic battle of fennel against sorghum had been won or lost.

For decades now the history of *mentalités* has been seeking to trace pagan survivals. In the consciousness of the peasants of earlier times these survivals coexisted with official Christianity, which was itself inculcated from above by the church hierarchy and the parish priests. Ginzburg has found some of these mysterious survivals. In the sixteenth century, that is, 1,600 years or thereabouts *after* Jesus Christ, they still functioned as living dogmas. A hidden corner of Friuli served as a conservatory of ancient cultures. Ginzburg links these paganisms to the decayed fragments of a 'peasant religion' or a 'cultural form', that was both vast and diffuse. We find traces of it from the Baltic countries to Lombardy, and, between them, in Sweden,

Germany and Switzerland. Is this really an old foundation of German, Baltic and Slavonic mythology which has slid itself like a wedge under the stratum of Latin clarity, south of the Alps? In Livonia, about a century later, the good sorcerers, disguised as werewolves, armed themselves with iron whips. In fantasy they would descend into Hell, if need be, there to combat the evil-doing sorcerers (infernal and yet human, 'real' and known each by an individual name), who were armed with broomsticks. The beneficent magicians thus succeeded, in the form of werewolves, in saving the crops of their village fields, threatened by the forces of evil. In this case, it was not fennel against sorghum but iron rods against wooden handles.*

Furthermore, the belief in night battles fought between rival sorcerers, the camps of good and evil, which would either stimulate the crops or destroy them, was linked with an ancient cult of the dead, which, again, had little to do with official Christianity. According to the records consulted by Ginzburg, the *Benandanti* had the distinction of having been born with cauls on their heads, a sign of good fortune and a promise of fecundity. They talked with the dead. They beheld the processions of those no longer among the living. They fought with them. They even faced the 'wild hunt', a monstrous cavalcade led by demons. In this hunt they saw passing before them the phantoms or ghosts of whores, wicked men and children who had died unbaptised. Faced with this procession, the *Benandanti* did not merely attack the evil magicians. They fought against the dead (which comes to the same thing) or, at least, they strove, by violence or by some other method, to pacify their ghosts.†

* In lectures at the Collège de France in October 1982 Carlo Ginzburg also mentioned in this connexion similar myths found in Ossetian and Hungarian folklore.

† Carlo Ginzburg suggested, in his lectures at the Collège de France in October 1982, the following model of a division of labour. In Friuli, the *Benandanti* ('those who go to do good deeds') are a group of men who, fennel in hand, undertake to do battle (in a dream-myth) against the bad

The objective was always to ensure fruitfulness for the corn or the grapes. To this end the *Benandanti* flattered, or else beat down, the macabre and maleficent powers operating from the beyond, which were capable of destroying cultivated plants. The church in Friuli in 1580–1650 was caught unprepared by such phenomena. It understood little of these strange beliefs, which had nothing in common either with book-knowledge or with Catholic dogma. They were the tattered remnants of an extensive culture – oral, pagan and popular – which had spread to the four corners of Europe and over the four seasons of the year. The inquisitor showed himself indulgent towards the *Benandanti*, neither burning, nor torturing, nor hanging them. Convinced of the validity of his own systems of thought, he nevertheless endeavoured to get them to admit that the night battles with fennel against the wicked magicians armed with sorghum were merely local versions of the classical *sabbat*, when the witches were supposed to kiss the backside of the Devil in the form of a black or green goat. This canonical *sabbat* had, to some extent, emerged fully-armed from the brains of the ecclesiastical judges, but it was also grafted on the old-established traditions of the souls' journey, when the witches left their bodies in order to engage in the rites of a shamanism not officially known by that name – an involuntary shamanism. What matters for us in this case is not so much the letter of Ginzburg's analyses as their spirit. He has established that there survived in the world of the countryfolk some myths that could not be reduced to the official Christian ideology, myths that were focused upon an emotional striving to ensure the fecundity of the harvests, or else, conversely, upon baneful influences

---

sorcerers armed with sorghum. They include a group of village women, who also practise the magic flight of a soul out of a body sunk in cataleptic sleep. These women, however, do not encounter the sorcerers with the sorghum, but, instead, the nocturnal funeral procession of the dead, or their ghosts, who form, as Varagnac puts it, the last age-group of traditional society.

directed against that fecundity, and also having at their centre journeys of souls transformed into animals (werewolves) and contact with the powers of a mythical beyond, often identified with the country of the dead.

More than European tradition is involved here. Through his work on Africa, and in particular on the Azande, Evans-Pritchard[7] has distinguished the behaviour of witchcraft, as opposed to that of other magical rites or special spells. In the specific case of the Azande, witchcraft is merely a substance present in the bodies of witches, who may be unaware of the power they possess and exercise because of it. This substance produces a harmful effect on other individuals, conveyed through psychic channels, and it can cause death. It is hereditary, and there are lineages of witches.

Finally, among this African people witchcraft is sometimes accompanied by transmigration of souls, or, at least, the witch's soul travels independently of his sleeping body, so as the more easily to harm his victims. Ginzburg encountered elements of the same sort in Friuli, and refers to shamanism in connexion with them.

Among the Azande the local aristocracy includes no witches. This absence is to be preferred, since a highly-placed caste would be hard to combat, given the power it already wields, were it to engage in such culpable activities. The soothsayers and counter-witches who normally struggle against sorcery would be incapable of overcoming an adversary of such stature. As a general rule, therefore, witchcraft involves the lower strata of society. Nevertheless, it is not necessarily accompanied by a class struggle. Yves Castan puts the matter simply: 'the demons fly low'.[8]

Evans-Pritchard also stresses the locally confined nature of the cases he studies. Witches do not attack a person who lives far away from them. If one wants to escape from their offensives, the best way is to move a respectful distance out of reach of their magical onslaughts. Witchcraft, moreover, is often impersonal and involuntary. As has been said, witches are in many cases unaware that they possess a dangerous nature, and it is hard to get them to accept that it exists and operates from their persons.

Evans-Pritchard argues that among the Azande, to explain matters in terms of witchcraft means to stress the bond that links an individual with a misfortune that has come upon him. Imbued as we are with the scientific spirit, we merely employ, in this connexion, words such as 'chance', 'bad luck', or, where a large number of cases are concerned, 'the law of probabilities.' But the Azande are pre-Pascalian in their way of thinking. By implicating the witch they establish elaborate relations of cause and effect where we, miserably, can talk only of 'chance'. This attribution is quasi-political in character. It elucidates *the event*. It is particularly useful in relation to death, which, for us, given the lack of *ad hoc* explanations, has become really the Unnamable. For death is physical, yet corresponds also to a moral and social phenomenon. It must always have its causes. Witchcraft appears at the right moment, among the Azande, to furnish these causes. It should be added that, according to Evans-Pritchard, the facts of witchcraft, such as combinations of misfortune, relations between individuals and personal antagonisms, are often detected through dreams. The witch is combated in a variety of ways, and especially by means of oracles, which announce or denounce him. Then, after this more or less solemn annunciation or denunciation, the counter-witch, or un-bewitcher, comes forward. He utilises various techniques to destroy the sinister powers of the witch and undo the harm inflicted. Paradoxically, the un-bewitcher operates like a witch in relation to the witch whom he has to combat. For example, when Witch Number One has destroyed the crops of Counter-Witch Number Two, the latter undertakes, in his turn, to bring about by magic the death of Number One. Number Two thus becomes the witch feared by Number One.

Witchcraft is not without its social utility. According to Evans-Pritchard, it imposes on people an attitude of mutual kindness, inspired by reciprocal fear of reprisals or spells. The fear of being bewitched is the beginning of wisdom. Meritorious actions are performed so as to avert a damaging aggression. La Rochefoucauld or Nietzsche could not have put it better. After all, it is preferable to do good for bad reasons and out of fear of witches than to be simply or straightforwardly wicked. . . .

I should not have gone on so long about Evans-Pritchard's ideas if they had not contributed to advancing the anthropology and history of witchcraft in Europe. The difference here is essential, to be sure. Among the Azande evil spells are universal and permanent. In what are called the civilised countries they are marginal, even ultra-marginal. And yet certain interpretative principles discovered by Evans-Pritchard in this connexion may find interesting application in our continent.

While studying the witches of 1960–70 in the *bocages* (wooded areas) of western France, Jeanne Favret-Saada fell under the beneficent influence of Evans-Pritchard, which she turns to uses of her own.[9] Favret-Saada sees witchcraft as a mortal combat waged by four actors: the person bewitched (A), who is a suffering victim; the witch (B), who is unaware of his maleficent nature, or who at least refuses to admit its existence, but who is considered to have 'produced' A's misfortune; the announcer or denouncer (C), who undertakes to inform A of the presumed intrigues of B; and, finally, the un-bewitcher or counter-witch (D). The last-mentioned effects the cure, at the outcome of which (if all goes well), A will be healed and, concomitantly, the power or force of B will be weakened. Be it noted that D, in un-bewitching A, is obliged to attack B, or, in other words, to bewitch him. That is to say, D functions as counter-witch towards A, but as witch towards B, who, in his turn, assumes the role of the bewitched in relation to D.

The ideas of Evans-Pritchard have also entered into the historiography of the sixteenth and seventeenth centuries on both sides of the Channel, as we see from the works of Macfarlane and Muchembled, on the witches, male or female, of

Essex and northern France, in the times of the Stuarts and of the first Bourbons.[10] For Robert Muchembled, the activity of witches and counter-witches is part of peasant strategy concerned with the exercise of checks upon authority within the village community. This strategy is effected through threats of *actual* death (I am thinking of the witches whom their enemies managed to exterminate by direct lynching, or whom they caused to be legally burned as a result of sentence by a court). Muchembled carries his analysis further. He considers that the seventeenth-century witch-hunt was caused, *inter alia*, by the disintegration of the peasant community in that period, and the separation thus brought about between the rich (individualistic) farmers and the poor agricultural day-labourers or farm-hands. The lynchers of witches detected and then persecuted their victims among the rural proletariat, and especially its female and aged elements. The latter were accused of magical machinations, so as the better to gratify a passion for domination. On this point I shall not follow Muchembled all the way. There were to be other periods – in the eighteenth century, for instance – during which the peasant community would be weakened, suffering ruin through the emergence of a group of well-to-do farmers, and yet these periods would not *necessarily* be marked by the appearance of any specific witchcraft or counter-witchcraft. The changes in rural society or in the peasant community were slow and long-drawn-out. They cannot always be correlated with the precise period of the witches, or, rather, of the witch-burnings, between 1550 and 1650.

Historians of witchcraft have also invoked, with justification, changes in the cultural and religious spheres. These took place both outside the peasants' world, in the society which surrounded and dominated that world, and also inside it. Where the middle or upper classes are concerned, those from which the magistrates, lay or ecclesiastical, who judged the witches were recruited, the fluctuation in Christian culture is easily definable. During a first phase, that of the 'long sixteenth century' (roughly, from 1500 to 1620), the intellectual élites, or semi-élites, were subjected to the tremendous waves of the Protestant Reformation and the Catholic Counter-Reformation. They became better-informed in theological matters than they had been before, and were therefore more alarmed about the power wielded by the Devil over this wretched world here below. They accepted the myths of the *sabbat*, half-popular and half-learned, which had been invented or knocked together in the years 1375–1450. They diagnosed the presence of Satan among the witches, pursued them even into remote parishes, and burned them, whereas their predecessors (inquisitors or others) in the early fourteenth century had treated with scorn the magical practices of countryfolk, which were looked upon by the literate of those days as insignificant or beneath their attention. In the 'popish' regions on the edges of the Catholic world (Aquitaine, Netherlands), the anti-Huguenot vigilance of the authorities was turned also upon the witches. They saw the Devil everywhere, and burned first the disciples of Calvin and then the sectaries of Satan, or those claiming to be such.

However, about the middle of the seventeenth century (a very loose dating), the scene changes again. The judges, whether Protestant or Catholic, are still good Christians, but from now on their religion has to be enlightened and purified. It absorbs Cartesian, rational and scientific ideas which at once undermine belief in the conjuring tricks performed by witches. It wishes henceforth to see a hailstorm as the doing of Providence rather than of the Devil. Malebranche integrates Descartes and Reason into a pious orthodoxy and helps the judges to de-fuse the anti-witchcraft paranoia. As for the Devil, he frightens less and less, especially among the judicial élite. 'Good Christians say, these days, that one ought to give the Devil a shake now and then. That tempter seems to have lost his real power to do ill since people have ceased to tremble before him and contemplate him in fascination and dread'.[11] A few generations later the magistrates take a step further and become Voltairians, and fear of witches now seems to them all the more absurd and superstitious. The rise of rationality thus ousts the disordered

religious acculturation. These fronts advance, from the Renaissance onward, over the judicial élites and over the peasant masses. Their differentiated progress reflects geographical and chronological disparities which themselves vary, depending on whether the groups affected are urban or rural.

In addition, Robert Muchembled, who is well acquainted with the records of northern France, emphasises the psychological processes[14] affecting the witch, whether she be young or not so young. At first, she is unaware of the character attributed to her. She does not notice that she is maleficent. Then, gradually, she yields to this circumstance. She bends beneath the influence, or, rather, beneath the unbearable pressure brought to bear upon her by the peasant community and the *iuges de fief* (magistrates of low rank). She gives in to them. She confesses, against her will, that she is a witch. In the end she perhaps believes in her own guilt. In any case, as a result of torture and of self-conviction imposed from without, she decides to tell the judge what he wants her to tell him. Yes, she went to the *sabbat*, held by night on the heath or on the hillside. Yes, she did kiss the backside of the Devil, or of the goat. And so on. Thereafter the witch glides into all sorts of fantastic narratives imposed on her by the judges, who have read the writings of the demonologists. Naturally, the accounts of the *sabbat*, as Carlo Ginzburg has shown, contain fragments of ancient paganism and peasant shamanism. But these fragments are now integrated by demonology into manuals of instruction. The examining magistrate has only to whisper the contents of these pages to the witch for her to regurgitate them in the form of confession.

We thus possess two models, I and II, separated in time. Each is rooted in very diverse realities and marked by a varying chronology. The first model, described by Ginzburg, is the more archaic, linking the oldest of our witchcraft cases to the Middle Ages, or even to a barbarous Antiquity. It never dies. Its roots are in fathomless and rich mythologies which, by their very rusticity, are alien or anterior to Christianity. The other model (II) is more modern and is illustrated, at long intervals of time, in the respective writings of Robert Muchembled and Jeanne Favret. In this context the African studies of Evans-Pritchard can offer useful pointers. Nevertheless, they constitute only an introductory guide to phenomena which are both dated and located, concerning a European witchcraft that gradually takes on a new form. This 'modernity' is already strongly apparent in the seventeenth century (in the Cambrésis and in England), and is destined to last in the *bocages* into the twentieth century. This model presents us with a de-paganised form of witchcraft, in some cases treated as criminal or diabolical by the Church and by believers. Above all, the model can be increasingly reduced to the diagram of a conflict between forces, the schematism of a strategy of powers, in which small farms or peasant holdings are set against each other – without there being any need for us to talk, in dogmatic fashion, about class struggle. The witchcraft that conforms to model II becomes demystified or dries up; it even becomes geometrical, allowing the mythical element in it to dissolve, as though a Max Weber is taking the place of the Great Pan. Between Ginzburg and Favret an impoverishment is observable. This is due to the facts, not to the writers who describe them, both of whom are substantial scholars.

After putting forward this notion of two models, a rather general notion derived from recent research, I should like, in connexion with Françouneto, to consider a number of cases – two, especially, which belong to the sphere of southern-French witchcraft. One of them is near to folklore, being the story presented by Jacques Jasmin in his poem. The other is more factual. It, too, is set in the old diocese of Condom. These two cases illustrate the models mentioned, indicating their adaptation to a particular region. Finally, they lead us to make a comparison with Béarn, outside the Condomois, where we have found our material so far.

The first case emerges from the pen of a hairdresser, or, rather, a wigmaker, from Agen. Jacques Jasmin is undoubtedly the greatest poet produced by the lands which make up Lot-et-Garonne.* In that *département* rivalry for such laurels was hardly intense, but this fact should not detract from his merits. Jasmin, a genuine worker-poet, lived for a long time by his razor and his curling-tongs until his growing fame brought with it a certain material prosperity. He wrote in Gascon, or in Occitan, or in the Agenais dialect – whatever you prefer to call it. His style did not lack charm, though it was spoilt by mawkishnesses *à la* Lamartine. As an inhabitant of Agen, Jasmin knew the traditions of the quarters where the poor lived, together with those of the town's suburbs and the countryside around it. He had no difficulty in communicating in the local dialect with the villagers of the neighbourhood. The linguistic chasm between countryfolk and townsfolk in the *pays d'oc*, at the level of the plebeian classes, had not yet opened: both groups still spoke Occitan. In 1842 Jasmin published a story, dated 1840 and put into verse by himself. He called it *Françouneto*[15] – in French 'Françounette' or 'little Françoise', being the Christian name, or the nickname, of the young heroine of the story, who, during her lifetime, was accused of sorcery. The wigmaker had found the plot of his story among the small farmers of the hamlet of Estanquet. This place is about six kilometres south of Agen and is included in the commune and the parish of Roquefort, which, before 1789, formed part of the old diocese of Condom. The investigation which I carried out on the spot, interviewing the oldest inhabitants, and also in the public records of Roquefort and Agen, shows that this local tradition concerning Françouneto does indeed exist. It was not invented by Jasmin, and, furthermore, it reflected some actual events, though these have, in the light of documentary evidence (see Part Three), to be placed in a later period than our author supposed. Jasmin situated them in the time of the warrior Monluc (about 1563–64). In reality, they occurred,

* He shares this honour with François de Cortète, an Agen playwright of the seventeenth century.

most probably, between 1650 and 1700, perhaps in the 1660s – let us say, in Colbert's time, the minister's name serving here merely as a chronological frontier-post (on this dating, see pp. 115f. below). Subsequently, we can assume, between 1670–90 and 1830–40, the passing-on of the story by word of mouth, through five or six generations of the same family (the one that originates in Françouneto, who married a man named Pascal). The process of passing-on follows the channels both of direct descent and of spiritual kinship, that is, of godparenthood (see below, pp. 136f.). The plot consists of a factual nucleus derived from the seventeenth century. It includes also a number of accretions which are hard to separate from the nucleus, accretions corresponding to the ideas held by successive passers-on of the oral tradition, especially their notions concerning witchcraft. To these accretions must be added Jasmin's own contribution. As one familiar with and immersed in the real life of the locality, this worker-poet, close to the peasants, had his own ideas about witches. Some would prefer to examine the court file wherein were recorded the alleged misdeeds of Françouneto the witch. However, no such file ever existed. In its day, the case never reached the courts, and the flames of a witch-burning pyre were never kindled. Besides, the very substance of a popular memory established over a period of 170 years is itself something precious to the historian. We are lucky, in this case, to have available the unadulterated development of a peasant tradition, totally separate from any educated culture. At most we can say that, in its final phase, this tradition emerges at the level of a semi-educated, semi-popular culture, namely, that of Jacques Jasmin himself. The entirely non-judicial aspect of the story presents a great advantage, in that magistrates did not have an opportunity to inject into this narrative their stereotyped concept of the *sabbat*, often derived from demonological treatises dictated sometimes under torture to defenceless peasants. Our text is relatively free from that sort of adulteration, although cultural percolations are always possible in so sensitive a domain.

Let us first look at the facts, or, rather, at the story. A pretty girl named Françouneto ('little Françoise') has grown up in a family of humble peasants, or game breeders, and lives in the outlying hamlet of Estanquet, not far from the village and *château* of Roquefort. She is the queen of local dances and festivals. Alas, all who dance with her collapse after going once round the floor, exhausted by the pace of her little steps. They are madly in love with this girl, to the extent that they lose the strength of their arms: suddenly, they become incapable of ploughing their fields or pruning their vines or trees. Little by little, the threat that Françouneto presents to the powers of men and of men's hands becomes more explicit. During a votive festival with dancing, held for the local church of St Jacques, two young men who are in love with the girl quarrel over her, from jealousy. The one she prefers, Pascal, seems to have got the better of his adversary. But, at the end of the fight, his arm is cut, drawing blood, and this deep wound incapacitates him for six months. He was a smith, and he is now ruined because he cannot strike accurate blows on his anvil. Even his mind is temporarily deranged. It is as though his farrier's hammer (*marteau*) is no longer in his hand but in his head. The young man has gone *marteau* ('cracked').

For the moment, no one (except Pascal's mother, announcer or denouncer Number One) appears to accuse Françouneto. But Christmas comes, and then the first days of the New Year. Local tradition (to which Jasmin alludes) associates this particular period of the winter with danger from werewolves and witches. It is the special time for these night-persons to move about the countryside round Agen and threaten the safety of travellers. These observations in Jasmin's poem have a wider implication. Throughout France and beyond, in the north as in the south, Christmas and the twelve following days are seen as a critical period, a joint or hinge in time, when werewolves and witches enjoy free rein. It is not good to come face to face with these creatures in a chance encounter.

The young people of Roquefort and the neighbouring

villages organise an all-night festival for the night of 31 December to 1 January. This festival is dedicated both to work and to pleasure. The persons taking part engage in winding yarn (elsewhere it could be cracking walnuts or husking chestnuts). Then, when these chores are over, they eat, drink and dance. The inevitable happens. A young man named Laurent, son of a well-to-do farmer in the village of Brax, wants to play with Françouneto the innocent game of hunt-the-knife. The blade is hidden by the girl (in her bodice?). The boy, half-joking and half-serious, and in any case very much in love, runs after our heroine. He stumbles, falls and breaks an arm.

This time, Françouneto calls down upon herself the hostility of everyone. Has she perhaps the evil eye? To make matters worse, a new personage comes on the scene at the end of this ruined evening, after Laurent's mishap. He functions both as announcer-denouncer (in this respect following Pascal's mother) and as un-bewitcher, in so far as he seriously weakens the power of the witch. This twofold activity implies possession of magical powers. He is called 'the sorcerer from the Black Wood.' The dark forest thus named is to be seen still upon the heights of Roquefort, away from the centre of the village and far from the hamlet where Françouneto lived.

With a sense of the dramatic, the sorcerer of the Black Wood announces bad news to the gathering of young people, who are now greatly alarmed. First, he tells them that the young dancer is of Huguenot birth, at least on her father's side: her father disappeared in a mysterious way soon after she was born. The girl's Protestant, or sinisterly magical, heredity is to be dreaded also on account of her maternal grandmother, whom the villagers likewise charge with heresy and witchcraft. (Note that such a succession as this – grandmother, father, daughter – amounts to assuming the existence of lineages of sorcerers, bearers of a monstrously supernatural heredity. Such lineages are to be found here and there all over the various regions affected by witchcraft.)

Secondly, the man from the Black Wood asserts that

Françouneto is a witch. Her father gave her to the Devil when she was born, in a pact that may have been signed with drops of blood. Consequently, any man who is so bold as to marry her will die during the wedding night. The Devil will wring his neck.

Satisfied with the effect produced, and his address of malediction completed, 'Black Wood' vanishes into the night as suddenly as he arrived; simultaneously, all the lights which had until then been generously illuminating the ballroom go out.

The happy atmosphere that had prevailed when the festival began is now no more than a memory. Françouneto, overwhelmed by the calumny, swoons and falls full length on the floor.[16] A logical series of events now follows. The young men's minds become clear, or so they imagine. 'Facts' crowd back into memory. Every time there was rain or hail, people in Roquefort are now saying, the standing crops throughout the parish, whether corn or vines, were destroyed – yet the little plot of land cultivated by Françouneto and her grandmother would flourish more than ever, and the harvest obtained by these two women would be magnificent,* amidst the surrounding general disaster. They did not even have to take the trouble to dig or to plough. These miracles smell of witchcraft. Supernatural powers and black magic begin to be thought of in connexion with our heroine. To complete the picture, after the (male) sorcerer of the Black Wood, there comes, a little later, a local (female) fortune-teller, who also announces that Françouneto's betrothed will die if he is so unfortunate as to contract, or to consummate, marriage with the Accursed.

The charges levelled at Françouneto thus emanate from wizards of both sexes. They are soon taken up by the generality

* It should be mentioned that the land adjacent to what Roquefort tradition calls Françouneto's house is highly fertile, being at present used for growing melons or strawberries, both of which require good soil. This furnishes the indispensable 'ecological' foundation needed for the villagers' allegations.

of the inhabitants of Roquefort, both young and old, who all shun the young girl. She is blamed under four heads:
(1) She takes away the strength of young men and eventually kills them, or tries to.
(2) She strikes at the act of reproduction. This is a typical feature of witchcraft: see the rites of the *aiguillette*[17] in Languedoc and elsewhere. On her wedding night, Françouneto may make sexual relations impossible for her partner, since the Devil will slay him.
(3) Not only does she annihilate sexual life, or life itself, she also turns her destructive attention to the wealth of other cultivators of the soil,[18] wiping out their crops by drawing down hail or frost upon them.
(4) Finally, she increases her own strength or wealth, and those of her lineage, at the same time as she reduces those of others. The two processes are correlative; they are communicating vessels. While other people's harvests are ravaged, those of the witch Françouneto insult the world's misery by their opulence.

Françouneto is thus placed at one of the intersections which are a feature of the rural network of powers and enmities. It is believed in the village, or the villagers are made to believe, that she plays an infernal game in which, for her to win, others must lose. Regardless of questions of witchcraft, this thinking in terms of gains and losses that balance each other was once widespread in traditional societies. It implied that the distribution of wealth – more for some, less for others – took place, or seemed to take place, on the basis of a fixed amount of goods, which did not increase. 'Growth', by contrast, was to be characteristic, for a whole period, of our industrial society, enabling everyone to increase his share without, as in the past, having to rob Peter in order to pay Paul. The American anthropologist Foster has conceptualised this 'creationist' attitude of old societies as 'the theory of limited goods'. It was not specific to the rural world: in the seventeenth century Colbert spoke similarly to Louis XIV, saying that 'in order to increase the amount of money and the number of ships at the disposal of the Kingdom of

France it is necessary to diminish by that same amount the quantity of both in the possession of neighbouring states.'[19]

As an unconscious witch, accused of reducing the strength of others in order to increase her own, Françouneto fits well enough into the models proposed by Muchembled and Favret for their respective centuries. Nevertheless, her case is more complicated than that of the pseudo-sorcerers of the *bocage*, as pertinently described in our own time by Favret. She blooms in a phase of the *ancien régime* much earlier than the reign of Louis XV. She is immersed in a culture which is Christian (more precisely, Catholic), in a period when the Counter-Reformation is still vigorous and a deep-going religious acculturation of the countryfolk is under way. The new priests now attacking what they see as the 'paganism' of the countryfolk are stern evangelists of very different breed from the colourful *curés* with mistresses who had decorated the villages of France in the distant Middle Ages. Moreover, the 'popish' community of Roquefort stands at the frontier of heresy, being close to the Protestant town of Nérac. Françouneto is therefore stigmatised by her fellow-villagers as a semi-Huguenot – here we perceive how they have been Catholicised. And she is held to have been manipulated by the Devil – here we perceive how they have been ultra-Christianised.

At Roquefort this new impregnation with Catholicism has penetrated well below the stratum of the better-educated peasants, those who *ipso facto* possess greater, or less faulty, knowledge of matters religious. For example, Françouneto's chief accuser, who, in learned terms, ascribes to her the crime of complicity with the Devil, is merely an ordinary sorcerer, or un-bewitcher, spoken of as being 'from the Black Wood', where he lives in a cave amid the trees. Note that he is paid by his clients for the services he performs as sorcerer or counter-sorcerer, and in this respect he is like his fellows generally, under the *ancien régime* and later.[20]

As for Françouneto, she is isolated more and more by the village community. At the outset of her misadventures she operated, apparently, as an involuntary and unconscious witch. In this respect she did not differ from her colleagues, or many of them, as they are described by the historians and sociologists of witchcraft.[21] Today we should say, given such a level of unawareness on her part, that Françouneto was certainly not a witch, even, and especially, if her neighbours formally alleged that she was. However, the verbal aggression directed at her from everyone in the village grows more intense. Her inner resistance fails her. Eventually, she herself becomes convinced, overwhelmed as she is by the thrusts aimed at her by everyone. 'Yes, I am under the influence of the Devil, or, at any rate, I am a noxious woman who can cause the death of others and, above all, of the one I love.' The young girl yields to the pressure of the community. These processes of autosuggestion under constraint are typical, and illustrated by other records, in France and elsewhere, relative to witchcraft.[22]

In the next phase of the narrative, Françouneto seeks to rid herself by religious means of this identity as a witch, this shirt of Nessus that is sticking ever closer to her body. At Easter she goes to Roquefort's extraparochial church, which is dedicated to St Peter (see below, Part Three). When she arrives there she is still subject to the boycott maintained against her by her fellow-villagers, all except Pascal. As for the priest of the church, he shows himself to be of no service to Françouneto, and one of his colleagues, in the following May, proves no better.

In that month of May, Françouneto takes part in the local pilgrimage to the shrine of the Virgin at Bon-Encontre, eight kilometres from Roquefort, on the other side of the Garonne. In this Marial sanctuary Françouneto is at first well received. There is nothing surprising in this difference in the treatment she gets, between St Peter's church and the one at Bon-Encontre. From a variety of observations we find that a witch is looked at askance in her own neighbourhood because the harm she can do usually takes place within a narrow radius, among her neighbours. Farther off, however, in places ten or twenty kilometres away, she is not necessarily feared or hated.

She may even be welcomed to some extent, for two reasons. First, at so great a distance from her closest environment she is no longer within the normal radius of her destructive capacities, which affect particularly her own community. And second, the witch's ability to cure people, especially by means of herbs, her knowledge, which embraces a wide range of secret matters, her power to un-bewitch (for the one who can do ill can also do good,[23] can also take spells away) – all this means that the reception a witch can expect in a place remote from her home is often warmer, or less hostile, than what she would obtain in her own village.

At first, therefore, during the Marial pilgrimage in May, in the course of the service held in the miraculous chapel of Bon-Encontre, Françouneto's situation seems to be eased. But then a fresh catastrophe occurs. The celebrant presents the statuette of the Virgin to Françouneto for her to kiss. Everyone hopes that Our Lady will command something beneficently wonderful to happen. Alas, just as our heroine's lips touch the sacred effigy, a violent storm breaks, with lightning and hail.* The candles on the altar are blown out. The scandal created is tremendous. As is to be expected, the damage spreads spontaneously, to Françouneto's own village, where the baneful supernatural powers she wields involuntarily make themselves felt to the full. All the crops in the locality, grain and grapes alike, are destroyed by the hail, save those favoured ones that grow on the holding which belongs to Françouneto and her grandmother. This time, the fury of the villagers is no longer restrained. The local populace riots against the young girl and

* Françouneto is, as we shall see in Part Three, very probably a witch, or alleged witch, who actually lived in the seventeenth century. But the idea that a pious kiss (of peace, or to a holy image) can have a baneful effect if it be given by an unworthy woman (witch, priest's concubine, etc.), is much older. See, in this connexion, a thirteenth-century document given in *The Exempla of Jacques de Vitry*, edited by Thomas Frederick Crane, Kraus reprint, 1967, of an 1890 publication (The Folklore Society, XXVI, p. 101). This reference was kindly given me by Claude Brémond.

her grandmother. Their house at Estanquet is surrounded by the angry peasants who brandish flaming torches. They want to burn the house: they want to roast them both, or at least to drive them far away from the district. We see the beginning of a pogrom or a lynching carried out by the community against the presumed authors of evil spells: such scenes are often to be found in the archives of the *ancien régime*. A melodramatic episode follows in which some elements (and these not the best) seem to have been added by Jasmin to the oral narrative which served as his point of departure. These apparent additions concern the stratagems of a soldier named Marcel. Nevertheless, what is essential is preserved. The smith Pascal, who still considers himself betrothed to Françouneto, decides that, for love, he will marry her, risking, if need be, death and hell. During the wedding night the neighbours in the hamlet of the newly-married pair imagine that they hear loud cries and see shadows dancing across the walls. When dawn comes, however, the bride, fresh and in good colour, dispels these anxieties. Risen from the marriage-bed and standing on her doorstep, she distributes, as custom requires, fragments of her garter, which is a way of conveying that the night had passed very well. The village seems relieved. No witch has ended her life at the stake. All's well that ends well.

This is how Jasmin tells the story. Yet the situation is not as simple as it seems. For a certain number of Roquefort's inhabitants the problem remains. The witch, or presumed witch, is still alive, free and present among them. She has contracted a pleasing love-marriage. She has been integrated into the honourable society of married grown-ups, but that will in no way prevent her from continuing her attacks (even if these be involuntary) upon the vital forces, wealth and crops of her fellow-villagers. Ethnologists have familiarised us in this century with situations of the same type. Among the Azande one can meet persons who are well-respected, honoured even, and who nonetheless are sorcerers, and fearsome ones at that. The fact that they do harm involuntarily does not in the least mitigate the danger that radiates from their persons, and in a way constitutes an aggravating circumstance. And yet these persons continue to enjoy general respect; as Françouneto will, now that she is happily married. We are thus faced with a Françouneto who is triumphant and cured of the subjective feelings of guilt that for a time she had suffered, under the pressure of the villagers, but who may represent a persisting danger to the community.

The story of Françouneto originates from an actual series of events which took place at Roquefort, most probably in the seventeenth century, and not in Monluc's sixteenth century as Jasmin claims. The poet was perhaps confirmed in this chronological error by the legends current among the people of Roquefort in 1840. They may have mixed up their centuries, as often happens in oral traditions.[24] It is in any case rather futile to try to separate that which in the story of Françouneto relates to a *real* series of events in the seventeenth century from that which results from the *intermediate* tradition of the eighteenth century and, finally, from that which is due to Jasmin's own creative work. This itself was inspired by the knowledge he had acquired, in his everyday life, of the stories about witches in the Agenais and the Condomois – for these were still current in his lifetime, in the gossip of the peasantry, and they were sometimes reflected in rural customs.

I shall again be told that what would be ideal would be to find, lying behind the poem *Françouneto*, the seventeenth-century records relating to the case. And I shall repeat that this is not possible, because the affair never came before the courts. This is, indeed, what makes it interesting, since we remain wholly within the intimate culture of the peasantry, and suffer less risk of the story being contaminated by judicial or prefabricated stereotypes.

Although we lack any judicial records of the case, we can nevertheless compare it with other cases which occurred in this same region of the Condomois under the *ancien régime*. It is a question of discovering on the spot not only the classical portrait of the witch, whereof Françouneto is merely one specimen among others (even if more attractive than the rest), but a portrait of the witch as a person who is either willingly or unwillingly harmful to others; who may be a gainer at others' expense, one who destroys other people's strength, wealth and sexual power, while enhancing the strength, life, wealth and power of herself and her family. We need to find another Françounette (or Françounet) who is structurally a sister or brother of our heroine. Such a discovery would confirm the soundness of Jasmin's knowledge, as a serious collector of local traditions and as an intuitive reconstructor of a regional model of witchcraft, or, rather, of witch personality, a model to serve as an 'identikit' portrait of such personality.

I have tracked down such a homologous case (thanks, in the first place, to Yves Castan) in the public records of Haute-Garonne and Gers. The event took place in 1785–87 or thereabouts, in the big village or *bourgade* of Montesquiou, in Gers, situated like Roquefort within the borders of the former diocese of Condom, an episcopal unit which disappeared along with the *ancien régime*. We are thus still in the Condomois, a *pays* or *pagus* typical of the *ancien régime*, in the same geographical setting as Françouneto.

The persons in this case whom their neighbours suspect of having cast evil spells form, in the classic manner, a lineage of sorcerers[25] whose family name is Mimalé. Here we do not have a maternal grandmother, a father and a daughter, as in Françouneto's case, but a son, or even children, together with their father and mother. The mother is, of course, like Françouneto, at the feminine pole of the plot. This lady, Gérarde Mimalé, *née* Bonet, is even accused of possessing the mandrake (*mandragore*). 'The woman Mimalé', says a neighbour, a 27-year-old carpenter, 'is able to do all that she does in her work only because she has the mandrake.' Similarly, a *bordier* (small farmer) of thirty-four says regarding Jean Mimalé, Gérarde's husband: 'If all he had was his work on his land, he could not do all that he does.' The likeness of the expressions used in connexion with the husband and the wife is striking.

Originally, in the folklore of the West, including south-western France, the mandrake is a plant which brings good luck. One needs, however, to be able to uproot it, for its root is forked or split. The old writings of Du Cange (quoting facts from the fifteenth century) and Olivier de Serres (sixteenth century)[26] present this mandrake to us in mythical fashion, as a preservative against poverty or a guarantee of success in business. In the south-west,[27] and especially in Périgord, it leads its possessor to the discovery of a treasure. To find it and collect it one needs to employ the supernatural powers of a witch. Note that, according to the peasant traditions of the south-west, the mandrake is not necessarily vegetable in form. It may also, notably in the Landes, close to the Condomois and the Agenais, be embodied in an animal. The common feature, whether it be the plant or the creature called *mandragore* or (in Gascon) *mandago*, is always the faculty of producing a treasure. *Mandragore*, as *lou mandago*, says the excellent folklorist V. Foix, in his *Glossary of Witchcraft in the Landes*,[28]

> is Mammon, the demon of riches, the goose that lays the golden eggs; it is the *Magot*, that mysterious animal which brings plenty to those who are so lucky as to possess it. Ask the peasants what is the origin of some fortune, inexplicable on the face of things, and they will invariably answer: *qu'a lou mandago*, 'he or she has the mandrake' . . .

(That is, indeed, what the people of Montesquiou say about the woman Mimalé: 'she has the mandrake', so that her modest work possesses wealth-multiplying properties.) The *mandago* of the Landes, according to Foix, can also be a rat, a fox, a squirrel, or a goat (with a cornucopia for a horn). These animals procure in various ways *le louis d'or*, provided one can catch them (Landes folklore of the eighteenth and nineteenth centuries).*

* The reader may perhaps be surprised that I am invoking Gascon folklore of the nineteenth century in relation to events (the Mimalé case) which took place at the end of the *ancien régime*. But M. Bordes's fine thesis on witchcraft in south-western France has shown the extraordinary continuity in

Frédéric Mistral,[29] the encyclopaedist of the Provençal or Occitanian world, confines himself to defining the *mandragore* as a plant, but he, too, sees it as always producing treasures:

Mandragore [he writes]: plant used in magic . . . sorcerers use its root to make the 'hand of glory' (*man de glori*) which has the property of doubling every day any amount of money placed beside it. *A la mandragouro* is said of someone who is successful in everything he does. *Vau un mandragouro*: 'it is a source of wealth.'

Taking account of these convergent definitions, it seems that the Mimalé family 'have the mandrake'. From what their neighbours say, they grow rich to an extent that far exceeds what their work alone would make possible. Such enrichment can only be supernatural in origin! It is true that the Mimalé family are, or become at the end of the eighteenth century, comfortably-off property-owners at Montesquiou. Persons of the same name are to be found living in this *bourgade* as far back as the beginning of the seventeenth century. Our Jean Mimalé, husband of Gérarde Bonet and father of Pierre Mimalé, all three accused of witchcraft, is the son of Jean Mimalé senior and Jeanne Lussan, who were married on 21 November 1742; they were both natives of Montesquiou, and their record in the register is accompanied by the marks of three illiterate witnesses. Jean Mimalé junior, our man, was born on 4 November 1745 and baptised the next day. His godfather and godmother, Jean and Pétronille Mimalé, were illiterate. His mother died giving birth to him. On 4 November 1766 Jean junior, being twenty-three years of age, married Gérarde Bonet* the daughter of a peasant couple living in a nearby village. Of the four witnesses of this marriage, two are, respectively, a carpenter and a

---

this region between the witchcraft cases of the sixteenth to the eighteenth centuries and the folklore concerning witchcraft current in the nineteenth century and explored by excellent Gascon folklorists.

* The parish registers show that her name was Gérarde and not Bernarde, as she appears in Y. Castan's transcription, his only slip of the pen in the large file he so kindly lent me.

master-surgeon, and can sign their names. The Mimalé family is thus starting to climb into slightly more distinguished circles (while the village is becoming literate). At least four children are born of this union: Pierre, Guillaume, Jean-Jacques and Jean-Baptiste, christened on 25 January 1768, 19 May 1770, 30 January 1774 and 24 July 1779. Of the six persons who, altogether, stood godfathers and godmothers to these four babies, only two are literate. The Mimalé family is rising, but only at a humble level. At the time of the happenings of 1786–7, in connexion with which the Mimalé couple were accused of witchcraft, Jean Mimalé junior, the head of this household, was aged forty-three. He was to die in 1804 (5 Messidor, Year XII), having almost reached the age of sixty. At that time he was living in the tiny hamlet of Thérou, perched on a hill situated a few kilometres from Montesquiou: there we shall find his eldest son, Pierre Mimalé, in the record of the land survey of 1820, as the cultivating owner of 17 hectares and 25 ares, made up of 60 strips, these ancestral lands being worth 308 francs according to the cadastral estimate.[30]

In 1982 I visited the farmhouse which used to belong to the Mimalé family, but is now owned by another local family of farmers. It is a fine structure of yellow stone and wood, with a main building, barn and out-buildings, the whole probably dating from the eighteenth century or even earlier. The Mimalés were thus included in the honourable stratum of prosperous farmers in this village, well above the mass of labourers. Only those persons named in the land-survey as 'proprietors', the value of whose property was estimated at a thousand francs, were above them in the scale of wealth. These Mimalés were never fringe-persons. They sprang from the peasant bedrock of the community, and moved themselves up to a modest extent during the eighteenth century. Their 'mandrake', or what was alleged to be such, had helped them to lift themselves into the estimable stratum of the *labourage* (well-to-do-farmers), but no higher. Their accusers (those who described them as evil-doing sorcerers), the Lahille and Bénac families, were persons (according to the land-surveys) either on the same social level or markedly beneath it, with the status of small farmer or day-labourer. The picture so dear to our demonologist historians of the poor witch, marginal and weak, persecuted by the rich notables of the village, thus fails to correspond to reality in the case of the Mimalés. If there is any class(?) struggle in this case, it is operating in the reverse direction from the accepted schema! In any case, regardless of sociological considerations, the neighbours, who include Bernarde Lahille, call the dangerous Mimalé trio (father, mother and son) 'the three devils.'

Let us recall the facts as they are given us. We have seen that Françouneto destroys other people's crops while obtaining excellent harvests on her own little holding, though she does not even so much as cultivate this, either with hoe or with plough. The situation is exactly the same with the Mimalés, whose self-enrichment by means of the mandrake, or hand of glory, we have already noted. 'They afflict the crops [of others] with sterility', says a memorandum by a lawyer which is annexed to the record of the proceedings.* However, our trio live in a cattle-raising area, less exclusively devoted than Roquefort to arable farming. They therefore do not confine themselves, as Françouneto did, to harming 'non-animal' production, such as the growing of cereals and grapes, on other people's land. They also attack the cattle, thereby complementing the Françouneto type. Françoise Lahille lost a cow in an accident for which the Mimalés were responsible. Bernarde Lahille, their neighbour,

* The Castan file, already mentioned. See also Castan, *Honnêteté* ... p. 585. This memorandum reproduces (in order to ridicule them) the popular charges brought against the Mimalés. The charge of doing damage to crops is indeed classical in witchcraft cases in the Condomois and in the Agenais, and whether in a Catholic or in a Protestant milieu. See the *arrêt* of the Nérac court against certain sorcerers in Clairac (in today's *département* of Lot-et-Garonne) who belonged to the Protestant religion, and who were 'convicted of having caused harm to a number of persons (who died of it) and of having taken and cast powders on fruit, cattle and persons' (P. de Lancre, *L'Incrédulité et Mécréance du sortilège* ..., Paris, 1622, p. 829. This reference was kindly supplied to me by M. Hanlon, a Canadian scholar).

complained that they had caused a lot of harm to her cattle and poultry. Françoise Lahille, recalled by the court, cites a *bordier* (a small farmer) of thirty-five and a soothsayer (specialising in the detection of witchcraft), according to whom the Mimalés had caused the deaths of a litter of eleven piglets. Charles Roujan, a *bordier* of fifty-five, and like the Lahilles a neighbour of our trio of witches,* declares, after consulting the same soothsayer: 'There are three persons who are determined to destroy my cattle. They are neighbours of mine whom I do not wish to name.' Typical, too, is the testimony of a 27-year-old carpenter:

> A neighbour wanted them [i.e., the alleged victims of the Mimalés] to go, five or six together, to seek out the local parish priest and ask his permission to bring in a man who would ascertain whether or not they [the Mimalés] were sorcerers. The soothsayer offered to expose the evil-doer . . .

The conclusion of the carpenter's investigation, corroborated by the soothsayer, was this:

> The husband [Jean Mimalé] casts a spell which causes cows to fall over a cliff, and the wife gets all her work done for her through the mandrake.

This document is concise and meaty. The priest plays only a very minor role in it, as a momentary link in the investigation carried out by the villagers. The soothsayer, an essential figure, helps to confirm the basic intuition, namely, that the Mimalés destroy other people's wealth (cattle) through their machinations, while increasing their own by means of the mandrake. Explicit also is the testimony of one Joseph Bénac, a small peasant of Montesquiou, whose arms had been satanically weakened by the Mimalés, in addition to which

* It was a Roujan, or Rouzan, who, with another neighbour, reported to the municipal authorities the death of Jean Mimalé, on 5 Messidor, Year XII. In any case, the Roujan of the Castan file is already presented in 1787 as a 'neighbour' of the Mimalé trio.

his mare fell from the top of a rock owing to bewitchment by those three, while his bull's neck was twisted and vermin were devouring his cattle.

Similarly,

the woman Commageaille [another small peasant] consulted the soothsayer [regarding the sickness of her cattle and the death-rate among her pigs]: the soothsayer named the Mimalés and the sickness passed off.

To conclude, the file on this case recalls that the Mimalés were accused of 'bewitching the crops, the persons and the cattle', or of 'causing harm to people and to the cattle and other animals belonging to others' (but not to their own stock).

At the same time, the mandrake possessed by the woman Mimalé offers to these persons suspected of witchcraft the prospect of prosperity without hard work on their family lands. As in the case of Françouneto, there is a total contrast between 'them' (enriched) and 'the rest' (impoverished). The well-being of some causes the ill-being of others.

We have seen that Françouneto breaks the arms and debilitates the strength of men. She ruins them and makes them briefly mad. She destroys their crops. Finally, she is capable of causing their deaths in the more or less immediate future. So then, we have: onslaught on the upper limbs (right or left); madness and ruin; and the threat of death. This same threefold sequence we find, within the bounds of the same former diocese of Condom, in the case of our Mimalé trio at Montesquiou in about 1785–6. Bernarde Lahille, whom we have already met, after mentioning the attacks by these three 'devils' on the cattle, poultry and other wealth of various persons, notes

that it is said about them that one ought to take care when eating and drinking in their company. A man ate at their place once and came away with his hands all yellow, which caused him great suffering.

The file on the case supplies some details on the victim who suffered in his upper limbs from the doings of the Mimalés. He was Joseph Bénac, a small peasant of Montesquiou whose meagre fortune was probably less than that, adequate though modest, of the Mimalés.* As is observed ironically in a lawyer's memorandum[31] which, though favourable to the Mimalés, records objectively the complaints brought by their accusers:

Joseph Bénac, of Montesquiou, shows his bare arms, covered with satanic marks, to persons who are as much worked up as he is: he complains of fire in his belly and of fits of madness, says that his bull's neck has been twisted, that vermin are eating up his farm animals, and that his mare would not have fallen off a rock but for a spell cast [by the Mimalés].

In addition, Joseph Bénac personally confides to a land-worker of forty-six (in other words, an agricultural labourer who may possess a smallholding, somebody of similar social position to Bénac himself) that

this house [i.e., the Mimalés' house] has always had a bad smell – remember the row that was kicked up there for some time when he got married.

(The reference is to the wedding of Jean Mimalé, master of the house, to Gérarde Bonet, which took place on 4 November 1766: we see that this matter of witchcraft goes back at least a score of years.) And Bénac goes on:

If that man Jean Mimalé comes to your door, don't let him in . . . I have had this trouble, and if I had not taken care, my whole body would have been peppered

(and not only his arms). Another worker of thirty-six (we are still in this semi-proletarian milieu of Bénac's, lower than that of the Mimalés) confirms, as to the words used, what Bénac

* From a comparison – for a much later period, to be sure – between the belongings (very few) of the Bénacs and those, more substantial, of the son of our Mimalé, see the Roquefort land-survey of the 1820s. It will be objected that this applies to a generation after the one we are concerned with. However, I unfortunately do not have at my disposal the land-survey or tax-roll of Montesquiou for the 1780s.

reported, although asserting a sound scepticism regarding the 'facts' alleged:

Bénac told me that the woman [Mimalé] had caused him to go mad, but I did not believe him, as Bénac was not in his right mind, being affected by wine – he could not control his tongue, and just mumbled.

Finally, this same Joseph Bénac was directly interrogated by the court, being summoned before it on a charge of spreading calumnies against the Mimalés, who complained of being accused of witchcraft as a result of his talk. During this interrogation Bénac retreated somewhat, out of caution, although on the basic issue he repeated his statements, mentioning in this connexion the warning given by the local soothsayer:

Joseph Bénac said that he did not remember what he had said, since he had been ill for eighteen months, losing his reason. He went to consult a man who was called a soothsayer. This man gave him a medicine which made him suffer dreadfully, but cured him. The soothsayer told him that the man who had given him the illness was a great rascal, and, if he liked, he would name this man. The respondent declined, but then went again, with others, to call on the soothsayer, and the latter still said that their troubles had been wished on them.[32]

This wished-on evil (*mal donné*) thus affects body, soul and possessions, but in particular, as we have just seen, it affects the whole arm from the hand to the shoulder, this upper limb being, as a rule, the source of wealth in agriculture and in the crafts carried on by the manual workers of the village. Already in the sixteenth century the witches of Ariège were in the habit of paralysing people's arms[33] merely by touching them. We thus have here an old-established Occitanian or Gascon belief.[34] A *bordière* aged twenty-seven whose testimony is included in the files of the judges of Montesquiou and Toulouse reported that a servant told her

not to let the woman Mimalé put her hand on my shoulder. The soothsayer advises people to keep right away from that family.

(The idea of boycott as a way of dealing with witches thus appears here, too.) Françouneto had attacked (involuntarily, but that matters little) the strength in the arms of two men at least. The Mimalés likewise, in one way or another, got at the arms, or at the work of the arms, of two persons, namely Joseph Bénac and the servant quoted above. The latter declares (in support of her remark regarding the shoulder) 'that the woman Mimalé had prevented her from reaping the corn.' In order to achieve this paralysis the woman Mimalé had said to the land-worker of twenty-seven: 'You will reap the Devil and you still won't have done with him.' The servant who had been prevented from reaping shared her direct suspicions: 'There is certainly somebody behind that.' Then Mimalé answered her: 'Don't worry, you'll cut all right.' 'And, from that moment, the servant was able to do it' – in other words, she could again cut the corn. The woman Mimalé thus appears as a true witch, or alleged witch – as being fundamentally ambivalent. She can heal just as well as she can cause harm. She can undo the ill she herself inflicted on the reaper of Montesquiou. As has been said already, in the world of the Latin and Romance cultures, in the records of witchcraft cases in the sixteenth century, 'the one who can cause harm can also heal.'[35] We are in the presence, here too, of a very old stratum of thought. An additional point: the servant who was first struck, then cured, lived in the same hamlet of Thérou as the Mimalés. The Mimalés, then, as is often the case with sorcerers, attack their nearest neighbours. Besides that servant, the Mimalés did harm to another fellow-resident of Thérou, 'the woman named Berville' whom Jean Mimalé 'caused to go on all fours.' This woman applied to the soothsayer, or oracle, who told her who was responsible for the curse laid upon her. According to another testimony, from a servant of twenty-seven, the soothsayer succeeded in curing the woman Berville.

There is another feature in common between Françouneto, the Mimalés and also, incidentally, a witch in sixteenth-century Ariège, namely an attack upon, or threat to, a marriage, either of other people or of the witch herself. The marriage is upset by the possibility of evil spells harboured in the person of the wife. Françouneto's wedding was under a curse from the start, and her husband, it will be recalled, was doomed (in principle) to death without delay, as the sorcerer from the Black Wood made clear. Despite the official happy ending of Françouneto's wedding, her first conjugal night spent with the smith who had just married her was indeed marked by strange occurrences. The inhabitants of the three hamlets thought fit to gather at Estanquet to observe the nocturnal phenomena which would not fail to occur on the occasion of so dangerous an espousal. And they were not disappointed. They saw shadows dancing along the wall, they thought they heard loud cries: and they were reassured, when morning came, only by the bride's appearing on her threshold to distribute fragments of her garter.

The woman Mimalé was much older than Françouneto. She was a witch grown old in harness. And yet, twenty years after the event, the local people were quite explicit about a particular matter. Joseph Bénac, the man with the peppered arms, declared, as I have mentioned, to a land-worker:

> Their house [i.e., the Mimalé house] has always had a bad smell – *remember the row that was kicked up there for some time when he got married.* If that man Jean Mimalé comes to your door, don't let him in.

The word used here was French *train*, Occitan or Provençal *trin*, meaning uproar, din or racket.[36] We are reminded of the 'loud cries' that people thought they heard during Françouneto's wedding-night.

The affair had no other sequel. The two marriages, one celebrated at Estanquet and the other at Montesquiou, apparently entailed no disagreeable consequences for the young couples in the years that followed. Nevertheless, the 'hellish din' that accompanied the wedding night (as was alleged) shows that the marriage of a witch is not always a commonplace event. According to southern tradition, indeed, it can happen that the witch is sufficiently dangerous to kill her husband. This prospect of murder was, in Françouneto's case, merely mentioned by the soothsayer or fortune-teller of the locality, but not actually implemented. One of the principal witches of Ariège in 1562, however, Mathe de Ga, did indeed, according to her judges, consummate this infernal-conjugal logic. She 'confessed' to killing her bridegroom with poison, or, rather, with a magic potion introduced into his bread and his porridge. This wretched woman has her place in the line which leads to the Françouneto case. Like Françouneto, Mathe was accused (falsely, she said) of causing hail to fall on the crops. Her colleague, Arnaude de Barrau, the second witch in the same village in the county of Foix, paralysed her victim's arm, like Françouneto later.[37]

The baneful powers possessed by persons like Françouneto or the Mimalés are fraught with grave risks for their own marriages. But what about the marriages of others? This question is not raised in the oral tradition referred to by Jasmin. In the case of the Mimalés, however (and this observation has general application), it seems that the noxious faculties of the witch (male or female) can be directed against marriages in general, and not merely marriages contracted by the witch (female) herself. A woman named Bernarde Dubertrand said that

> Mimalé wanted to kill them, her and her husband, and that they [the Mimalés] were the cause of her husband's ill-treatment of her, but since she went to the soothsayer things had been different.

He who can do the greater can do the less: the sorcerer can kill a couple of people, or he can, more simply, set them against each other or inflict all sorts of trials upon them, such as impotence, frigidity, sterility, domestic quarrels . . . Here we come again upon the complex of the *aiguillette*, that charm directed above all against marriage, sex and fertility which figures so importantly in the spell-casting of southern France in the sixteenth and seventeenth centuries.[38]

Attacking the sexual life of a couple, whether or not this be sanctified by marriage, means also harming what is the usual product of that activity, namely, a child. In this sphere the witches of the South were not idle: babies were suffocated or beaten in the cradle (in Occitan, *brès*) by these women. Their little bodies bled when the guilty witch passed by, thus automatically denouncing her. On this point investigations into the doings of the witches in Ariège in 1562 and the testimony of Father Amilha, a missionary who specialised in studying rural superstitions in the seventeenth century,[39] are unanimous, and provide plenty of convergent evidence. As a baby, Françouneto was not yet a witch, but she was already bewitched owing to her father's devilries, and suffered from machinations like those reported from Ariège:

> When you were in your cradle (*brès*) [her grandmother told her][40] we heard every night, up there, a strange noise, and, afterwards, always found you out of the cradle, and on the edge of your little bed we saw three drops of congealed blood. . . . We had a Gospel read aloud, and all of that went away.

The Gospel read aloud was considered to be an antidote to evil spells.[41]

In Françouneto's case, as in that of the Mimalés, the witch's house is seen as being dangerous. In Jasmin's poem it is marked by signs that are both good and bad. The garden adjoining this house is always fertile and blooming; but when hail descends upon the neighbours' crops, and the people of Roquefort decide to slaughter our heroine and her grandmother, they also prepare, not unreasonably, to burn Françouneto's house and barn, for they regard these buildings as hateful or threatening. Finally, it is in this same house, or around it, that the 'nocturnal row' is heard, the din that accompanies our heroine's wedding night. The same is true of the Mimalés:

> Their house has always had a bad smell – remember the row that was kicked up there for some time when he got married. . . . It is said about them that one ought to take care when eating and drinking in

their company. A man ate at their place once and came away with his hands all yellow, which caused him great suffering.

(From the testimony, already quoted, of Joseph Bénac and Bernarde Lahille.) This banning of the guilty persons' house* goes along with the boycott which is more commonly applied to them, transforming their case into a *cause célèbre* in the region: 'In short,' says the file of the lawyer dealing with the Mimalé affair, who expresses himself in the true spirit of the Enlightenment,

in short, this is the legend of the day and the erroneous belief of a whole district: men, women, priests, all see Mimalé, his wife and his children as werewolves, sorcerers, creatures who spread illnesses (and diseases of animals) and cause crops to fail. . . . The village soothsayer assures them that this is so and everyone believes him: they are pointed out and named. . . .[42]

In Françouneto's case, this crescendo of boycott and notoriety is observable from beginning to end of the story, with the evening party (the *Buscou*), her encounters with fellow-villagers, the ceremonies at the churches of St Peter and Bon-Encontre, and the near-pogrom that almost ends the affair.

In both of these cases, the role played by the priest as potential religious adversary of the sorcerer is not absent but is some-

* The house of the sorcerers (in Occitan the equivalent of 'house' is *ostal*, which can mean both dwelling-place and lineage) is threatened by persecution, but it also enables its members, strengthened by the cohesion of their house, to resist such persecution. At Montesquiou the Mimalés, wife, husband and grown-up sons, stand together in their *ostal* against their enemies who denounce them as sorcerers. Françouneto is at a younger, more tender stage of life than the woman Mimalé. But, helped by Pascal, her fiancé, soon to be her husband, who will become, and is already, objectively, the pillar and head of her house, Françouneto is in a position to put up a victorious resistance to her foes on the basis of an *ostal* or household in formation – an *ostal*, or a pugnacious couple, which, in the case of the Mimalés (and this is the only difference), has been formed long before. In Françouneto's case we are therefore very far from having what might seem at first a silly sort of 'happy ending.'

what overshadowed by the intervention of the soothsayer, un-bewitcher or counter-sorcerer. At Roquefort as at Montesquiou, rural witchcraft operates at deep levels, which, though affected, have not been wholly overturned by the superstructures of official or educated Christianisation. As against that, the typically peasant Pan-touched rituals of pilgrimage, little regulated by the church hierarchy, openly confront the dangerous powers of witchcraft, without however always proving victorious over them. In *Françouneto* one of the essential crises of the story occurs during the Marial pilgrimage to Bon-Encontre, which had constituted a vital part of the peasants' religious life in the heart of the Agenais and on the borders of the Condomois from the end of the Middle Ages (see *infra*, Parts II and III). In the case of the Mimalés the same antagonistic relationship of pilgrimage *versus* witchcraft is indicated, discreetly but plainly enough. Regarding that trio of sorcerers:

> a land-worker of forty-six heard that when one of the villagers was about to set out for the church, to pray to be relieved of his illness, he suddenly saw two persons appear in his room. He was the only one who could see them and he suffered worse pain than before.

Setting out for the church, to pray to be relieved of his illness, means that he was preparing to go on a pilgrimage of healing. In these circumstances the Mimalés who, like werewolves (we shall come back to them), are able to move around miraculously while remaining invisible except to their victims, showed themselves to be more powerful than the therapy of pilgrimage, normally the antidote to sorcerers. The same applied to Françouneto. Even against her will, she proves to be more powerful than the regional pilgrimage, although this is dominated by the Virgin of Bon-Encontre.[43] Françouneto unleashes a deadly hailstorm when, sacrilegiously, she kisses this effigy of Our Lady.

At the end of the arm there is a hammer, a sickle, or a knife for pruning vines ... The witch not only takes away the strength in men's arms: in Françouneto's case she renders the smith's hammer useless, 'crazy', and she runs off with the knife of one of her dancing-partners. The woman Mimalé attacks the arm of a reaper, but we may speculate whether her magical power may not extend to making ineffective, and then once more effective, the sickle itself, and the edge of its blade, which a tiny slip would indeed be enough to blunt.* Observe the procedures followed by Madame Mimalé. She prevents a servant reaping and then tells her: 'You will reap the Devil,' after which she gives back to this servant both her strength and the cutting power of her tool – all this being accompanied by the simple words: 'Don't worry, you'll cut.' It seems, therefore, that the maleficent power of the Mimalés, like that of Françouneto, is directed at the workers' tools no less than at the hands that grasp them.

Witchcraft occurs in certain special locations. First, we have the lineage of the sorcerers: grandmother, father, daughter in the case of Françouneto; father, mother and children in that of the Mimalés. Secondly, we have the house where these people live (see *supra*). As we have seen, the Occitan word *ostal* (used by Jasmin when referring to his heroine's little farm) synthesises those two concepts, meaning both house and lineage. Furthermore, social intercourse provides witchcraft with favourable opportunities. The village beanfeast and hop, embracing drinking, eating and dancing, offers Françouneto twice, with a six-months interval, the desirable occasion for breaking the arms of her suitors, Pascal and Laurent – or so public gossip alleges against her. The Mimalés are twenty years older than Jasmin's heroine, so that the cycle of festivals is behind them: as they are at least in their forties, dancing is no longer their amusement. But eating and drinking with them (as with Françouneto) is already a dangerous experience. I have already quoted in this connexion the testimony of Bernarde Lahille, saying that Joseph Bénac, who wined and dined in company with the Mimalés, came away from their house with his hands all yellow

* Letter from Y. Castan, already mentioned.

and his arms peppered with holes.

Françouneto and the Mimalés are accused of paralysing, weakening, even killing men's bodies, but they are also responsible for deranging the minds within those bodies. Françouneto has 'crazed' Pascal to the point that he now seems to have a hundred hammers beating in his head. He has become *marteau* ('cracked') for a certain period. Similarly, Bénac, magically afflicted with pain in his arm, like Pascal and Laurent, complains that the woman Mimalé made him mad. . . . He was sick for eighteen months, losing his reason.

The soothsayer indirectly points to the one who was responsible for this bout of madness: Jean Mimalé, without a doubt. Unquestionably, that Jean is a 'great rascal'! The Mimalés' victims call in a soothsayer to help them. He is a surgeon who lives at some distance from Montesquiou. He demands a payment of six *livres tournois* for his consultations. He withdraws into a room, then comes out with his diagnosis, accusing the Mimalés of responsibility for the various ills from which their (alleged) victims are suffering – losses of cattle, madness . . . It may be that he cures this madness, using a remedy which inflicts cruel suffering. The counter-sorcerer of the Black Wood, backed up by a fortune-teller, is certainly different from this surgeon-soothsayer. However, he too detects the witch in Françouneto and he too demands payment for his diagnoses and his machinations against the girl, receiving his money from the soldier Marcel. 'Black Wood' lives at a distance from the Roquefort hamlets, in the forest that bears his name. After making a special journey, he does his work in a room, or at least in some enclosed space, when he struggles openly against our heroine. Functionally, then, and even in points of detail, he occupies exactly the same place as that of the soothsayer hired by the good people of Montesquiou.

'[The Mimalés'] house has always had a bad smell – remember the row that was kicked up there for some time when [Jean Mimalé] got married', says Joseph Bénac, in a document I have

mother. On the other side, the grandmother in question *dreams*, twice, of the fire-pogrom to which she and her grand-daughter are in danger of falling victim. And, indeed, men bearing bundles of wood that they had set alight were to come intending to burn the two women alive in their house. In this affair, Françouneto, the girl armed with flowers who destroys crops, plays the part of a *bad* witch, dangerous to the community; the pogromists, armed with flaming firewood and urged on by the counter-sorcerer from the Black Wood, function as *good* fighters whose purpose is to destroy the evil witchcraft at work in their village. True, we have not yet arrived at, or we are no longer in the presence of, the impressive conception of the Italian *Benandanti* of the sixteenth century, with its dream-battle between the good sorcerers, armed with fennel[48] and the bad sorcerers, armed with sorghum, who endanger the crops. Nevertheless, in the Agenais, this dream-battle in which flowers confront burning pieces of wood also refers us back to an old agrarian mythology which we shall shortly have occasion to speak about.

More generally, there is evidence of the role of *dreams* in witchcraft of south-western France, and also in nearby western Spain. During the epidemic of witchcraft in 1 the Basque country, on the southern slopes of the Pyrenees, witches dream that they are going to the *sabbat*, while childr have *counter-dreams* of denunciation, as a result of which first set of dreamers are hauled before the courts.[49] Wha Françouneto's case is merely dreaming by an individual, the inhabitants of a village, appears in the Basque count dreaming on a mass scale, channelled in a particular way, fo their own purposes, by the authorities.

Has Françouneto the evil eye? The outcome of her 'activity' (gallants crippled, crops ravaged by hail) might cause one to believe that. Jasmin alludes to the matter, in passing, in a phrase of double meaning. At the 'Buscou' ball, when the suitors are gazing at our heroine and when she is preparing to break the arm of a boy who is in love with her, the narrative notes that 'the eye of the girl who bewitches the boys flames and sparkles as she sees how they are bewitched' (second section of the poem). This eye which makes eyes is more dangerous than it may seem.

There is a veiled allusion to the evil eye in the Mimalé case, too, although love plays no part in this. Françoise Lahille complains about the harm done by the evil trio to her cattle. She mentions that a neighbour,

> seeing Mimalé's wife coming towards her, said *would you like to bet that she will turn her head, have a good look at her*: and he saw the woman [Mimalé] slowly turn her head as she passed. . . .

This passage seems to imply an exchange of glances, or the possibility of an exchange of glances, which in the case of Gérarde Bonet-Mimalé, is fraught with danger.

The 'evil eye' had long been practised in the Agenais, as in the Condomois. In 1654 the wife of Pierre Combet, a craftsman of Clairac (in the present Lot-et-Garonne), complained to the ordinary court of Clairac that Marie Barast had looked at her daughter Jacquette, and merely by that look had caused the child to go into convulsions and die within a few months. Furthermore, this Marie Barast was doubly maleficent, because her breath, too, had the power to kill little creatures.*

Another feature in common with Françouneto seems well established. The Mimalés, like her, are involuntary and even unconscious sorcerers – if, indeed, they deserve to be called sorcerers at all. They assert their complete innocence, rejecting the supernatural identity ascribed to them. Nevertheless, as a researcher who is impressed by ethnology, I cannot rest content with recording these protestations of guiltlessness, even if they do correspond to the outlook of the Enlightenment, in which is rooted to this day the ideology of those historians who are rationalistic, Whig or liberal. I need also to look at the Mimalés with the hate-filled eyes of their neighbours, through the possibly distorting spectacles that they wear. True, the

* According to G. Hanlon's thesis, Vol. II, pp. 551–3.

Mimalés are able to defend themselves and hit back, differing in this respect from Françouneto, a weak girl, and her grandmother, broken down by old age. The Montesquiou 'sorcerers' are a couple in the prime of life, and able to call on the help of grown-up children. The Mimalés are not prepared to let themselves be influenced or intimidated by the accusations of their neighbours. They are well aware that, under Louis XVI, they are not up against the hostility of the courts, as they would have been in Louis XIII's time. And so they defend themselves, they react, they fight, and, in the end, they win the day.[50]

This brings us to another point of similarity with the case of Françouneto, in that, as we have seen, she emerged victorious from the trap into which her enemies wished to thrust her, just as the Mimalés won a splendid victory. Official justice found in their favour. They got the better of their opponents and slanderers. The 'happy ending' which closes the poem *Françouneto* is therefore not necessarily an invention of Jasmin's or a pious legend. (We shall see that, historically, there is every reason to suppose that the Françouneto case is derived from actual facts. Some witchcraft cases did, in fact, end well.)

The Mimalés hauled their slanderous neighbours before a court, and got them sentenced – supreme disgrace – to pay a fine of 223 *livres*. In a way, and if I take the line of liberal or Whig historiography, I can say that this verdict is cheering, and testifies to the progress of the Enlightenment. The forces of village obscurantism are hewn in pieces. The unjustly accused family cleanse themselves of the calumnies to which they had been subjected. They may hope that the *Parlement* of Toulouse will, in its turn, non-suit the anti-Mimalé faction, who have seen fit to appeal. And, indeed, this is what happens. In passing, let us note that the judges of Languedoc show themselves on this occasion to be highly enlightened: they do not deserve, or deserve no longer, the cartloads of scorn heaped upon them by Voltaire on account of the Calas case. Our southern magistrates, even in out-of-the-way Montesquiou, seem to have been converted to the ideas of progress and reason, in face of the pressure of rural backwardness. The latter, in a just turning of the tables, now knows the taste of defeat. Our thoughts turn to Françouneto as she proudly distributes the fragments of her garter on the morrow of her wedding night, before flabbergasted neighbours who no longer even dare to call her witch.

Let us now try to take up a different standpoint, that of the neighbours of Françouneto or of the Mimalés. In the latter case, the defeat suffered by these good people before the court is shattering. The simple fact, so far as they are concerned, is that the sorcerers have *won* their case, have overcome their victims. The 'winners' can now continue to terrorise the community without even having to admit to themselves that they are dangerous, harmful, terrifying people. Yet an admission of that sort, a confession of guilt like that, was the A.B.C. of counter-sorcery in the seventeenth century. If they had lived under Richelieu, the Mimalés would soon have ceased their protestations of innocence, whether false or sincere. They would have joined the camp of their accusers. Persuaded by autosuggestion or by torture, they would have ended by confessing their guilt. From there to the stake would have been a step quickly taken.

This comparison has the merit, it seems to me, of bringing out all the ambiguity of the 'happy ending', or pseudo-'happy ending', of *Françouneto*. Who knows whether this young woman, happily escaped from the clutches of her accusers and neighbours, is not going to become, in her turn, once the honeymoon and the love-kisses are behind her, and she has reached the prime of life, a Mimalé, a mature and powerful witch, known to be such, who will once again frighten her neighbours just as she did when she was young? Now, Françouneto will no longer be a weak girl: to protect her against the anger round about she will have a strong husband, and soon there will be grown-up children as well. What is more, the traditions that are favourable to her have come down to us through her own lineage.* They tell us nothing of the feelings

* See, in this connexion, the analysis I give, *infra*, in Part Three of this book.

of frustration and hatred which may still have filled her neighbours, in her lifetime, whenever they passed her house.

Comparing the Françouneto case with others, and in particular with that of the Mimalés, means bringing up also the difficult problem, rich in interest, of the werewolves. On this matter *Françouneto* makes no more than a mere allusion. The evening dance-party, the 'Buscou', in the second section of the narrative, is held in winter, on the eve of and during Christmas, 'when the werewolves and sorcerers (*fatchilhès*) who cause house and cottage to tremble' are supposed to perform their *pavane* (i.e., their dance, or even their *sabbat*) behind barns and elm-trees. Are these *fatchilhès* the masculine counterpart, in the same etymological family, of the *fados*, who are feminine, 'witches', 'fairies'?[51] In this context the frontier between human being and supernatural entity is easily crossed. In his *Trésor du félibrige*, Frédéric Mistral mentions that in the *pays d'oc* the *fados* and *fatchilhès* live near water-points – lakes or springs – and also near caves whose essense, by tradition, is sacred. Our sorcerer from the Black Wood entertains the idea of living in a woodland grotto. Moreover, these hybrid creatures, who have one foot in the supernatural world of folklore, make themselves known, among other times, during the cold season, and, for preference, during the twelve days between Christmas and Epiphany. After 1566, in the case of the Agenais and Gascony, as a result of the historical alterations in the calendar, this twelve-day cycle came to correspond to the joining of the old year with the new, around the night of 31 December–1 January. More generally, in both parts of France, *pays d'oc* and *pays d'oïl* alike, the period leading up to Christmas is considered to be a dangerous one, propitious to the exercise of maximum power by sorcerers and also to the baneful wanderings of werewolves.[52] One and the same person can be both sorcerer and werewolf, either casting spells or putting on a supernatural animal's skin. Oral traditions like this can be found in the *Bocage* area of Normandy, in the Limousin, in Picardy, the Charentes and the Agenais.[53] More precisely, the Occitanian south-west puts the emphasis on the instant presence of fairies during the night of 31 December–1 January. (Here we have traditions which could not have crystallised in the general setting of the twelve-day cycle until the end of the sixteenth or in the seventeenth century, when the new calendars which made the year begin in January and no longer in March had become firmly rooted in local habits.)

On the eve of 1 January in Hautes-Pyrénées, they prepare a meal for the fairies in an out-of-the-way room, the doors and windows of which are left open, because it is thought that the fairies visit the houses of persons who believe in them on the night of 31 December, bringing them happiness in their right hands or misfortune in their left hands.* Then comes the dawn of 1 January, with the new year. On that morning, at sunrise, the head of the family takes the bread which had been offered to the fairies and dips it in the water or the wine that was on the table, and they breakfast on this bread.[54]

The same custom is found in the Landes, which also form part of the Occitanian or Gascon south-west. In those parts, on New Year's Eve, each household leaves on the table bread, wine and other food, so that the 'white ladies' may have a meal. 'If they find nothing to eat, beware of the woes that will rain down upon the unbeliever and his family.' In the Franco-Provençal region (Savoy and Jura), closely akin to the Occitanian region, the fairies who visit people's homes on the night of 31 December–1 January also preside over the activities of spinning flax and hemp.[55]

In short, the night of 31 December–1 January seems to be really strategic. The tradition collected by Jasmin gives prominence at this night-time turning-point to the battle waged between the two sorcerers, male and female, one accused of sinister doings and breaking of arms (Françouneto), the other intervening in order to un-bewitch, since he who can do ill can

* See, in *Françouneto*, the ambivalence of this fateful night of 31 December, when conflict is joined between the maleficent sorceress heroine and the vigorous counter-sorcerer from the Black Wood.

do good also (the man from the Black Wood), with as background both textile activities (winding of yarn) and the consumption of a variety of food and drink – wine, flatcakes, porridge, etc. In all this the tail of the werewolf is not far away, with its capacity for disguise and movement, under cover of darkness or by miracle. The tradition collected by Jasmin emphasises, as we have seen, this disturbing proximity (beginning of the second section of the poem). Furthermore, Françouneto herself, as a hail-maker, belongs to a 'family' of sorcerers whose activities are traditionally linked with those of werewolves. A little comparative history will not come amiss at this point. In the frontier region between Switzerland and France, which embraces the Jura, Franche-Comté, French-speaking Switzerland and some of the German-speaking cantons, at the intersection of the French, German and Franco-Provençal cultures, the two essential or correlative charges brought against witches in the sixteenth and seventeenth centuries were (1) disguising themselves supernaturally as werewolves, and (2) causing hailstorms which destroyed the crops.[56]

Around Françouneto, who causes hail to fall and who is particularly dangerous during the twelve-day cycle, there is certainly an odour of the werewolf, sniffed by the good folk of Roquefort and Estanquet, whose suspicions are relayed allusively in the traditions collected by Jasmin.

This odour becomes simply unbreathable in the case of the Mimalés who, in the pattern of their witchcraft, are so closely akin to our Françouneto. The Mimalés, in fact, are werewolves, or are held to be such, with all the consequences that this entails.[57] According to the advocate's memorandum attached to the documents of their case, this case 'is the legend of the day and the erroneous belief of a whole district: men, women, priests, all see Mimalé, his wife and his children as werewolves, sorcerers . . .' Then follow the charges relating to the losses of crops and cattle and the revelations concerning this family made by the local soothsayer. Later, this memorandum goes on in rationalistic style, somewhat distancing itself from the case:

There are doubtless guilty persons, and these guilty persons are Mimalé and his wife – guilty not of magic, for we are no longer in the days when ignorance and superstition dominated excessively credulous judges, in the age when Louis XIV in his wisdom forbade the courts to entertain complaints of witchcraft, but of having put citizens in danger, of having given substance to their false opinions, of having brought trouble into the villages by providing reality for their illusions concerning ghosts wearing the skins and uttering the howls of werewolves as they bewitch the crops, individuals and animals: and yet it is they [the Mimalés] who have complained to the court of Montesquiou, accusing their neighbours of having for two years past charged them with witchcraft. . . .[56]

Finally, the labourer Joseph Bénac, who claims that his arms were wounded by the Mimalés through magical means, is judicially requested 'to prove, besides, his allegation that the Mimalés dressed up in skins and ran around the countryside by night acting the werewolf.' These precise charges were formulated by the villagers and were repeated as such, but not, of course, endorsed, by the court. They render intelligible the comments made by the villagers themselves about the Mimalés. For example, Françoise Lahille, who complains that her cattle have been killed or threatened, says mysteriously, regarding the 'magic trio', 'He who wears a bad coat needs only put it off'. These words of Françoise Lahille's are repeated almost exactly by a *bordier* of thirty-four:

Ah, that wretch Mimalé, *his is a very bad costume*, he would do well to pull it off. If all he had was his work on his land he would not be able to do all that he does.

Finally, a land-worker of forty-one

heard that when one of the villagers was about to set out for the church, to pray to be relieved of his illness, he suddenly saw two persons appear in his room. He was the only one who could see them, and he suffered worse pain than before.

The bad coats or costumes which the witnesses cautiously refer to and which, they say, the Mimalés would do well to 'pull off' are simply the *skins of werewolves* which the members of this family, according to the advocate's memorandum and to the allusions in the court's verdicts, were accused (by their enemies in the village) of having put on expressly in order to commit their misdeeds as sorcerers, and also to enrich themselves by using their magical powers or their mysterious mandrake.[59]

In acting thus the Mimalés were far from isolated cases in the south-west. The werewolf figures as 'the white wolf' in Gascon folklore, especially in the Landes right down to the nineteenth century. In the same region (Gers-Béarn-Labourd), he even assumed 'the animal's skin'[60] in the midst of the 'Voltairian' eighteenth century. The werewolf figures woefully in the repression of witches in the Bordelais in the seventeenth century.[61] He is present in Switzerland and the southern half of France since the fifteenth and sixteenth centuries at least.[62] There he circulates along with other animals of the same sort into whose form the soul of a human being temporarily inserts itself. Be it noted in this connexion that the werewolf is not necessarily a 'wolf' in the zoological sense of the word: in the Landes he can be a dog, a donkey or a horse.[63] In Quebec he can even be a bustard.[64] In any case, the werewolf comes within the scope of the broader definition that Carlo Ginzburg has given of phenomena of this kind: metamorphosis into an animal, followed by a magical journey by the soul thus metamorphosed, this journey being usually preceded by an ecstatic or cataleptic trance, during which the soul, in animal form, temporarily leaves the body of its owner.[65]

Ginzburg links these facts with the general notion of 'shamanism'. The judges of Montesquiou and Toulouse, who are at least to some extent men of the Enlightenment, hint to us that the Mimalés *disguised* themselves as werewolves in order to frighten their fellow-countrymen, but the natives of Montesquiou do not see it that way. They hold firmly and spontaneously to the version which today we call 'shamanic.' Proof of this they see in the supernatural power to do harm which they ascribe to the members of the Mimalé family, metamorphosed now and again into animals. Proof also is offered by the appearance, magical and pain-causing, of two of the Mimalés in a room where a sick man sees them. He is the only one among the persons present in that enclosed space who is able to see them: these two Mimalés who have miraculously appeared are therefore, without doubt, creatures which can move about in supernatural fashion and by their magical techniques can worsen the sufferings that are the usual lot of their victims.

We are now in a position, bringing the different pieces of evidence together, to sum up the cases of witchcraft that have interested us, so far, in a vaguely defined Condomois.* These cases have been taken, on the one hand, from *Françouneto*, in which village tradition intersects with literary creation, and on the other, from certain cases or facts of a comparable order drawn from peasant practice in the same region. The Mimalé episode should not, from this standpoint, be seen as an 'isolated' event but, like *Françouneto*, as an exemplary, many-sided and complex fact – a 'total social fact.' It brings together all sorts of features that one finds dispersed in a number of episodes of southern witchcraft, from Ariège to the Landes and from the Gironde to the Jura, and even to Vaud and to north-western Spain.

Let us briefly recall the principal points in our comparison, by summing up what has just been said. This sort of witchcraft that we find in the Condomois, and more widely in the *pays d'oc*, is the work of specialised lineages. It is characterised, first, by an attack launched against the life-cycle, from beginning to end. The cradle of the newborn baby† and then the nuptial bed are the targets of aggression in various forms, the consequence of which is, at best, the sterility of the married couple and, at

* Remember that both Françouneto, at Roquefort, and the Mimalés, at Montesquiou, lived, under the *ancien régime*, within the former diocese of Condom.

† It should be mentioned that attacks on babies, including acts of cannibalism, were included by the inquisitors in their overall conception of the *sabbat*.

worst, the death of their baby, or of other couples' babies. The physical and mental integrity of the persons attacked is under threat, and especially their arms, the source of wealth (the tools – sickle, mattock, knife – wielded by these arms can be made temporarily unusable). These attacks on people's arms take place especially during times of social intercourse, when the witch and her victims are eating and drinking together. Such social intercourse would normally be harmless, but it becomes dangerous in such company. In the case of the Mimalés, who are adults, it is a matter merely of consuming bread and wine with them, but in that of young Françouneto it involves also a series of dances and deafening revels which take place at an evening party and are appropriate to the age-group to which this witch belongs.

The evil-eye phenomenon is no more than hinted at in the two cases, without being expressly indicated. Odours and flowers define a dangerous area within which the action of the sorcerers is most intense. Dreams explain behaviour or give foresight, both among the sorcerers and among the unbewitchers.

The attack on persons is accompanied by an attack on property, and in the first place on the fertility of land. The sorcerers harm both cultivation (by means of hail) and animal husbandry (by means of diseases and mysterious accidents which kill or wound cows, pigs or horses). On the other hand, the suspected sorcerers manage, with or without the mandrake, to increase their own crops by as much as they reduce those of others. As Carlo Ginzburg rightly observes, they thus preserve the function of fecundity, but apply it to the enhancement of their own property and, contrariwise, to the impoverishment of the community. Being capable both of destroying and of creating wealth, by virtue of an impeccable logic they develop wealth for their own benefit while diminishing it for others. They operate in a world of *neighbours*, their powers being exercised only within their immediate environment. The antidote to them is the counter-sorcerer or soothsayer, who is perhaps only their mirror-image, together with relics and amulets, and also the pilgrimage, the specifically agrarian variant of rites of Pan ceremonies. In the cases which interest us, this last is ineffective in relation to the spells that emanate from the sorcerers, or that overwhelm them. The Church and the clergy are much concerned to impute Devil-worship to our sorcerers, yet, as it happens, these imputations, although undeniably correct as to their form, are not absolutely central to the phenomenon of witchcraft, as one might suppose if one's investigation of the matter were to be restricted to reading the works of demonologists very remote from the sources of peasant culture.

Finally, our witches, whether named Françouneto or Mimalé, seem to have been unjustly persecuted or ostracised, thanks to a local notoriety which they could well have done without. They were made the victims of harassments, which might have turned into pogroms, aimed at convincing them that they were indeed sorcerers, although unaware of that fact at the outset (or even innocent of such an identity). To conclude, the suspects emerge victorious from the accusations brought against them. At the end of their experience is not the stake but a happy marriage or a successful law-suit.

All the same, the 'werewolf' phenomenon remains to be considered. Though barely perceptible in the case of Françouneto, it is amply explicit in those of Mimalé and some others. It links our protagonists with an ancient basis of paganism, or rural shamanism, which has been well-established as existing in Occitania, Valais and northern Italy. In the *pays d'oc* there is, in fact, a very strong tradition concerning 'journeys of souls.' The latter leave, in animal or human form, the living (but sleeping) body to which they belong and pay a short visit to the realm of the dead, from which they bring back information and also some riches. Disguised as lizards, they emerge from the mouths of the sleeping persons in whom they have been residing, in order to go and collect, or merely to visit, a treasure hidden on the other side of a river, in the fleshless skull of a long-dead donkey, and then they return home. Or else, wearing the skin of a werewolf, they go in search of evil to be done to others and prosperity to be won for their own families. The Mimalés are still very close to these old memories of shamanism, which flourished in mediaeval Ariège or modern Condomois, fading but not dying out between the sixteenth and eighteenth centuries. Our Françouneto, who lived between 1660 and 1690, was, however, somewhat deprived of her original flavour by the writer who brought her back to life in 1840. In the form of her story that has come down to us, orally-transmitted and then worked up in literary form, she is allowed to convey only a muffled echo of her distant past. She has not completely cast off her moorings from the ancient shamanist mythology of the south, which spread unhindered over Gascony in late mediaeval and even early modern times. From the literary standpoint, Françouneto is richer than the Mimalés, but existentially she is poorer. She already enters (with Jasmin giving a shove?) into the abstract schema of a relation of forces and powers among the strategies of rural antagonism, as these have been defined by Muchembled, Favret and Macfarlane for the Cambrésis, the *Bocage* and Essex. And yet Françouneto's memory is not defective. If her traditions dressed her in the cast-off clothing of a werewolf, too, our heroine would feel quite comfortable like that. (See the important work by J. Duvernoy, *Le Registre d'inquisition de Jacques Fournier* . . ., and *infra*, p. 187.)

Such differences are of merely outward significance: Françouneto and the woman Mimalé are truly of one blood. Together, they give us the identikit portrait of a Gascon witch, equipped with all her attributes and accessories. In other, less complete, cases these features are scattered, like the fragments of a broken mirror. The portrait remains valid beyond the strict limits of the Condomois of classical times. It would not be hard to find a Mimalette or a Françounette in seventeenth-century Béarn, just across the way from Condom.

Here, in fact, is an example from Béarn. In May 1609, during the night, the peasant Ramonet de Lola (of the village of St

Armou, in what is now the *arrondissement* of Pau) hears a frightful din of bleating, coming from his goat-shed. He had been worried for several days before this, having already lost a goat and a heifer. His brother Odet suggested to him ('announced', as we should say) that there was some sort of witchcraft behind it all. When Ramonet, awakened by the noise, reaches his goat-shed, he sees a she-goat by the light of the moon. She hurls herself at him, spits in his face, scratches him, and gives him such a hard bite on the little finger of his left hand that he fears he has lost it. He will retain the once-bloody mark of that bite for a long time. With his still-usable right hand, Ramonet grasps his 'dagger', a sort of knife or half-sword, and kills the goat, striking several blows, one in the lower belly. Then he comes to, surrounded by his neighbours, who have run quickly to the spot. The body of his wife lies beside him, stabbed with many wounds! Some of his neighbours confirm that she was a witch. Others, however, do not agree, and accuse Ramonet of premeditated murder of his wife. He goes away. Some years later, he returns to live in the same place, and is not made uncomfortable. Eventually, however, a judge, more scrupulous than others, brings him to trial and sentences him to exile.

In a number of respects this case of Ramonet and his unfortunate wife coincides with the Mimalé–Françouneto model, typical of the neighbouring Condomois. The leading characters belong, like the Mimalés, to the stratum of well-to-do farmers, higher up the social scale than game breeders like Françouneto. Ramonet and his brother are both referred to by the names of their respective houses. The murderer, having followed the plough from the age of fourteen, possesses sheds with goats and heifers in them, and he wears a dagger with something of a sword about it. This indicates a certain degree of social pretentiousness, characteristic of a well-off peasant.

The 'witch', Ramonet's wife, is called Marie de Sansarric and comes from Argelos, another village in the present-day *arrondissement* of Pau. Like her equivalents at Roquefort and Montesquiou (Françouneto's father, Françouneto herself and the Mimalés), Marie de Sansarric attacks the different phases of the life-cycle. Like those others, she endangers the lives of little children.

Jeanne de la Them [Ramonet tells us, in this connexion] gave birth to two boys. My wife [Marie de Sansarric] offered them her breast a few days later, and at once they became very ill, one of them dying the second day and the other the third day after that. . . . [Another time], my wife breathed into the mouth of a little child, who became bewitched, could not speak or shed tears any more, and died soon afterwards. The father and mother of that child bear witness to this.

At a later stage of human life, Ramonet's wife strikes a blow, of course, at marriage, or (what, in this case, comes to the same thing) at love. The Mimalés sowed dissension among other couples. Françouneto caused the arms of her suitors (one of whom became her husband) to bleed, or to break. By doing this she brought upon herself the vengeance, which might have proved fatal, of a third suitor.

Marie de Sansarric, for her part, does not beat about the bush. Disguised as a goat, she bites her husband's finger, drawing blood, despite the warm affection he says he feels for her; to defend himself, he has to kill his wife with dagger-blows. As a result he is doomed to suffer further on account of his dead wife, being exiled twice as retribution for killing her.

We also find in the case of Ramonet's wife the very familiar theme of the onslaught on the arm, which we have already observed in the cases of Françouneto and the Mimalés, and also among the witches of Ariège in the sixteenth century. Marie de Sansarric attacks people's arms at both ends – shoulder and finger. Ramonet claims:

My late wife was reputed to be a witch. She looked at a neighbour named Quintere de Toulouse, and while she was looking at her this neighbour felt a great pain, coming down from the top of her head to her eyes and *on to her shoulders*, from which she remained quite benumbed and unable to rest until, the next day, she went to see Jeanne de la Coste, a woman living in the same place, who understood such witcheries and by means of some prayers removed the spell.

In passing, let us note the richness of this fragment of text. An attack on someone's shoulder is directed against a neighbour by means of an evil eye. This can also cause an outbreak of madness (see Françouneto and the Mimalés, too, on this point), since it affects the head and mind of the victim, who for a time is the prey of numbness and bewitchment. A soothsayer with healing powers is called in, and successfully applies antidotes of a religious nature. All these elements are already familiar to us from the happenings at Roquefort and Montesquiou.

As I have said, the witch attacks the arm at its other end, too – in Ramonet's case, his little finger. She bites it so savagely as to draw blood and to leave upon it the classical mark of witches (possibly of Devil-worshippers). Luckily, it is Ramonet's left hand that Marie attacks. With his right hand still usable, he is free to plant his dagger in the lower belly of his better half, whom he takes for a supernatural goat.

I have already noted the importance of the shedding of blood, in connexion with Ramonet's little finger. Françouneto also bled (passively) when, as a newborn baby, she was devoted by her father to the Devil. Then she (actively) bled the wrist of her suitor when she took her first witch-like action against Pascal. These two or three operations were certainly magical in character.

Social intercourse, sometimes with dancing and always with eating and drinking, was at the heart of the intrigues of the Condomois witches. In the same way, a person comes to eat in Ramonet's house, when he is away, at the table presided over by Marie the witch, wife of the future murderer. 'Soon afterward', the guest falls to the ground in a faint. Marie raises him up and rubs his head with her hands. This makes him feel better. In this instance the witch uses the twofold power of doing harm and then cancelling the harm has she just done. The woman Mimalé, similarly, first paralysed the arm of a reaper, then, in kindly fashion, gave her back the use of her arm and her sickle. Françouneto and the Mimalés cause crop-failures or animal diseases on their neighbours' farms, while at the same time inducing prosperity on their own. Their powers are aimed in both directions, good complementing evil.

I have already mentioned the presence of the evil eye in the case of Ramonet's wife as in that of the woman Mimalé and that of Françouneto. In the first case, where Marie de Sansarric is concerned, just as in witchcraft in the Agenais in the seventeenth century, the evil eye is merely one weapon among others which also 'emanate' from the witch's body. Marie's eye attacks the head, the eyes and the shoulders of a neighbour, but her spittle is dangerous to Ramonet, her breath can kill a child, and her mother's milk can cause the deaths of two babies – a paradoxical form of commensality through the breast.

Françouneto and the Mimalés acted through baneful flowers and (in the case of the Mimalés) through the sickening odour of their house. Marie is, instead, a specialist in magical poisoning. She kills a neighbour's dog to which she has given bread. With her own milk she causes the death of a baby. This bread and this milk are therefore fatal. The advocate of Marie's victim is not in any doubt: he says that 'weregoats', like Ramonet's wife, have poison in their teeth, just as vipers have.

The attack on human life (infantile, adult, sexual) is accompanied in Marie's case by the characteristic offensive against property in land or animals, as with Françouneto and the Mimalés. She leaves behind in her neighbourhood a long, macabre trail of dead dogs, goats and heifers, including some of those in her husband's sheds, since she treats him as an adversary.

We find around Marie the usual fauna of announcers, denouncers, soothsayers, un-bewitchers and healers. They go for the young woman just as their counterparts in the Condomois raged against Françouneto or the Mimalés. First of all, Ramonet's brother detects the machinations of the witch. Then the neighbours join in: they announce, or denounce, her activities and a healer comes on the scene to de-fuse the spells, and so on.

There is no need to dwell on the religious context. The charge of Devil-worship is regularly levelled at Ramonet's wife in the speeches of the advocate and the procurator (which have been preserved), just as in the complaints brought by the peasants.

I have mentioned the lynch-and-pogrom atmosphere which was stirred up around the Mimalés and which actually exploded against Françouneto and her grandmother, although it did not get so far as actually killing them. Against the wretched Marie lynching was carried to its ultimate conclusion, with the killing of the witch by her husband, acting as executioner.

At Roquefort as at Montesquiou, the house and the lineage, otherwise known as the *ostal* in the dual meaning of the Occitanian term, are hereditarily infected with witchcraft. As for Ramonet's wife, her house is maleficent: the goats go mad in their shed. The evil-doing heroine of this story has no difficulty in passing through the door of the conjugal bedroom, even though it is bolted. A lineage sprung from the womb of Marie would be suspect in advance. Otherwise, why should Ramonet feel obliged to kill his wife by stabbing her *in the lower belly*? Why should he mention the poisonous quality of her breast-milk? As a mother of blood and as a mother of milk, Marie has to go. She could only engender wicked creatures.

I have mentioned the unconscious character of the sorcerers of the Condomois. They often do ill without wanting to or knowing what they are doing. Marie de Sansarric, too, has many backers in the village, who take sides against the murderer Ramonet. In the end, the husband himself can never decide which feeling is uppermost in him – passionate love for his wife or hatred for the witch. He is ambivalent because she is two-fold. Perhaps she is a witch, some say a willing witch, but others question that, or say she is not a witch at all. Françouneto and the Mimalés are *winners*. They end by overcoming the hatred of the rural society around them. In her own way, Ramonet's wife is also a winner, or at least a half-way winner. True, she dies under her husband's knife. But she is not brought to judgement, or burned, and for good reason. That is already important. Above all, a more obvious victory this time, when she is beyond all that, she succeeds in getting her husband condemned many years later to perpetual banishment – just as the soldier Marcel has to leave the district after the failure of the measures he has taken against Françouneto. From this standpoint, Marie de Sansarric is even stronger than the Mimalés. They, at least, had in their favour the big trump-card of being alive when they caused their enemies to be sentenced to pay a heavy fine. Ramonet's wife is able to go on doing harm from beyond the grave. A remarkable woman, no doubt about that. A dead hand ruling the fate of the living.

Above all, Ramonet's wife is no pre-fabricated personage emerging ready-made from the stereotyped *sabbats* dictated by magistrates. She is a true 'weregoat' – not just a hinted-at werewolf like Françouneto or a partial (though certain) werewolf like the Mimalés. In the notorious night that is to culminate in her murder, Marie de Sansarric rises from the conjugal bed and from her sleep, passes supernaturally through the bolted door of the bedroom, transforms herself into a goat, and bites her victim, drawing blood and leaving a mark. Furthermore, she has shown herself capable, like every self-respecting creature of her sort, of doing both evil (harming) and good (healing) – the latter, just by rubbing the head of a man she had harmed. In her, then, we recognise the canonical features of the werewolf, shaman and nocturnal traveller, able to leave in dreams his or her sleeping body and to assume, in a magical trajectory, the body of an animal, and able also to confer either well-being or the reverse on persons in her immediate environment.[66]

Though Françouneto, followed by the woman Mimalé and Ramonet's wife, beings who logically synthesise in their persons the thousand-and-one facets of the local form of magic, with complete structural isomorphism and geographical contiguity, we have been able to take the measure, in the depths of the countryside, of a certain kind of witchcraft in south-western France. This, as it existed at a particular moment, revolved around the mortal combat between peasants, both men and women, but was also heir to mythical structures and narrative schemas derived from a distant past. The peasants shrewdly applied both of these to persons whom they accused, for one reason or another, of sorcery. On that matter our old public records are rich in information.

Up to now I have been seeking to fit Françouneto into a Gascon witchcraft culture that existed during the seventeenth and eighteenth centuries. My approach has been more synchronic than diachronic, and more typological then genealogical. However, ultimately one has to look into the origins of structures.

Is it possible to go further back into the past? To inquire not merely who Françouneto is, but whence she comes? To find her antecedents, her roots? The mythical schemas applied to Françouneto by fellow-villagers who were also her enemies might then be traced to their remoter, though not to their final and primordial, origins. What is the use of trying to find an absolute starting-point?

For this investigation of ancestry we possess at least one useful fact to work on. Françouneto is a hail-maker. She is accused of bringing down the deadly hail, just like the sorcerers of Berry in the nineteenth century, or the hail-makers of Ariège in 1562 who, like her, attack the arms or the babies of their victims.

Meteorologically speaking, hail is a selective phenomenon. It attacks one person's vine while sparing his neighbour's meadow. We can understand that suspicion of witchcraft should early have seized upon this particular form of inclement weather. Without going back to the Flood, let us note that, from time immemorial, persons held to be sorcerers were thought to have provoked hailstorms in order the more easily to transfer to X the wealth that the hailstones had destroyed on Y's farm, or else had carried off by supernatural means. In 829 AD a capitulary of Louis the Pious attacks persons who are considered to be sorcerers:[67]

It is said, that these persons are able to trouble the air by means of their spells, *to bring down hail*, to foretell the future, *to take away crops and milk in order to give them to others*, and to commit many other misdeeds of the same kind. These guilty persons, men or women, must be punished when exposed, for, disastrously and recklessly, they do not shrink from entering the Devil's service.

As we see, the *maleficium* (causing hailstorms, transferring crops from one farmer to another, serving the Devil) goes back a long way before the classical age of our witches, Françouneto included – even a long way before the fourteenth and fifteenth centuries, when more articulated and substantially learned conceptions of the *sabbat* were formulated. But the latter assimilated or digested the good old *maleficium*, or rural spell, with eventual devilish connotations, much more often than they invented it. There were 'hail-makers' in the ninth century and even earlier. The contrary would be surprising, since of one thing we may be sure, at all events – that hail was known to fall under the Carolingians. Having said that, Louis the Pious is certainly far too ancient a personage – the gap is one of eight centuries – for us to be able to locate through one of his capitularies, however typical this may be, an ancestress for our Françouneto.

A more recent document will bring us closer to the heroine of Estanquet, chronologically and, in particular, geographically. On 23 August 1326, in his papal see of Avignon, Pope John XXII expressed the wish that the trial of Bertrand d'Andiran, canon of the church of St Caprais in Agen, who was accused of magical practices, be brought to a conclusion. Bertrand had called upon demons and evil spirits.[68] He had made various magical invocations with a view to causing thunder, lightning, storms, hail, attacks by demons, deaths of human beings and other harmful events. To this end he employed magical techniques based upon forbidden arts and sciences. These consisted of writings, various books, vessels made of glass, earthenware and wood, and other bizarre instruments with which or in which Bertrand composed or combined powders of all kinds and stinking liquids, as well as other mixtures, all of them serving, most certainly, to call up devils, who in turn would bring on hailstorms and thunderbolts.

Finally, this Bertrand was the close friend of a priest and a layman – the former being from the town of Limoux, the latter a mere villager – who, together, removed the heads and arms from corpses hanged on gibbets and brought them into Agen.

These two fellows were arrested with their macabre booty by the watchmen on the ramparts of Agen. The layman was burned after making a full confession, and the priest was consigned to the episcopal prison.

Let us try to sort out from all this what were the specific activities of Bertrand d'Andiran. In this unravelling we shall leave aside the man's relationship with the corpse-stealers. Their crime, if it was one, was not his doing and he was not specially punished for that (although, perhaps, his magic may have necessitated contact with the dead?). Bertrand, a townsman, was a sort of alchemist; he read books and compounded mixtures in glass vessels. Such activities would hardly be within the range of a mere peasant of the neighbourhood. Having established that fact, we note with interest that the production of hail, lightning, thunder and thunderbolts, with diabolical accompaniments, is an activity carried on in the suburban or rural parts of the Agenais in the seventeenth century, since Françouneto damages a church tower and some crops by means of lightning and hail, and that this same production of storms and hail is an activity carried on in the *town* of Agen in the early fourteenth century. This comparison is all the more interesting in that the church of St Caprais in Agen, where Bertrand d'Andiran worked, was patron of the parish of Roquefort, the home of Françouneto. It will not be exaggerating to say that in Gascony as in the Franco-Provençal zone (Jura, French-speaking Switzerland, northern Alps, etc.) the production of hail and storms is, between the fourteenth and seventeenth centuries, a magical, witch-like and already diabolical activity that is very well established. It did not wait to appear until the myth of the *sabbat* had crystallised, after 1350 or 1400.

Françouneto and Bertrand d'Andiran are both inhabitants of Agen or its environs. They meet in a sinister environment of lightning and hail. This conjunction is not due to any mysterious coincidence. With three centuries between them, it is just that these two are situated in a long series of supernatural activities, concerned with hail and storms, which are specific, in the Agenais, to the rural witch and even the urban magician. Every town in the south of France, Agen included, remained to a large extent involved in agriculture and wine-production, and consequently with an economy vulnerable to hail, between the fourteenth and the eighteenth centuries.

In this connexion, Monseigneur J. M. Vidal, who edited the Papal document on Bertrand d'Andiran,[69] mentions the traditional activity of the *tempestarius*, the magician or sorcerer who is able to bring about dangerous bouts of bad weather:

> In some places, instead of punishing these men, it was decided to take them into paid service. Moissac, for example, in 1448, had its *tempestarius*, whose job it was to control the weather in the region, or, at least, to keep storms away from it – *vira la malino*, as it was put in the local idiom.[70]

Pursuing the same line of research, but in a different area, let us now leave the Agenais and Gascony for Switzerland and the diocese of Lausanne. The Alpine borderlands thus evoked are essential to a history of witchcraft, for in these mountains Teutonic and Romance cultures, Germanic and Franco-Provençal traditions come into contact in ways that are fertile at both the popular and the learned levels. Hail-makers and werewolves swarm there, from way back. Here it was that crystallised, between 1375 and 1450, on a foundation of elements both rural and scholarly, the new conception of the *sabbat*, which was destined subsequently to enjoy immensely wide diffusion, through treatises on demonology and through their readers, many of whom were priests or magistrates. We shall meet, in the German-speaking marches of the diocese of Lausanne, a person named Stedelen. He helps us to decipher, historically, the genesis of that stereotype of witchcraft which the good people of Roquefort were one day to apply to Françouneto or those like her.

The trial of Stedelen, a native of Boltigen, in the Simmenthal,* diocese of Lausanne, was 'conducted by a secular judge, Pierre de Greyerz (Gruyères), who represented the authority of Bern.'[71] The date of the case lies between 1397 and 1406. Stedelen, 'a great sorcerer', had confessed to his *maleficia*: for example, he had caused seven successive miscarriages or still-births to be suffered by a certain woman.[72] In the peasant home of this woman and her husband, with its adjacent accommodation for the farm animals, Stedelen likewise caused all the mares to miscarry. These catastrophes took place, naturally, in the same years as those of the miscarriages suffered by the mistress of the house. Stedelen achieved his aim, he said, by placing a lizard under the threshold of the wretched couple. It was only necessary, he added, to remove this lizard for fecundity to return to the inhabitants of the unfortunate household. Investigation was accordingly carried out under this threshold, but no lizard, or 'serpent', was discovered, doubtless because it had been reduced to dust. Nevertheless, care was taken to remove the soil and dust found there. At once, 'in that same year, fecundity was restored to the wife and to all the mares belonging to the farm,' which had previously been attacked by Stedelen. (Incidentally, we see that the sorcerer had, in this case, acted against the household of a fairly well-to-do peasant, the owner of farm-animals, including mares.)

Moreover, this Stelelen possessed, when he wished, a remarkable capacity. He could remove from his neighbour's fields, without anyone noticing, a third of the manure, the hay or the corn. After removing these materials he transferred them, still by magical means, to his own holding (*ad proprium agrum*). Our sorcerer was thus himself a peasant, too, since he cultivated arable land (*ager*). Stedelen also caused formidable downpours of hail (*grandines vastissimas*) and harmful storms, accompanied, in the approved manner, by lightning (*cum fulminibus*). He threw into the water, unnoticed by anyone and, in particular,

* A Swiss valley in the eastern, German-speaking part of the former diocese of Lausanne, north of the Bernese Alps.

by the parents who were present, children who were walking near this water. He spread sterility among human beings and horses alike. He injured his neighbours in their property and in their persons. He caused horses to go mad or become frantic while being ridden. He moved through the air from one place to another. He gave off foul odours when they were about to seize him. He induced an ungovernable trembling in the hands and in the souls of those who sought to take him prisoner. He made manifest things that were hidden from others. He foretold the future, or some parts of it. He struck with a thunderbolt someone he wanted to kill. Finally, he procured many other disasters, which descended like plagues (*pestifera*).

We do not know whether Stedelen belonged to an actual lineage of sorcerers. In any case, he did belong to a symbolic, or pedagogic, lineage, being the pupil of one Scavius and the fellow-pupil of one Hoppo, who together made of him a master of spells. Scavius succeeded, before the eyes of his friends, in changing himself into a rat or a mouse: in this way he escaped from, or slipped supernaturally out of the hands of, enemies who sought to kill him. They had managed eventually to dispose of Scavius only by taking him by surprise: he was pierced with pikes and swords through a window, when he least expected it.

Stedelen is relevant to our subject. This personage who, across time and space, comes to us out of the cold of the Alpine borderlands at the end of the disturbed fourteenth century is absolutely homologous to the three or four Gascon witches we have described at length in the preceding pages. He is even closer to Françouneto than are Marie de Sansarric or Gérarde Mimalé.

Let us recapitulate. Like our three women, or members of their lineages, Stedelen attacks the marriage-bed and its fruit, doing this in his own way, through miscarriages. He also attacks his neighbours. Not content with destroying *in utero* the results of conjugal love, he also causes small children (*infantes*) to disappear, by drowning them in supernatural fashion. Finally, he kills people, by thunderbolts or other means.

While attacking the human life-cycle, Stedelen, like the Gascon witches, also harms the fecundity of the soil. This quasi-professional abortionist indulges in the malicious delight of causing mares to miscarry. Moreover (and here we are again very close to Françouneto in the second section of her story), he transfers products (wheat, hay) and fertility (manure) from other people's fields to his own. Like Françouneto, he does not confine himself to vaguely manipulating 'the inclemencies of the weather' (rain, snow, storms), he is a master of the thunderbolts and hail. In this respect he is the exact equivalent of our Gascon witch. At the same time he is, in this matter, quite in line with local practice for, in the Alps and the Jura, both Germanic and Romance, there are innumerable hail-makers who also operate as werewolves.

Like our three Gascon ladies, and especially Françouneto, Stedelen makes men's hands useless, and disorders their minds, as also those of mares. The Gascons did their wicked work with poisons, odours and flowers. Stedelen, too, gives out odours, but his are frightful: they put off, or render helpless, enemies who are after him. Finally, like two of the three Gascons, Stedelen engages in the werewolf activity (change into animal form and magical flight). He moves supernaturally through the air. He does harm through a familiar in the form of a lizard. Scavius, his master, practises at one and the same time the change into animal form (as a rat) and the supernatural or disguised movement, thereby managing to slip through the fingers of those who try to catch him. Like the three Gascons, Stedelen operates in a world of neighbours, of familiar's and of people who are peasants like himself. He belongs, as do the Gascons, to a lineage of sorcerers, though, in his case, it is not a lineage of blood but a symbolical, pedagogical one.

Stedelen's confessions were wrested from him by torture, and this means that, in him, we are not necessarily dealing (far from it) with a genuine sorcerer. Françouneto, too, is unwilling to admit that she is a witch, and she succeeds in avoiding the label they want to stick on her. We are confronted in both cases with a stereotype which ill-intentioned persons from the rural community or the magistracy try to fix upon an individual concerning whom it is of minor importance whether he or she is guilty or not. In Françouneto's time the stereotype is already well defined. It includes rural elements (hail and various spells) and elements of scholarly origin (the witch-to-be gives herself to the Devil).

In the years 1380–1450 matters are even clearer, for we are then present, if not at the birth, then at least at the crystallisation of the stereotype – that crystallisation of which Nyder, who reports the Stedelen case, is, more generally, one of the advocates. This new cultural complex involved authentically ancient elements, drawn from the rural and popular world: *maleficium* directed against human beings at every age and in a variety of situations, and other *maleficia*, effected through hail and storms, directed at men's belongings, whether in the form of animals or in that of plants (grain, hay, vines). Be it noted in this context that Stedelen, like Françouneto and the Mimalés, is also capable of promoting fecundity, but only for home use, since he selfishly transports to his own field the agricultural riches he has taken from the lands of others.

The authentically rural elements incorporated in the stereotype of the sorcerer and the *sabbat* also include the manipulation of hail and thunderbolts together with the emission of evil odours and the use of the old peasant myth which for convenience we call that of the werewolf, a myth close to classical shamanism (change into animal form and magical flight).

As against this, the crystallisation of the stereotype relating to witches that takes place between about 1350 and 1450 also includes factors that have nothing to do with the mediaeval peasantry. They are drawn from a learned form of Christianity, or from the arguments this doctrine formerly used in relation to heretics, lepers, and Jews.[73] The country sorcerers served, in their turn, as a receptive target for these deadly arguments. I have in mind charges such as ritual cannibalism (eating of babies), the organised formation of sects of sorcerers grouped in hellish hierarchies under the suzerainty of Satan, and, soon, *sabbats*, with humble kisses on the Devil's backside bestowed by the new sectaries, thus inspired by a sort of 'feudalism' in bad taste. From this standpoint we see that Stedelen and the three Gascons stand much closer to the ancient rural roots of the *maleficium* than to the superstructure, learned or calumniatory, which the demonologists imposed upon it, to the extent of developing it in an exaggerated way in their treatises.

Stedelen and our three witches, among hundreds of others less known to us, have their feet firmly planted in the soil, or even in the dungheap. Their heads barely emerge among the learned and pernicious constructions of which inquisitors and judges were so fond. The witch-stereotype of which our four characters bear the mark is made up, so far as they are concerned, of a rural substance much anterior to the definitive late-mediaeval crystallisation of the stereotype.

However that may be, independently of these beginnings, the stereotype took shape, to last for several centuries, during the terrible last phase of the Middle Ages when destructive plagues and frightful crises forced the men of those days, whether ignorant or educated, to re-think or re-interpret their destiny, the tragedy of their lives. They helped themselves to do this by drawing on ancient elements in their culture (the werewolf, the hail-maker) and also by using the cogitations of the most learned men of the time, who produced ideas that were new and deadly. Each of our characters personifies, in one way or another, this cultural and stereotyped complex, but all of them stress the rural and ill-educated aspect of the phenomenon, in which mere spell-casting bulks biggest. Stedelen is a sort of conservative mutant who belongs to the initial phase of crystallisation (around 1400). Marie de Sansarric illustrates the full force of the phenomenon (around 1600–09). Françouneto, fortunately for her, is already on the forward slope of the decline, now beginning (around 1600–1700), in acceptance of the stereotype which threatens to overwhelm her. The Mimalés coincide, if not with the reduction of witchcraft to folklore status, at least to the de-criminalising of country magicians, as this was resolutely practised by the magistrates under Louis XVI. Hence the contrasting outcomes of these cases. Stedelen was burnt by order of the judges. Marie de Sansarric was stabbed by her husband. Françouneto was saved *in extremis* through a man's love. Finally, the Mimalés were able to thumb their noses at those who defamed them.

It took three centuries to neutralise that toughly-resistant stereotype, which was for so long a bringer of death.

PART TWO

Françouneto

prose translation of the French version of 1842

Dedication to the town of Toulouse
1840

When I saw breaking the pale dawn of this month which brings to blossom the flowers of poetry and of may and flax, I said softly to myself: 'O Toulouse, Toulouse! How I long to visit your green lawns and deck with buttercups the tomb of Goudelin!' And, buttercups in hand, as soon as I saw that day had come, I set out for you, as pilgrim and troubadour.

At first your famous Capitole, your palaces and your many churches, your great name as the 'City of Learning', made me crouch with fear. But when your people and your gentlefolk, like worthy sons of the Garonne, made our resonant language ring in my ears, I felt my fear waver and vanish. I spoke in my language, too, you listened, and then, at a great festival, you named me 'Son of Toulouse and brother of Goudelin'.

Great God! Am I like him, then? Goudelin, who lies in the Capitole? How proud I am to be compared to him! In my vainglory I would wish that his songs and mine may cause us, one day, to be taken for twins!

Meanwhile, O Toulouse, filled with hope, I plait the corn-stalks of my gratitude and bring you my wreath. Oh, it is not very big, elsewhere I should even blush to reveal the poverty of what I have to offer. But in this place I have no fear: I am your son, I am bold, for I know that, everywhere, a mother is always indulgent towards her child!

Françouneto

Section One

The votive festival at Roquefort – The prettiest of all – The soldier and the shepherds – A kiss and a slap – Pascal's courage – Marcel's fury – A great oath.

> But, great gentlemen, if you wish to depict shepherds
> as they are, then become peasants yourselves!

It was in the time when, in this place, Blaise the Bloody fell upon the Protestants with great back-handed blows and hewed them in pieces: when, in the name of a God of mercy, he deluged the land with blood and tears. But now he was tired. No more was the musket or the culverin to be heard firing on the hillside. That wretched man had, in order to uphold the Cross, which was in no more danger then than now, slaughtered and strangled enough people to fill up all the wells. The land towards Fumel and Penne was loaded with corpses. Almost all – children, fathers, mothers – were dead. His executioners drew breath, and the tiger himself, exhausted, got down from his horse and returned to his warlike castle with its threefold bridge and moat, knelt down to make his prayer of devotion and took communion, while still covered in the innocent blood with which he was at last sated.

Meanwhile the shepherds and the young shepherdesses, though they at first took fright at the mere name of 'Huguenot', nonetheless still carried on their flirtations, and in a hamlet at the foot of another castle, one Sunday, a troop of lovers were dancing at the votive festival of Roquefort. They hailed, to the sound of the fife, both St Jacques and the month of August, that lovely month which, every year, by the warmth of its sun and the freshness of its dew, causes the figs and the grapes to come to ripeness.

Never was seen such a splendid festival! Under the great parasol of leaves where each year the people meet, every space is full and more than full. From the height of the rocks and from the depth of the valleys, from Montagnac and Sainte-Colombe, crowds flock in abundantly. They come, they come! And still the sun is blazing down. All will find room, for there, you know, the meadows serve as chambers and the mounds as stools.

How pleasant! The heat makes the air quiver. There is nothing more agreeable, though, than to see all these fife-players piping away, while the dancers spin round. See the waffles and cracknels being brought out of the baskets! Oh, look! Cool lemonade! How eagerly they drink it, gushing from the bottle! What a crowd round the Punch-and-Judy show! What a crowd, too, round the merchant who is beating cymbals together! Crowds, crowds everywhere! . . . But who is this arriving? Oh, good! Here comes the young queen of the fields! It is she, Françouneto! A few words about her, if I may.

In town as in country, you know that, everywhere, there is one pearl of love above every other. Well, all together join in naming this girl as the prettiest of all in the canton.

But do not suppose, gentlemen, that she is melancholy, that she sighs, that she is white as a lily, that her eyes are pale, half-closed and blue, or that her body is thin, bowed by languor like the willow that weeps beside a clear stream. You would make a big mistake there, gentlemen. Françouneto has two lively eyes like two bright stars. It seems that one might pluck roses by handfuls from her rounded cheeks. Her hair is brown and curly. Her mouth is like a cherry. Her teeth would make snow seem dark. Her little feet are shapely. Her legs are slim and light. In short, Françouneto was the very paragon of beauty, grafted on to a beautiful woman's body here below.

All this, in the families that were now arriving by fits and starts, though it made the girls furious, made the boys sigh. Poor boys! Oh, they loved her, all of them, to the point that their fingernails would drop off. All gazed at her, adoring her as a priest adores the cross. The girl enjoys this and her brow beams with pleasure.

And yet a feeling of resentment starts up within her. Her bouquet of honour lacks the finest flower. Pascal, whom everyone praises, Pascal, the handsomest and the best singer, seems to avoid her and to look on her without love. Françouneto bears a grudge against him for that, and thinks she hates him, whenever he comes into her mind. But in her terrible vengefulness she only waits for the moment when she can dart the glance that will enchain him. What else would you have? From the beginning of time, a girl so greatly desired becomes coquettish or conceited. And all of that was to be seen already in this girl. She was a little bit conceited, and was turning into a coquette – but not a cunning coquette, although, whereas she loved no-one, more than one boy thought she loved him.

Her grandmother often said to her: 'My child, the country is not the town, a drawing-room is not a meadow. You well know that we have promised you to the soldier. Marcel loves you and counts on marrying you. So, restrain your flightiness! A girl who wants to have every man ends by having none!' Oh dear! the mischievous creature quickly gave her grandmother a caress, jumped up and uttered the well-known saying: 'I've time enough to fall in love, grandma: meanwhile, she who has only one has nobody!'

All this resulted in making many girls jealous and many boys grief-stricken and wretched. Yet these shepherds did not compose such songs, both learned and moving, as others, dying, would go and carve on a poplar or a willow. Oh, heavens, no, they could not write. Besides, these innocent creatures, whose heads were turned by love, preferred to suffer long and stay alive. But how many tools were grasped the wrong way round, how many vines were badly pruned, how many branches poorly lopped, how many furrows cut crookedly!

Now that you know the crazy young thing, do not let her out of your sight. Oh, how she spins round! Alone with Etienne she dances the rigadoon of honour. Everyone drinks her in with his eyes, his mouth agape. Everyone makes eyes at her. The little sly-boots, not missing any of these tributes, dances all the better for them. Lord, when she straightens up, the wild thing, with her lizard head, her Spanish foot and her wasp-like waist, when she glides, turns and leaps, and the breeze stirs her blue kerchief slightly – oh, yearning to plant two kisses on her cheek, all lips are twitching.

One of them will achieve that aim, though, for the custom is to kiss one's partner on leaving her when she is tired of dancing. But a young girl is never tired until she wants to be, and, already, Guillaume, Jean, Louis, Pierre and Paul have been discarded, out of breath, without having won the right to kiss her.

Another takes their place, it is her intended, Marcel. He is Montluc's favourite, a huge man, wearing a sword, a uniform, and a cockade in his hat. Straight as the letter i, with a fine gait, he has a good heart but a bad head – reckless, getting into everything at random, boastful, always up to his tricks, unwelcome as caterpillars, Marcel, who is mad on Françouneto, pesters all the girls, trying to make her jealous; and if he so much as touches one, the conceited ass exaggerates as he talks of his success.

He has behaved like this to such an extent that now the girl wants to see no more of him. He knows this, gets jealous, and, always clumsy, proclaims that she loves him, does everything to make this believed, and, the other day, in a certain place, he exclaimed, as he smashed a glass, that he would not let anyone else kiss her.

1. Jacques Jasmin at 44, by Sébastien Cornu, 13 May 1842 (Agen Museum; photograph René Dreuil).

2. Solemn procession of the Consuls of Agen, together with *Angèles*, to the miraculous Virgin of Bon-Encontre, by Fournier, 1707. Below, left, the miraculous finding of the statuette of the Virgin (Agen Museum; photograph Pierre Capot).

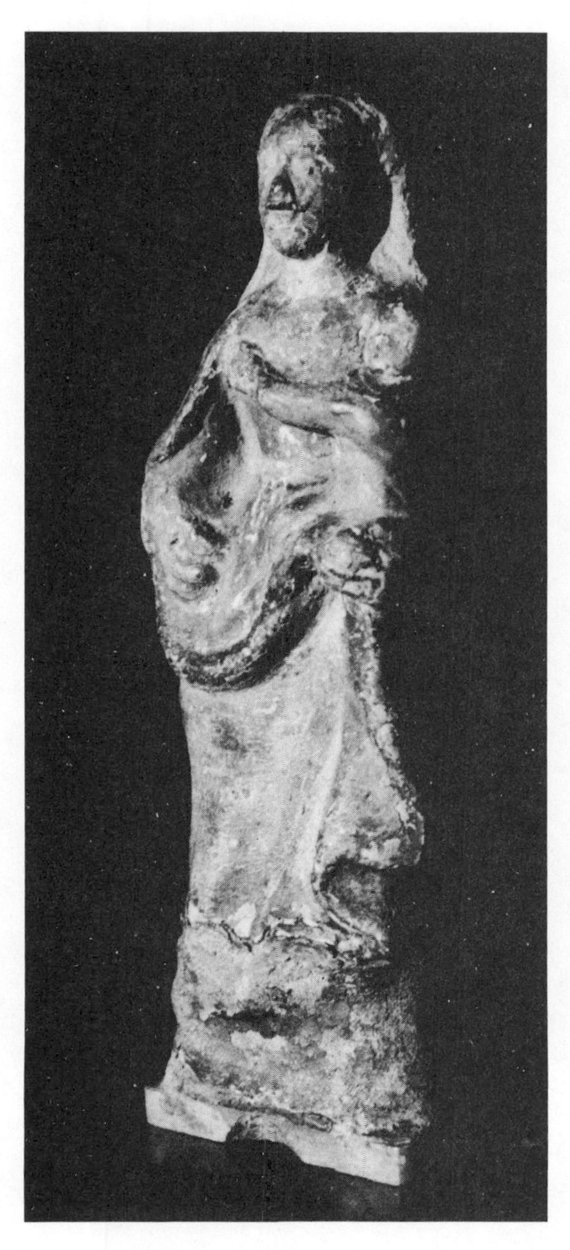

3. Mediaeval miracle-working statuette of the Virgin, kept at the shrine of Bon-Encontre, about five kilometres south-east of Agen (photograph René Dreuil).

120

4. Marriage contract of the Comtesse de Laugnac, whose maiden name was Serène de Durfort, 8 March 1618 (Archives départementales, Lot-et-Garonne [ADLG] B 53, fol. 120 recto).

5. 'The Mandrake', by Abraham Bosse (1602–76).

You can imagine how, as they watch them dancing, the crowd, among whom the Devil is at work, pushes forward, one person bumping into another, all keen to see if the handsome soldier will win the contested kiss. At first the dancer smiles at his intended, saying 'please' with his eyes, but she answers nothing and only bounds the more. Marcel, cut to the quick, sees that she has to be brought to heel, and the vainglorious fellow, who is one of those who like better a kiss taken in public than twenty given willingly in private, makes play with his knees and his shoes, hastening the dance. Oh, just to tire her out, the soldier would give his sword, his hat, his woollen galloons – even golden ones, if he had them!

But when the game is not to her liking, how strong a weak girl can be! This one, instead of succumbing, gets him out of breath, exhausts him. Marcel mulishly loses his temper. Suddenly he turns purple, can dance no more, is about to fall down. Zing-zang! Pascal rushes forward and occupies his place. And he has only taken two steps and changed sides when Françouneto laughs, has had enough, stops dancing, and standing before the shepherd, leans her cheek forward for him to kiss. Oh, he doesn't keep her waiting!

At once the crowd cries out, and hands clap like flails, applauding Pascal, who is quite embarrassed by all this.

What a spectacle for the soldier, who really loved Françouneto! He trembles at that kiss. Rising and eyeing Pascal from head to foot, he exclaims in a thunderous voice: 'You took my place too soon, peasant!' And the brutal fellow, following up the insult, slaps Pascal's cheek, and smartly, too.

Alas, how quickly troubles can wither the sweetest happiness! Kisses and slaps! Glory and shame! Light and darkness! Fire and ice! Life and death! Heaven and hell! All this shakes Pascal's ardent soul. But when a man finds himself so basely treated, to avenge an insult fearlessly he does not need to be a gentleman or a soldier. No! Just look at him! The storm is not more terrible. His eyes dart lightning, his voice thunders, and his clenched fists bring down upon Marcel, before he can turn away, a whole rain of blows. Of what use is it for the soldier to rear up and half-draw his sword? Pascal, who seems to have grown taller, seizes him round the waist, grasps him in his arms, and with firm strength throws him to the ground under his feet, broken and stunned.

'There! The peasant allows you to live!' says Pascal, releasing him. 'Finish him off, for you are covered with blood!' a thousand voices then shout to him. And, indeed, in his fit of rage, Pascal has wounded himself in the wrist, it is not clear how.

'Never mind! I give him quarter all the same. When he has been struck down, the bad man deserves pity.' 'No, no! Finish him off! Hew him in pieces!' the populace keep shouting. 'Stand back, peasants, for you are in the wrong,' cries a gentleman gleaming with gold. Everyone at once makes way for him. It is Montluc, who has come to see what is going on, accompanied by the Baron de Roquefort.

No more amusement now. The frightened girls have fled, two by two, like hares across the fields. And whereas, a moment after, the young shepherds were accompanying the handsome and brave Pascal with the sound of fifes, as though it were his wedding day, Marcel, angrier than ever, wanted a fight to the death and was blazing with fury, but a gesture from his lord kept him motionless. Then he ground his teeth and said in a low voice:

'They love her and do all they can to hinder my love. She lends herself to this, and makes a joke of it. Very well! By Marcel, my patron saint, they shall pay for it! And Françouneto shall have no husband but me!'

Section Two

The smith in love – A mother's woes – The unwinding party – Pascal's song – The sorcerer from the Black Wood – The girl sold to the Devil.

One, two, three months went by in festivals. But dances, games, harvest-homes and all gay pleasures came to an end with the leaves on the trees. With the coming of winter, everything took on a sad and aged look beneath the vault of heaven. Soon, no-one was brave enough to go into the fields by night. Filled with gloom, everybody huddled round big blazing fires. Werewolves and sorcerers, who cause both house and cottage to tremble with fear, were thought to hold their *sabbat* under the bare branches of the elms and around the ricks.

At last Christmas came, with its bright morning, and Jean the town-crier announced in the hamlet, waving his arms: 'Stir yourselves, girls, come to the Buscou, an evening party for unwinding yarn, on Friday, New Year's Eve!'

Ah, my dear, how the boys and girls spread around everywhere the news the old man had brought. This news was of the sort which, quick as a bird, lends wings to words. The air had hardly been warmed by the sun's rays when the news was being puffed in every direction, from hearth to hearth, from table to table, from stove to stove.

Friday came, and while drizzle fell, beside a cold forge a mother mourned, then spoke to her son, and this is what she said:

'Have you then forgotten the day when, in front of the shop, I saw you appear, to the sound of music, gloomy, wounded and covered with blood? Yet I, poor woman, have suffered enough as a result. That wound festered and for a long time we feared for your arm. Please don't go out this evening. I dreamt of flowers. What do they warn me of, Pascal? Of troubles and tears?'

'Mother, you are too fearful, in your eyes everything looks black. But Marcel comes no more now, so why tremble?'

'All the same, take good care of yourself! The sorcerer from the Black Wood prowls near here. You know the great misfortunes he caused us last winter. Well, it is said that a soldier was seen, the day before yesterday, coming out of his grotto at dawn. If it was Marcel, beware, my son! Every mother has laid relics on her son. Here, take mine – and, again, believe me, don't go anywhere.'

'Good Lord, I only want to go out for an hour, to see my friend Thomas.'

'Your friend! Say, rather, to see Françouneto, for you love her, too. You think that I don't see it. Oh, but I read it in your eyes. You don't want to upset me, so you sing, and act happy, but in secret you weep, you suffer, you are wretched. And I am sorry on your account, I am wasting away. Something tells me that a great unhappiness lies in wait for you. When she holds you, she takes possession of you. It is as though she is a witch. Now, with all her silliness, what does she want? What is she after? Riches? She has had twenty suitors and refused them all. But she seems taken with that rich man Laurent, from Brax. It is said that they will soon be betrothed. Oh, what a lot of embarrassment she will cause when she is with him this evening, that conceited hussy. Give her up, Pascal! It's for your own good. She would snap her fingers at a smith whose father is old, ill and poor. Because we are poor, as you know. We have lost everything. We have only one scythe left. Oh, things have been bad with us since you fell ill. Now that you are well again, boy, work! What am I saying? We shall continue to suffer Rest if you wish, but, for the love of God, don't go out this evening!'

And the poor, tormented mother wept as she implored her son, who, leaning against the forge, stifled a sigh within his downcast soul, and said: 'We are poor, that's true. I had forgotten all that . . . I'll go and work, mother!'

Two moments later the anvil was resounding, but even the simplest observer would have noticed, seeing the iron so often struck at the wrong angle, that if the smith who was striking it had one hammer in his hand, he had a hundred in his head.

From the Buscou, however, few were absent, and soon, coming from the four corners of the district, everyone sought to unwind his skein at the lovers' festival.

In a big room where a hundred reeling-machines, doubly laden, were already turning, girls and boys were tiring out their fingers, quickly winding bundles of thread as fine as hair.

Now it's over, white wine and flatcakes fall, seething, into glasses and bowls, giving off hot fumes which spark the gunpowder of enjoyment. Ah, if the prettiest girl were the hardest worker, I should already have mentioned Françouneto, but the queen of the games lags behind everyone else when it comes to work, and it is only now that she is going to queen it as she should.

Oh, how this dark-haired girl carries on! Now she is going to rule the crowd absolutely. You would take her for three women in one. She dances, she talks, she sings, she does everything. When she sings, you would think her a turtle-dove; when she talks, you would say she has the mind of an angel; when she dances, you would think she has a sparrow's wings. And she sang and talked and danced that evening in a way that would turn the soberest of heads!

Her triumph is complete, all eyes are upon her. The poor boys are helpless, and the eye of the girl who is bewitching them flames and sparkles as she sees how they are bewitched. Then Thomas stands up and, fixing eyes burning with love upon our coquette, he sings, in a soft voice, this new song:

The Siren with the Heart of Ice

I

Playful shepherdess, siren with a heart of ice, tell us, oh tell us, when we shall hear the hour sound when you will soften. You always act so crazily, and when you flutter about, the crowd you rule takes your road and follows you.

But none of this, my girl, can bring you happiness. What good is it to be loved when one doesn't know how to love?

II

You have seen our joy increase when the sun shines. Well, each Sunday when we see you appear, you give us more pleasure than the sun. We love your angelic voice, your swallow-like movements, your ladylike air, your mouth, your hair, your eyes.

But none of this, my girl, can bring you happiness. What good is it to be loved when one doesn't know how to love?

III

Our fields are sad when they are bereft of you. The hedges and meadows no longer smell sweet. The sky is no longer so blue. When you, crazy young creature, come back to us, languor flies away, everyone feels that he is returning to life, and we want to cover your tiny fingers with kisses!

But none of this, my girl, can bring you happiness. What good is it to be loved when one doesn't know how to love?

IV

Your turtle-dove, who has fled from you, teaches you a lesson. She is in the woods, where she forgets you, and where she has grown prettier since she has made love there. Through love everything throbs: follow where it leads, since it invites you. Otherwise, the best days of your life will be barren and lost.

Only Love, my girl, can bring you happiness: It is everything to be loved – but only when one knows how to love!

The singer has finished. The crowd, pleased with his song, shouts its appreciation and claps. What a fine song! How well it goes! Who wrote it? 'Pascal!' Thomas replies. 'Bravo! Good old Pascal!' the crowd exclaims.

Françouneto says nothing: but how she enjoys this, how proud she is! What it is to be loved by everyone, and to hear this proclaimed, and in a song, and in front of everyone!

However, she grows serious as she thinks about Pascal. 'What a fine man he is! He has everything in his favour, there is no-one like him . . . How he describes love! . . . All the girls love him, no doubt . . . And his song – how touching it is.' She knows everything already: but since he loves her, why does he hide himself away so much? Suddenly turning round, she says: 'Thomas, I long to see him and compliment him. Where is he?' 'Oh, he has to stay at home,' says jealous Laurent, who is bored with all this. 'Pascal won't be able to compose songs any more. Poor fellow, everything is going to rack and ruin with him. His father is confined to bed, almost an invalid. He is in debt all round. The baker won't let him have any bread!'

Françouneto goes pale and says: 'And he so good! Poor boy! How I pity him! He is in a wretched state indeed.' 'Ah, yes,' replies Laurent, pretending to be kind, 'they say he is living on alms.' 'You lie!' says Thomas: 'May your tongue stick fast! Pascal has been doing badly in his business since he was wounded in the arm on account of Françouneto, but he is better now, and, provided no enemy hinders him, he will get things back to normal by his own efforts, for he is courageous and hard-working!'

If anyone had taken a good look, he would have seen tears in Françouneto's eyes.

'Let's play hunt-the-knife!' two girls have cried. The young people sit in a row and the knife is hidden. Françouneto has it. One of the girls, it's Mariannette, winks and asks: 'Laurent, have you got my knife?' 'Why, no, young lady!' 'Well, get up, then, and look for it!' Laurent, looking hopeful, asks: 'Françouneto, have you got my knife?' 'No, sir!' 'Yes, you have, you fibber! You have! Get up! Give me a kiss!'

If a finch, caught in a net, finds a little hole in it, she will fly off into the osier beds. Like that bird, Françouneto escapes, and Laurent runs after her. Desire for her kiss inflames him. He wants it, he will have it – but the poor boy, just as he is about to grasp her, stumbles, slips, falls and breaks an arm.

Already the whole scene is sombre; but now, oh, what a dreadful thing happens! Suddenly they hear a door creak at the end of the room, and an old man with a beard down to his waist comes in like a ghost. Heavens, they are caught: it is the sorcerer from the Black Wood who stands before them! 'Rash creatures!' he says to the young people: 'I have come down from my rock in order to open your eyes, because your fate concerns me. You love Françouneto, you say. Well, unlucky ones, learn that her father, who was in a wretched state when she was in her cradle, went over to the Huguenots and sold her to the Devil. Her mother died of sorrow. And the Devil, who goes ever on his way, now keeps watch over the girl he purchased. Hidden from sight, he follows her everywhere, and you have seen how he punished Pascal and Laurent, who kissed her. You have been warned. Woe to whoever weds her! On the first night, when the bridegroom is about to lift the crown of flowers from her brow, the Devil will take possession of her. The Devil will even appear in person, and wring the husband's neck!'

The Sorcerer says no more. Sprays of sparks darting from his fiery hands brilliantly light up his face, covered with warts. Then he is seen in a ring. He spins round four times and orders the door to open. The door creaks and opens, and the bearded man vanishes.

No big words, no resounding and re-echoing comparisons could depict the way those girls and boys look, as they stand there, seemingly turned to stone. Only Françouneto gives sign of life. Beneath the misfortune that has come upon her the poor girl does not bow at once, for she hopes that they will look on it all as a joke.She laughs in a friendly way and takes two steps forward. But when she sees them quickly fall back from her, and they cry: 'Go away!' great sadness comes over her eyes and she cannot breathe. Suddenly, losing consciousness, she falls headlong to the floor.

So ended a party which had begun so gaily. On the morrow, New Year's Day, there was much murmuring about what had happened, and this continued for long after, spreading from cottage to house and from meadow to ploughland.

Ah, fear of the Devil, who nowadays can hardly find a victim, was terrible at that time, especially in country places.

Therefore, everything awoke, and everyone called to mind how, at Françouneto's house, people had often in the past heard the sound of chains clanking; how, then, her father disappeared; how her mother, broken by sorrow, died as a madwoman. And how, thereafter, all went well for Françouneto. No bad luck came her way. Her *faisande* [smallholding] without anyone to work on it, brings in more than a *métairie* [a farm held on a share-cropping lease], and when all the rest of the district is under frost or hail, her land is covered with grapes and corn.

That was quite enough. The youngsters believed it all. Girls, mothers and grandmothers improved upon it. Soon, the children trembled when they heard her name. And when the poor girl, bowing her head, went out on an errand for her grandmother, she found packs of them, shouting from afar, as they ran off: 'There she is, the girl sold to the Devil!'

Section Three

The girl of Estanquet – The bad dream – A grandmother's advice – The consecrated bread and the snub – Redress and love – First thoughts of love – Great sorrows of love – Appeal to the Virgin.

Around the hamlet of Estanquet, on the banks of that stream, so cool, whose clear water chatters over pebbles in the shade all year through, a pretty girl was picking flowers last summer on the greensward, and she made the birds jealous with the merry sound of her voice as she sang.

Why does she sing no more? Hedges and meadows are now green, and the nightingales come to tease her with their songs even in her very garden. Has she, perhaps, left her house? No, her hat of fine straw lies there, on its bench, but it is no longer decorated with a ribbon. Nor does her little garden look as it used to: her rake and her watering-can lie across the crushed daffodils. The branches of the rose-bushes fall, higgledy-piggledy, upon big stems of groundsel, and her much-praised avenues are choked with weeds.

Oh, what is happening? Where is that lively girl? Her house gleams through the bushy branches of the hazel-trees. Let us go near. The door is open. Let's not make a noise, they might hear . . . Ah, I see her grandmother asleep in the armchair. I see, also, behind the window, the girl of Estanquet. But she is weeping! What is the matter? Tears are falling on her little hand. Is there darkness in her heart?

Oh, yes, darkness indeed! For it is Françouneto, as you have already guessed.

There she is, then, poor girl, quite crushed beneath the blow that has struck her. She has gone to her room to weep, and her heart is never free from her sorrow. Girls often weep for nothing, and then go out for a stroll, but *her* woe is too great, and *her* trouble is one that is not softened by weeping. Daughter of a Huguenot, one of the forbidden church, and sold to the Devil! Oh, she is quite struck down by this news! To be sure, her grandmother tells her: 'Child, it isn't true!' But she does not listen. Only her father can refute the story, if indeed it is a lie: but nobody knows where he is, and when she sees that she is alone, she is filled with such fear that she believes the story.

'What a change of fate!' she said: 'I, who used to be so happy – I, the queen of the meadows, whose praise was so often sung, the one for whose pleasure all the boys would have walked barefoot into a snake's nest – I, to be despised and accursed, the terror of the district! . . . And Pascal? He, too, avoids me like the plague. Yet I was sorry for him in his frightful poverty. Now that he knows that I am unhappy, perhaps he isn't at all sorry for me? . . .'

She was mistaken, and today her sorrow is less than it was. She has learnt that Pascal defends her against everyone. That cheers her up. It is like two drops of balm for her aching young heart. And so, to make her misery less painful, she thinks of Pascal, often and always.

A cry wrenches her from her thoughts. She runs quickly to her grandmother, and finds her awake. She hears her saying: 'The wall isn't on fire? So it was only a dream. Ah, dear Lord, how glad I am!'

'Grandmother, tell me, what was the matter? What were you dreaming about?' 'Poor child, it was at night, and brutal men were setting fire to our house. You were crying, you were tiring yourself out as you tried to save me, but you couldn't, and we were both burnt. How I suffered, child! To comfort me, come here, let me embrace you!' And the white-haired woman holds tenderly for a long time, in her thin arms, the brown-haired girl who smiles at her, kissing and caressing her. Then, after a thousand kisses, the old woman says to her, with a loving air:

'Françouneto, on her marriage-day your mother stepped out, betrothed, from the château, and we all know that. Madame gave her this place as her dowry, and so it is not to the Devil that you owe your well-being. It is true that when you were in your cradle, my angel, we heard every night, up there, a strange noise, and afterwards always found you out of your cradle, and on the edge of your little bed we saw three drops of congealed blood. But I remember that we had a Gospel read aloud, and all of that went away. This shows you that you were not sold to the Devil. That's only a nasty bouquet they've picked for you.* Courage! You are weeping like a child. Come, girl, believe your grandmother! You are prettier than ever. Start to show yourself again. Go for walks. A person who hides from enmity only gives more opportunities to ill-wishers. Besides, Marcel still has the same tender feelings for you. Secretly, he has told me that you can marry him whenever you wish . . . You don't love him! . . . But Marcel would give you support in your vulnerability. I am too old to do that. Come now! Tomorrow is Easter Day. Go to Mass. Pray there better than you have ever prayed before. Take the consecrated bread and cross yourself. I'm sure that God will give you back all the happiness you used to enjoy, and will prove, to your face, that he has not struck you from the number of his own!'

The suffering visage of the old woman was so lit up with hope that, clinging to her neck, the girl promised to do as she was asked, and so silence returned to the little white house.

Next morning, when everyone was singing the joyous *Hallelujah* in the church of St Pierre, they were greatly astonished to see Françouneto there, kneeling and saying her rosary, her eyes cast down. But, poor girl, she prays in vain to be spared. No girl will spare her: because they have seen both Marcel and Pascal turn round towards her, seeming to pity her, the others give her a terrible snub. Not a single one of them remains near her, so that she finds herself left alone in the middle of a big circle, like someone condemned, who bears her shame imprinted on her forehead. And that is not all that the poor child has to endure. Marcel's uncle, the churchwarden, comes forward in his purple long-tailed jerkin and, with the lofty air of a councillor, offers the congregation consecrated Easter bread. Françouneto, who has promised to take home a piece of it for her grandmother, crosses herself and is going to collect a double portion. But the basket of Grace, which stops before

* That's only a nasty story they've made up about you – Trans.

everybody else, passes her by, passes without letting her take her share of the bread of heaven.

What a terrible moment! A snub even more cruel than the first!

This time, she believes that God has driven her from his temple. She trembles, thinks herself lost, and is about to collapse: but a man, a boy, Pascal, who has never removed his eyes from her, Pascal, who today is taking the collection, Pascal, who had grasped what was up when he caught a glance exchanged between uncle and nephew, draws near, noiselessly and without fear, and on his gleaming plate, decorated with a lovely bunch of flowers, before the gaze of everyone, presents her with some consecrated bread.

What a sweet moment for Françouneto! Oh, it makes the blood leap within her! Warmth returns to her body, her soul trembles. It is as though the bread of a risen God, by touching her, has restored her to life. But why is her brow all flushed? Oh, it is because the angel of love has blown a little of his flame on to the hearth that was already smouldering in her soul. Oh, it is because something strange and new, quick as fire, sweet as honey, has come alight and is growing in her throbbing heart. Oh, it is because she is alive with a new life. Now she feels it and knows it, now she understands its magic. The crowd, the priest, everything vanishes from her sight. In God's house she sees one man alone, the man she has at last come to love, the man to whom she now says: 'Thank you!'

Let us now leave jealousy, as it emerges from the church of St Pierre, to snarl around the streets and create a threefold scandal by exaggerating what it has seen. Let us not lose sight of Françouneto, who is taking the consecrated bread to her grandmother and then shutting herself away in her little room, to be alone with her love.

First drop of dew in time of drought, first ray of sunshine in winter, you are not so sweet to the sad earth as this first flame of love to the heart of the fond girl! Transported with happiness, she forgets her troubles and gradually lets herself yield to the bright new joy of love!

Then, far from the sound of jealousy, she does what we all do – she dreams, with open eyes, and without stone or hammer she builds herself a little château where, close to Pascal, everything shines, glows and streams with happiness. Oh, the wise man was right who said: 'A suffering soul is more loving than any other.'

Françouneto, already on fire with the love that has mastered her, feels that she is in love for always. Everything smiles upon her. But, alas, the sweetness of love all too soon turns to bitterness. Suddenly she remembers, trembles, turns to ice. At the onset of a dreadful thought her little château is demolished. Poor girl, she had dreamt of love, but love is forbidden to her. The great sorcerer said so. The Devil bought her, and any man so bold as to marry her, after that threat from Hell, must find in his nuptial chamber only a grave . . . She would see Pascal die beside her! Pity, O Lord, have pity!

And the girl, her soul torn apart by the cruel torments she has suffered, falls to her knees, bathed in tears, before an image she possesses:

'Holy Virgin', she says, 'without you I am lost! For the power of love is carrying me away, and I have neither father nor mother, and everyone says that I have been sold to the Devil. Oh, take pity on me! Save me, if it is true! Or, if they who say it are wicked, let my soul know that that is so! And if I dare offer my candle to Our Lady, then, kind Virgin, show me that you receive it with pleasure!'

When a short prayer is sincere, it ascends quickly to heaven. Sure, therefore, that she had been heard, the girl kept thinking about her plan. Often it made her tremble, and fear deprived her of speech, but often, also, hope shone in her lifting heart like a flash of lightning in the night.

Section Four

The *Angèles* at Notre Dame – An offering to the Virgin – A thunderclap and a candle blown out – The storm at Roquefort – The hamlet stirred up – The fire at Estanquet – Pascal's triumph – Marcel's fury – A terrible danger – A mother's power – A bad head and a good heart.

Now, at last, the day has come which she so greatly fears and yet desires, and now, as the sun rises, long columns of girls dressed in white advance from all directions, to the sound of the bell. Soon, Notre-Dame, amidst a cloud of perfume, proudly assembles thirty hamlets in one place.

How many censers, crosses, bouquets and candles! How many banners! How many *Angèles*! Here we see Puymirol, Artiques, Astafort, Lusignan, Cardonnet, Saint-Cirq, Brax and Roquefort. But, this year, the girls from Roquefort have pride of place. Crowds of curious people have come out to watch them arrive, because the story of the girl sold to the Devil is already known everywhere, and they know that today she is coming to pray to the Virgin to protect her.

Close to, people laugh at one's trouble: farther off, they are not so unkind.

Here, everyone's soul is filled with her sorrow, everyone sympathises as they look upon her. They all would like a miracle to happen so as to help her, and wish that the Virgin may save her. She sees this and is glad. Her hope is enlivened. The voice of the people is the voice of God! Oh, how her heart beats as she enters the church! All around, the indulgence of the Virgin is to be seen. Sorrowing mothers, unhappy young people, orphaned girls, women without children, all are kneeling, holding their candles, before the image of the Virgin that an old priest in a surplice places on their lips, after which he blesses them.

si
cr
Hu

At
her a

To se
clench
them, a
ing dew

What wa
Alas, she
she holds
gave her.

'Poor bouqu
was happiness
you in my bos
happiness. Goc
this, but farewel
doom you along
yet today I feel th
you is such that n
earth, either causes

her. But death means nothing to me, so long as it spares you.'

'Françouneto, what are you so sad about?' exclaims her grandmother. 'You told me, laughing, that the Virgin accepted your gift. You said that you were very, very happy. And now I hear you moaning like a soul in torment. You have deceived me! Something happened to you today!' 'No, no, be reassured, grandmother, there is nothing wrong with me! On the contrary, I'm . . . I'm happy!' 'Ah, good, dear heart! With that word you comfort me. Alas, your sorrow is digging my grave. I spent a dreadful day today. That dream about a fire that I had recently keeps coming back to me, against my will! And then the storms frighten me, you know. Why, all this evening, a trifle has been enough to make me tremble!'

Suddenly voices ring out: 'Burn, burn! Everything must be burnt!' And the chinks in the old shutter gleam. Trembling, Françouneto goes to the door. Oh God, what does she see? By the terrible light of her burning straw-stack, a whole crowd of angry people are howling: 'Come on, we must make them get out! Let's drive away the old woman as well as the young one! Both are the causes of our ruin! Girl sold to the Devil, away with you, or we will burn you!'

On her knees, Françouneto appeals to the mob: 'My grandmother can hear you! You'll kill her! Have pity!'

But these wretches, blinded as they are, when they see her crying out to them, bareheaded, imagine that she is possessed by the Devil, and merely cry the louder: 'Out!' Already, the worst of them, as they draw near the edge of the dwelling, are brandishing lighted pieces of firewood.

'Stop, stop!' someone shouts, and, immediately, an angry man rushes in front of them. It is good Pascal who addresses them thus:

'Cowards! To make martyrs of these women, to burn their house so as to cause them more suffering, after they have suffered so much already! Are you all tigers, then, all you people here? Go back! The walls are hot already!'

'All right, but let them leave the district. They are possessed by the Devil. They are both Huguenots! God is punishing us for letting them stay here. Quick! Let the other one come out, or she will be burnt alive!' 'Wretches! Who is it who is setting you on? Ah, Marcel is coming. He has a grudge against her, don't trust him!' 'You lie,' says Marcel, as he arrives on the scene. 'I love her more than you do, you boaster. What are you doing for her, you with your heart so tender?' 'I have come to help her! I have come to defend her!' 'And I to marry her, in spite of everything, if she will have me!' 'I, too!' says Pascal, and without the slightest hesitation, before the eyes of his dumbfounded rival, he turns to the orphan and says to her, in a firm voice:

'Françouneto, there can be no more rest for you! The rage of these evil men lies in wait for you in village after village. But here are we two who love you, two men who are willing to brave death and hell in order to save you. If you want one or other of us, choose!' 'Oh, there can be no marriage! Pascal, I kill with my love. Go away, forget me, find happiness without me!'

'Happiness without you! No, no! I can no longer be happy without you. I love you too much, and if it is true that the Devil is your master, why, to die with you would be better than to live far from you!'

There can be no doubt that a beloved voice masters our tender thoughts as it wishes, nor that, when we are in the depths of despair, we are ready to dare all, with unbreakable courage. For the girl, carried away by his words, declares, before all that crowd: 'Oh, Pascal, I love you, and I wanted to die alone. But it is your wish, and I can no longer resist; if it be our fate, well, let us die together!'

This puts Pascal in heaven. The crowd shudders. The soldier is overwhelmed. Pascal goes up to him. 'I am happier than you. But you are a true man. Forgive me! I need a best man to lead me to my tomb. I have no friends any more: will you do this for me?' Marcel is silent, thinking. It can be seen that a battle is raging in his heart. Then, suddenly, his eyes shine and his brows knit. Silent, he gazes on Françouneto, grows pale as death, straightens himself, gives a half-laugh and says: 'Since *she* wishes it, I will be your best man!'

A fortnight later a notable wedding procession was descending the slope of the green hillside. In front were the handsome married couple. Curious people have come from every direction and many a place, and line the path three deep. They tremble for Pascal. Marcel marches ahead of all. His face shines with secret pleasure, and there is something in his glinting eye which cannot be defined.

It might seem that this day is his triumph. In any case, it had been his own wish to join in the celebration. To crown everything, he is giving a great banquet and ball in honour of his rival, spending his money freely. Everything is there, as much as anyone could wish – except for the noisy pleasures, for nobody sings and nobody laughs.

The bridegroom on the brink of his grave. His best man, pushing him towards it, while smiling kindly upon him. The setting sun. All this arouses pity in the people's hearts and all are filled with sorrow. They would like to save Pascal, but believe it to be too late, and all stand there not as at his wedding but as at his funeral. Bewitched by love, on the edge of the chasm, the couple have sacrificed their lives. No sound distracts them, they hold hands, and their eyes display the happiness of their mutual love.

At last, night has fallen.

Suddenly a frightened, bewildered woman flings herself on Pascal's neck. 'My son! My poor boy! Leave her: I have just been with the fortune-teller. Oh, quit your betrothed! The sieve turned: your death has been announced, and the bridal bedroom already smells of sulphur. Pascal, don't enter it! You are lost if you stay! And I, who love you so much, what will become of me if you die?'

Pascal feels his eyelids becoming moist, but only grasps more firmly the hand he holds as a pledge.

The poor mother sees this and falls at her son's feet. 'Ungrateful boy, I will not leave you! And if you are so brave, you will walk over my body before you go into their house! So, then, a wife is everything and a mother nothing! Oh, woe is me!' And everyone bursts into tears.

'Marcel,' says the bridegroom. 'How unhappy her unhappiness makes me! But love has mastered me and proves stronger. The hour has come. If misfortune strikes me down, oh, take care of my mother!'

'I can't go on with it! Your mother has disarmed me!' cries the soldier, wiping away a tear. 'Triumph, Pascal, and congratulate yourself! Françouneto was not sold to the Devil. All that is only a made-up story. But give thanks to your mother. If she had not come, you both would have died, and I as well.'

'What are you saying?' 'The truth. Listen.

'You certainly know how much I love her. For her I would, like you, give all the blood in my body. I thought she loved me, she possessed my soul and all. Yet she rejected me, though she knew she had been promised to me. I saw that you two were barring my path. In love, as in war, a trick is permissible. I paid the sorcerer to frighten you. He invented a fearful tale, and chance did the rest, so that I thought she was already as good as betrothed to me. But when we two asked at the same time for her hand, and when she braved everything for you and was at once ready to say that she loved you, that was too much! I decided that I, she and you must all three die. I was going shortly to lead you into the bridal bedroom and there, before the bed which I had loaded with explosives, I would have said: "You have nothing to fear from the Devil!" But then I would have spoken of the torment consuming me and said: "Cross yourselves! You must die, nevertheless!" And I would have blown up the two of you, along with myself! But, by her cries, your mother disarmed my anger: she reminds me of my own mother, whom I have lost. Live, Pascal, for your mother's sake! You have nothing more to fear from me. Your paradise now descends to earth. As for me, having no-one, I shall go back to my trade as a soldier, to heal me of this terrible love. Perhaps a cannon-ball is to be preferred to the great crime I was going to commit!'

He falls silent and walks away. Shouts of approval are heard. The happy couple tremble. Already, the stars are appearing in the clear sky. Oh, I put down my brush now, to take breath. I had the colours with which to depict distress, but I have none for such happiness!

Next morning, as dawn was beginning to break, nothing stirred in the little white house. But the inhabitants of three hamlets, gathered in Estanquet, waited for the awakening of the young couple. Marcel had told all, with frankness, yet such was the fear of the Devil in those days that people still trembled for the bridegroom. Some had heard loud cries during the night, while others had seen shadows dancing on the walls. They think Pascal is dead, and so nobody has presumed to bring him the *tourrin.** But then, when, after a moment, music sounds before the little house, and they hear the old refrain of the *aubade* someone is singing in honour of the couple, and the door opens and the two appear, and the bride, blushing, presents, with friendly hand, to all the girls she sees, two pieces of her garter – why, then, fear gives way to shamefaced repent-

* The bowl of tomato soup traditionally offered to a bridegroom on the morning after his wedding-night – Trans.

ance. Pascal's happiness now arouses jealousy, and the poor boys whose souls are hardly cured of their first love, on seeing Françouneto there, a rose in full bloom, so happy and so pretty, say to themselves: 'Never again will we believe in sorcerers!'

PART THREE

Françouneto restored to her century

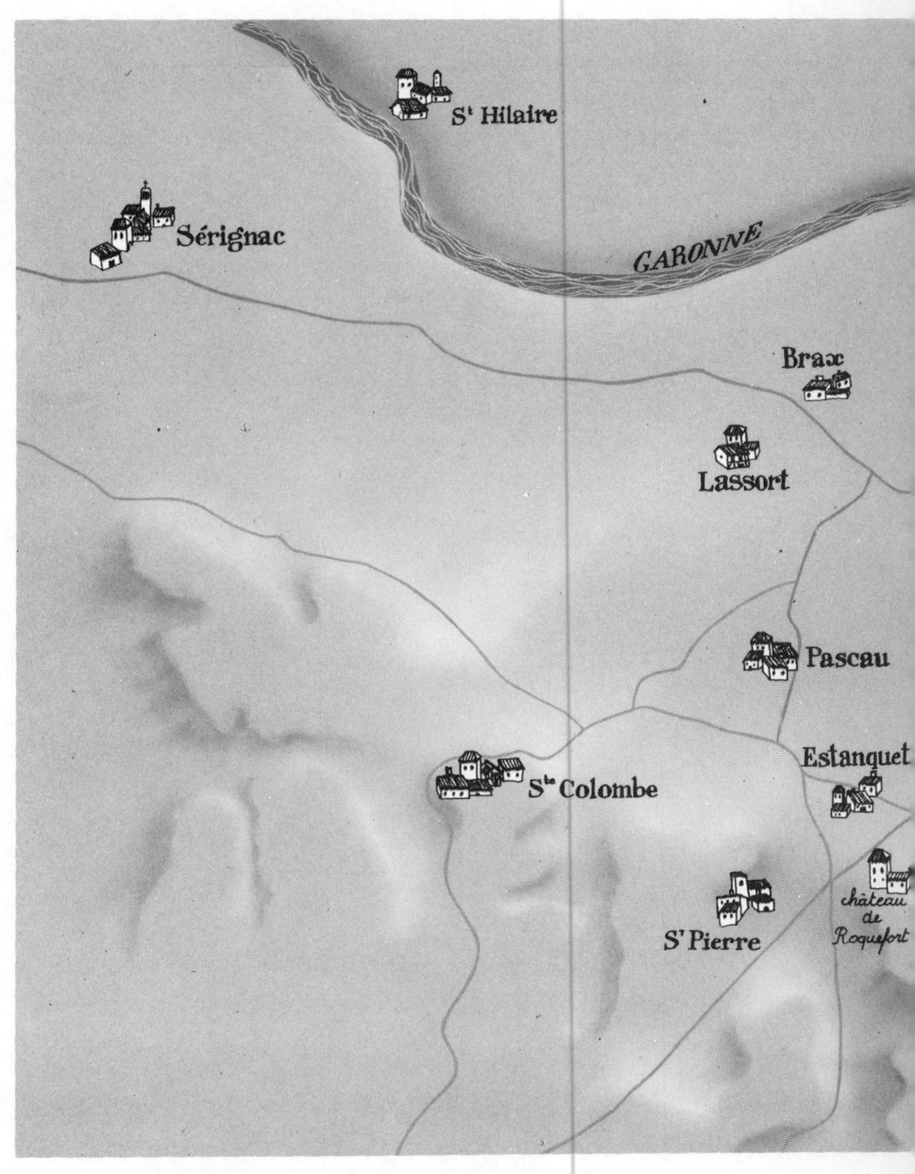

In this plan, composed on the basis of the land-survey of 1820–40, we see the buildings in the hamlet of Estanquet, adjoining the village of Roquefort, among which is Françouneto's house, quite well identified in local tradition, though it was completely demolished in the 1940s and its site is now occupied by ploughed fields [in this map, *actuelle maison de M. Pigeol* means 'where M. Pigeol now lives' – Trans.]. Map by Michèle Dehoky.

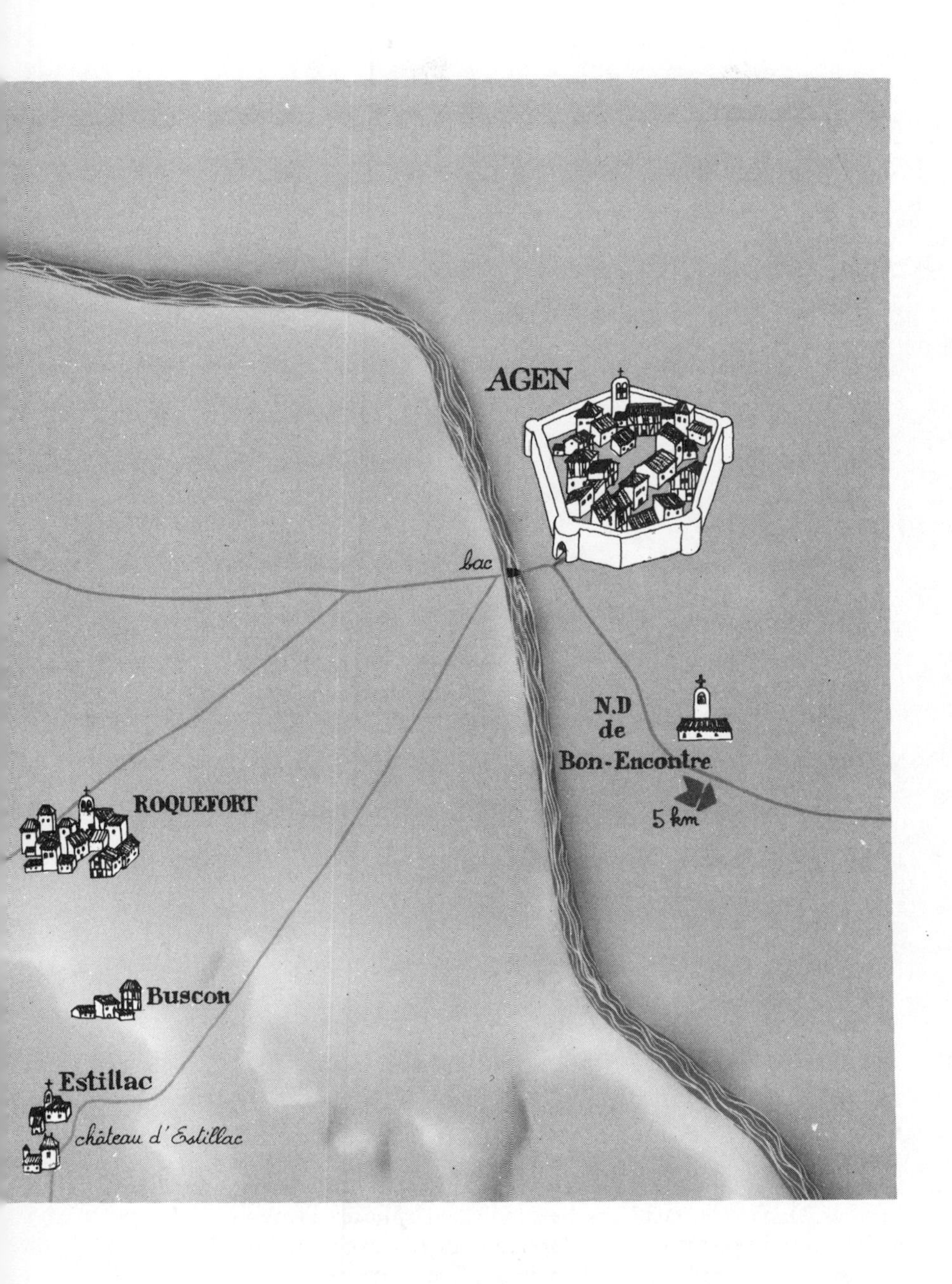
AGEN
bac
N.D
de
Bon-Encontre
5 km
ROQUEFORT
Buscon
Estillac
château d'Estillac

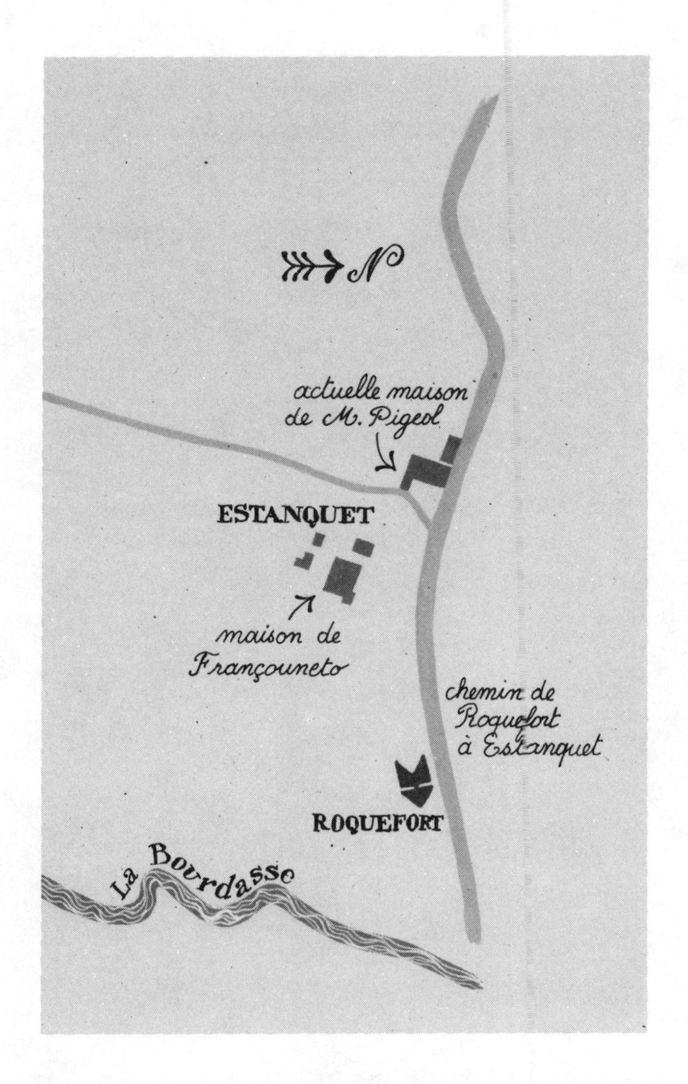

In this map, composed on the basis of eighteenth-century maps and land-surveys, I have selected places, here indicated by purely symbolic drawings, which were important in the story of Françouneto, including the hamlet of Pascau (=Pascal), of which only a place-name remains [in this map, *bac* means 'ferry' – Trans.]. Map by Michèle Dehoky.

The story of Françouneto, like the stories of the Mimalé couple and Marie de Sansarric, is most probably derived from an actual episode, even if at the time this was interpreted in supernatural terms. It was passed on to Jasmin by an informant from the hamlet of Estanquet. The poet took the episode from the oral tradition of the locality, passed down into the 1830s through five or six successive generations. Here the problems of chronology and of existence are one and the same. If one can date the historical occurrence of Françouneto in the sixteenth or the seventeenth century, on the basis of factual evidence, that proves that this heroine did exist, or, at least, that she has a basis in reality, even if only a slender one, which has been covered over from the start by the inventions of myth-making.

Jasmin places Françouneto in the age of Monluc (the 1560s). More precisely, if we follow the implicit chronology which is to be found at the beginning of the poem, the evil-doings and festivities which constitute the plot of the poem must be situated in the period following the massacres at Fumel (11 March 1562) and Penne (August–September 1562), and also after the peace of Amboise (March 1563). This treaty marked the end of fighting for several years and the temporary interruption of the Wars of Religion in France, more particularly in the southwest.[1] It could be deduced, for example, in view of these dates and this *terminus a quo*, that the Buscou festival took place on the night of 31 December 1563 to 1 January 1564, over a year after the massacres and seven months after the return of peace. Indeed, 31 December 1563 was in fact a Friday,[2] and the Buscou festival was held on a Friday, 31 December,[3] according to Jasmin, who was perhaps inspired, on this point, by the oral tradition which he collected.

When we think about it, though, this chronology, with the year 1563 at its centre, seems doubtful. Jasmin's poem makes the Buscou festival a New Year's Eve celebration. Yet it was only on and after 1 January 1566 (and not 1564) that, in the Agenais, the year was held to begin on 1 January. Before then, it still began on Lady Day (25 March). The registers of the municipal council of Agen (complete for the decades 1550–1580) are perfectly clear on that point.[4]

Thus, a New Year's Eve party for 1564 would have been held on 24 March. The years immediately following 1564 are ruled out, since they did not end on a Friday, and also because they were soon marked by the resumption of hostilities (September 1567). This throws us back to a pre-war past, well before the massacres of Penne or Fumel, and, especially, the Peace of Amboise which followed them.[5]

Actually, the Buscou festival, conceived as a New Year's Eve party, could have been held only in a period when the new calendar had been accepted sufficiently for it to enter into the folklore of local festivities. This was certainly not the case during the Wars of Religion (1562–1595). It becomes quite conceivable, though, in the seventeenth century.

Why, then, does Monluc appear in Jasmin's poem? The poet was a superior type of self-educated man, and had read (like all cultivated persons in his region) the *Mémoires* of Monluc.[6] When he turned up, at Estanquet, the story of Françouneto, which was current among the peasants of that hamlet, he noted that this text, which up to that time was merely oral, and contained mention of the Huguenots, was not precisely dated, and on his own initiative he placed it in the time of Monluc (1562–1564). Jasmin himself inserted the references to the massacres at Penne and Fumel, and the return of peace with the treaty of Amboise, which he knew about from Monluc's memoirs and from history books. He thus bestowed upon his subject, or thought he did, an historical dignity which now seems to us, on the contrary, to be greatly strained. When this fake chronology[7] has been set aside, the problem of the true dating of the story of Françouneto still remains to be solved.

In the following pages I am going to suggest a different chronology. My analysis passes through three stages:

(1) Establishing criteria of probability as regards period:
(2) Establishing criteria of factuality for the events described:
(3) Closing up a chronological bracket.

1. *Criteria for determining probability as regards period*

In this connexion we possess an important element in the text which Jasmin collected and then put into verse. This is the pilgrimage to the Virgin of Bon-Encontre, on the right bank of the Garonne, a few kilometres from Agen and two leagues from Roquefort, which is on the left bank of the river.

Regarding this Marial pilgrimage itself there is not much to be said that it relevant to our inquiry. It is a typical rural ceremony which dates from the thirteenth or fourteenth century, at least, to judge by the coins found under the old altar during archaeological excavations in the nineteenth century.* During the sixteenth century a pious legend which may have been brought over from Italy (from the Viterbo area), but which, in any case found many in the south-west to believe it, came to flower at Bon-Encontre. The miraculous terra-cotta statue of the Virgin of this shrine is supposed to have been revealed long ago in a bush, by some cattle, helped by a religious herdsman who made the most of this 'discovery'.

Whatever its origins, the pilgrimage was indeed taking place in the time of Monluc, but that proves nothing as to the actual chronology of Françouneto. Moreover, the sisterhoods of young girls, or *Angèles*, whom the poem shows us going on pilgrimage to the Virgin of Bon-Encontre are probably later

* For the references for this account of the Virgin of Bon-Encontre, see Sources and Bibliography.

than the Wars of Religion and belong to the period of the Counter-Reformation (see one of our illustrations). In the sixteenth century, and right down to the nineteenth, this holy place of Bon-Encontre specialised in the healing of illnesses associated with hysteria.[8]

The point that interests me is of a more precise nature. When did this Virgin concern herself with witchcraft cases comparable to what we read of in *Françouneto*? What was the outcome of the Virgin's interventions? Did they fail? Or did they succeed? (In the case of Françouneto, as we have seen, the heroine's encounter with the Virgin of Bon-Encontre results in a disaster, initially at least. Comparison with other witchcraft cases, broadly contemporary with Françouneto, would thus be of considerable interest.)

The first case of this kind that we know of is certainly later than the age of Monluc. In 1622 the Bordeaux judge and demonologist Pierre de Lancre published a book entitled *Incredulity and Disbelief in Sorcery*, in which, on page 399, he tells the following story:

There was a house in the town of Roquecor, belonging to people who were quite well-off for that neighbourhood, in which one or two spectres, draped in white, appeared to an aunt, a niece and a servant girl, who all saw them and gave similar accounts of what the spectres looked like and how they behaved, even down to details. The spectres, who said that they were souls in torment, became so tame in their attitude to these women that the latter were able to draw near to them and listen to what they had to say, without any fear. The women did all they could to please the spectres, finding no ill intention in them, nor any evil word, action or desire: on the contrary, the spectres spoke of God, the Holy Virgin and the saints with all the honour and respect that could be wished. Eventually, after leading these women from their house to the church, they transformed themselves into angels, and caused the masses to be said which the spectres had desired. They assembled all the people (who are easily attracted by such curiosities), and heard mass with attention and devotion, on their knees. They helped to decorate the altar, causing it to seem to these three women so adorned and bespangled that it was a little paradise. They helped the priest to robe, and lit the candles. They flew about the church like angels. And when the Holy Sacrament was elevated, two angels appeared, on the priest's right and left, gently and respectfully supporting the arm of the priest who was celebrating mass. When it came to the anthem, they went to their tombs at the time of the sprinkling of holy water, telling the priest that he was to say the usual prayers for the dead, and accompanying these prayers, in the presence of the whole congregation, although, in fact, only these three women saw them.

At last, after five or six weeks of such entertainment, showing themselves satisfied with the masses which had been said so that they might remove and return to the other world, they caused it to be known, through the women who saw them, that, for their last act, they wished to go on pilgrimage to Our Lady of Bon-Encontre, where there is a new monastery, served by monks of the Third Order of St Francis – a place of very great devotion. When the Bishop of Agen was told of this, he gave order that three learned men should each, separately, question one of these women, doing it reverently in the church and as though in confession, and being assisted by a man of understanding, to act as secretary and write down, so that there might be a record of so great a secret, what each of the women might reveal concerning the conduct of the spectres. One of the men so appointed was a Jesuit Father, one a Capuchin Father and one the lecturer in divinity in the Cathedral church of St Etienne, in the town of Agen, all being persons of high quality. When they had heard, digested and written down what each of the women said, separately, that they had seen, the investigators found that all three had seen and reported the same things. And, after all that, the spectres, seeming now to be souls well content and satisfied with what they had asked their relations to do, assembled everyone to watch their departure, and appeared to fly up into the sky. At the very moment when the spectres spoke, the women reported that they saw something like a trail of vapour or smoke in the air, marking the way that the spectres had gone, and as though aiming and moving ever upward.

I have put in my first volume on the Demons the true story as the said Bishop of Agen, a man of honour and most worthy prelate, told it to me, and the judgement passed on it by the learned theologians he commissioned. One of the latter did me the courtesy of subsequently bringing to my house the master of the lodgings where these apparitions occurred. I did not dare dissemble or disagree, as I was unwilling to give my own opinion on so strange an event, after three persons of such substance and merit had given theirs.

To speak plainly, however, I find the account that was sent to me, and their report and opinion, so brief and so little reasoned that, although I indeed share their view that these were evil demons who were aiming at the earth rather than poor afflicted souls who were aiming at heaven, nevertheless I believe that the matter deserves fuller investigation if we are to clarify an event so recent and so strange and unheard-of.

This affair took place long after the time of Monluc, since it is dated between 1611 and 1622.* The second date (*terminus ad quem*) is that of the publication of Pierre de Lancre's book: the first (*terminus a quo*) is that of the installation at Bon-Encontre of the Fathers of the Third Order of St Francis.[9] De Lancre speaks judiciously of 'the foundation of their monastery', and that took place in 1611. This was, of course, later than the actual beginning of the pilgrimage, which was at least three centuries old by that time. In these circumstances, during the first decade of Louis XIII's reign, the Virgin of Bon-Encontre was confronted by a supernatural phenomenon, coming from Roquecor,† of which it was not known whether the cause was white magic or black, or whether angels or demons were involved. In any case, the 'spectres' in question, who may have been angels having fun and not devils (whatever de Lancre thought), were not at all ill-disposed. They readily took part in the Church's propaganda, in Counter-Reformation style. In the end, after a few little tricks which, though in bad taste, were quite innocent, they amiably evaporated in the direction of heaven. The Virgin of Bon-Encontre, whose pious accomplices they may have been, even if they were practical jokers, had no difficulty in getting rid of them. In them she found no tough opponents such as Françouneto was to be – according

* I am grateful to M. Hanlon for pointing out this passage to me.
† This place is in the Moissac area.

at least to the reputation given to that heroine by her fellow-villagers.

The years immediately after 1610, during which the pretty affair of the spectres took place, seem, in any case, to match the pilgrimage to Bon-Encontre as it was to appear in the Françouneto affair. In the first place, the connexion between this local cult and the district of Roquefort and thereabouts is then established.[10] On 14 April 1613 a woman from Sainte-Colombe (a village adjacent to Roquefort) named Françoise Rivière, wife of François Lafargue, wanted to have a child but could not conceive. She commended herself to God and to the Virgin (of Bon-Encontre), and was cured of her trouble. As a mark of gratitude she repaid the miraculous favour she had received by giving what was vaguely described as a 'cordon' to the sanctuary.* In the very heart of Françouneto's home territory a fresh miracle occurred on 27 October 1616. A woman from Bordeaux was cured of blindness, this marvellous event being authenticated by three witnesses who represent the élite of our heroine's parish, namely, a sub-deacon, a doctor and a notary, all from Roquefort.[11] On 23 March 1626 the granddaughter of the *seigneur* of Sainte-Colombe, at the gates of Roquefort, was cured of paralysis. From the decade 1610–20, then, the district of Roquefort and Sainte-Colombe enjoyed special relations with Bon-Encontre, which the Françouneto affair merely underlines. These relations were to continue into the 1660s and '70s. On 10 June 1663 the document already quoted certified:

> a miracle last year at Roquefort . . . Young François Marcou was sick of a mortal illness. His mother knelt and made a vow in the chapel of Bon-Encontre, and the boy got well at once.

And again, on 27 October 1679:

> A Roquefort child had erysipelas. His mother devoted him to the Virgin of Bon-Encontre. He was cured forthwith.

* Possibly a specially-made attachment to the corner of a pall, to be held by a mourner during a funeral procession; or a girdle to be worn by the priest celebrating Mass; or a ribbon to decorate a statue? – Trans.

However, the Françouneto affair is not to be reduced merely to some link between Roquefort and Bon-Encontre. It involves an episode of black magic or witchcraft. We have already noted the phenomenon of 'grey' magic (half-white or half-black) in the case of the spectres of Roquecor exorcised by the terracotta Virgin not long after 1610. This time we have before us a real example of witchcraft, of the blackest sort, beginning in the Roquefort area and finding its solution at Bon-Encontre.[12] On 30 May 1655, at Laplume, a small town not far from our village, a merchant named Laffontant declared that

his baby, a boy, had taken milk from the breast of his mother, Françoise Laffontant, née Dufour, for eight days, after which he persisted in refusing to suck for five or six weeks. [He] believed that this misfortune had come upon their child through some spell or charm, and, not wishing to employ anyone to remove this spell, he made a vow to have a mass said at Notre-Dame de Bon-Encontre and to take the child there and present its clothes. [The baby] became well again, thanks be to God, and in gratitude [the father] has come this day [30 May 1655] to fulfil his vow, in testimony whereof he has signed his name.*

This passage is interesting. The region of Roquefort, if not the parish, is involved. The evil spell bears not upon a marriage, as in *Françouneto*, but on the fruit of a marriage, that is, a baby, and on the bond between the baby and its mother (breast-feeding made impossible). Recourse to a soothsayer who would be able, as for Françouneto and the Mimalés, to remove the spell, was proposed, but this method of counter-sorcery was rejected ('not wishing to employ anyone to remove this spell'). The pilgrimage of Bon-Encontre emerges, as in *Françouneto*, as the ultimate resource. In this case it proved successful, whereas in the story collected by Jasmin it was to fail – temporarily, at least.

The point is thus made by the facts themselves, as given by Jasmin on the basis of Roquefort tradition, that the Virgin of

* So Laffontant was literate.

Bon-Encontre may not always succeed. On these problems of Marial failure during the period 1611–1700, vital for the history of witchcraft, we have documentary evidence that reveals spectacular ill-success on the part of the terra-cotta Virgin. In this respect, too, the case of Françouneto is far from unique in seventeenth-century Agenais.

Here are the facts. In 1617 a magician from Lyons, 'a bad Christian', bewitched 'Serène de Bajamont, a young girl,' also called 'Serène de Durfort de Bajamont,'[13] a scion of the nobility of Agen. 'This spell was worked through a rose or a carnation.' Witchcraft through flowers! We have seen that this figures in *Françouneto* and also at Loudun (1632). In the following year (April 1618), Serène married the Comte de Laugnac. The wedding-night went off badly. The bride threw herself about, imitating animal cries. She seemed to be possessed. They took her to the chapel of Bon-Encontre, where, it was hoped, the Virgin would be able to drive out the demonic nuisance which had the new countess in its grip. This at once gave rise to scandalous gossip in Guyenne.[14] It became the only topic of conversation. Madame de Bajamont, a Huguenot and mother of the sick woman, even resolved to convert to Catholicism there and then,[15] in order to encourage the terra-cotta Virgin to apply her healing power more efficaciously. And so Serène the possessed spent the night in the Marial shrine of Bon-Encontre, accompanied by Catholic ladies and by Franciscan Tertiaries, who had been in charge of the pilgrimage since their installation there in 1611.

Among the religious who were present that day, or that night, was Brother Natal. He took advantage of the opportunity to whisper in Serène's ear. They recited the *Ave Maria* and the *Salve Regina*. During this long nocturnal vigil the bride howled and swooned. A Protestant satirist, hostile to the 'mummeries' of Bon-Encontre, claims that, nevertheless, her pulse remained normal. Then the power of the Virgin seemed to come into action. After a few hours, the young countess said: 'Praise be to God and to the Blessed Virgin Mary, I am healed.' From every corner of the little sanctuary rose shouts of: 'A miracle, a miracle! Great is Our Lady of Bon-Encontre!' Brother Natal urged Madame de Bajamont very strongly to remain Catholic and not to relapse into her former Protestantism. Alas! Three days later, Serène fell back into the state of diabolical possession in which she had been before. Worse still, two more victims were added to the list of the possessed, namely, the servants of the unfortunate countess. Sylvius notes that Natal had *touched the arm* of one of these girls.*

The suspicions aroused in the bridegroom, the Comte de Laugnac, and his mother-in-law, the former Huguenot, fell at once upon Natal. They accused this friar of having prevented the consummation of the marriage of their respective spouse and daughter. Natal was merely sentenced to do penance by the Bishop of Agen, but the *Parlement* of Bordeaux intervened. Natal was hanged and his body burned. Before his execution Natal made a full confession in which he accused his colleague Eusèbe, another friar and guardian of Bon-Encontre, of having plotted with him, because both were in love with the same girl (Serène?). However, the clergy of Agen persisted with their exorcisms. The countess's two servants, who had also been contaminated, were subjected to prolonged and theatrical sessions of exorcism in the churches of Agen, in the presence of large crowds. The demons who possessed them promised to come out if the Virgin of Bon-Encontre interceded, but then failed to do so, which once again brought ridicule upon the unfortunate terra-cotta statue in our little sanctuary.

A number of elements from this case recur in the story of Françouneto. A kiss, pious but ineffective, is given to the effigy of the Virgin (by Françouneto) or to the sacred vessels (by the countess's servants). Anti-Huguenot propaganda is subjacent, the countess's devils and those of Françouneto being accused

* In the witchcraft of the Condomois, the Agenais and Béarn, under the Ancien Régime, the vulnerability of the arm plays an especially important role (see *supra*, Part One).

of acting hand-in-glove with the Protestants. The candles are extinguished in *Françouneto* when her devil leaves the church to go and unleash the hailstorm. The same phenomenon is mentioned in the Laugnac case, at the moment when the demon leaves the body of the possessed servant-girl and, as he goes, puts out a torch blazing in the church. We note also threats of burning directed at the Huguenots or devils lodged in the various bodies: the fire would not fail to consume these bodies along with them! Such threats appear in *Françouneto* and also in the Laugnac case, during the exorcisms of the countess's servants.

The failure of the Virgin of Bon-Encontre is patent, in the Laugnac case as in that of Françouneto.

It never proved possible completely to deliver the two servants, who were named Guillemette and Marie. Guillemette was the first to die, then Marie.[16]

As has been mentioned, the Laugnac case gave rise to tremendous scandal throughout south-western France. It was the biggest case of witchcraft – or, rather, of possession – theatrical and urban in nature, to happen south of the Loire between the Gaufridy episode (Aix, 1611) and the troubles of Urbain Grandier (Loudun, 1632). In that connexion, Agen even had a certain bearing on Loudun. A priest named de Sourdis was Archbishop of Bordeaux at the time of the Laugnac case, and tried (in vain) to exert a moderating influence on the fanatical magistrates who succeeded in burning Brother Natal, charged with witchcraft at Bon-Encontre. Another de Sourdis, related to the above-mentioned, was Archbishop of Bordeaux in 1632, and he, too, attempted, though in vain, to calm public excitement during the Urbain Grandier case.[17]

At Bon-Encontre itself, where one of the monks of the establishment had actually been burned, the local Virgin showed herself so sickened and shocked that for five years (1618–23) she practically ceased to perform miracles. She did not resume her miracle-working functions, if we may judge by the manuscript register of her miracles,[18] until those five years had passed.

Serène de Bajamont had been since 1618 the unhappy wife of the Comte de Laugnac, whose name was Charles de Montpezat. Following the disasters which descended upon his wife and her servants, the count was even threatened by the demons who tormented the countess's body with being possessed in his turn. We can imagine his justified anger, and may suppose that he used his influence, rather stupidly, to ensure that Father Natal was burned at Bordeaux on 6 September 1628, by order of the *Parlement*.* The risk of conjugal possession thus affected first the wife and then the husband. The Roquefort tradition, transmitted through Jasmin's poem, tells us at length of a risk of this sort, since the future husband of Françouneto is twice threatened with becoming possessed and even killed by the Devil, just as his future wife had been possessed since babyhood.

From this standpoint the relations between the young Comtesse de Laugnac and the *seigneurie* and community of Roquefort are of interest, since we are here in Françouneto country. In 1625 the countess, who is also referred to by her maiden name, Serène de Durfort, or Serène de Bajamont, seemed at last to be thoroughly cured of her diabolical possession. She was more fortunate in that respect than her two servants, who were to die still possessed. On 12 April 1625 Serène, presumably now in good health, stood godmother at Agen to Gaston-Jean-Baptiste de Secondat-Montesquieu.[19] Now this baby boy, born into a family from which emerged, collaterally, the great Montesquieu, was the son of Pierre de Secondat, baron and *seigneur* of Roquefort. Young Gaston thus became the godson of a formerly possessed woman whom Bon-Encontre had not

* We know of this burning from a number of Agen documents. The records of the Bordeaux *Parlement*, however (letter from M. J. Valette, curator, 16 November 1981) show a gap for precisely this period. Was the destruction of the files due to the passage of time, or was this perhaps partly caused by human agency?

been able to cure at the first attempt. This Gaston was later to become the resident *seigneur* of our village of Roquefort, after the death of his father, Pierre. His lordship at Roquefort lasted from 1638 until his own death in 1693. The tradition collected by Jasmin mentioned on more than one occasion that Françouneto (or her mother) was, as was normal, in contact with and even under the protection of the Secondat family, the *seigneurs* of their village (see *Françouneto*, Section Three). Among the numerous four-sided links uniting Roquefort, Estanquet, Françouneto's family and Bon-Encontre we thus find some of a rather melodramatic kind: the sad story of the Comtesse de Laugnac, godmother of the local *seigneur* and a living witness to the momentary failure of a Virgin whose shrine was an object of pilgrimage, was known in Roquefort, in château and village alike.

To sum up. Jasmin made a pseudo-dating to coincide with Monluc's time, but the period lasting from 1611 to 1700 seems to be more likely for the true timing of the story of Françouneto. The parish of Roquefort had in that period numerous links with the pilgrimage to Bon-Encontre. These links related to spells which the Virgin of Bon-Encontre was able to remove when they were relatively benign (angels indulging in practical jokes, or a breast that could not function). But an exemplary failure and even disaster for the Marial pilgrimage occurred, resoundingly, in 1618, and cast its shadow over the following decades. The district of Roquefort was involved in this experience, for the formerly possessed countess, who was a living witness to the defeat of the Virgin, became also, in 1625, the godmother of the local *seigneur*.

We can appreciate that Françouneto's misfortune when she went on pilgrimage to Bon-Encontre might easily be interpreted as a serious temporary failure for the terra-cotta Madonna. In the shadow of their *seigneur*'s château and within the orbit of Agen, the villagers were familiar with the distressing experience suffered by the Comtesse de Laugnac, their *seigneur*'s godmother. Françouneto was not, of course, the Comtesse de

Laugnac. She was only a peasant girl. But she grew up and suffered within the huge and tragic (or tragi-comic) shadow of that countess, who, between 1618 and 1625, was first possessed and then imperfectly healed of possession.[20]

2. *Criteria for determining the factuality of the events described*

We now have a chronological bracket, as yet imprecise, from which we can start. The Monluc dating seems wrong. Many of the signs indicate that the Françouneto case is later than the period 1611–18, and probably earlier, though not much earlier, than 1700. That last date closes the great period of interventions, successful or otherwise, by the Virgin of Bon-Encontre against spells. To help us further, we possess two sets of facts: on the one hand, the names of the characters in the story, and, on the other, the heroine's house (Françouneto's *ostal*), which is still today well known among the inhabitants of the hamlet of Estanquet. Let us begin with the names of the personages.

This review will not take long. Let us first eliminate the soldier Marcel. If he really existed, he probably corresponded to someone whose actual name was Martial – a name found fairly often among the forenames, placenames and names of saints in the south-west in general and in the region of Auch or Agen in particular. The forename Marcel, in the *langue d'oïl* form, was unknown in the Agenais in the days of the *ancien régime*. Having said which, Marcel, or Martial, in the oral account which Jasmin later put into verse, appears only as a soldier passing through, though he has some local connexions. His uncle, the churchwarden who looks like a judicial councillor, would have been among the petty notables of the Roquefort community, but I have encountered him only in the version made by Jasmin.

Given merely his forename and the statement that he was a soldier, it would be hard to identify this isolated individual in the parish registers, the sole documents which survive from the old archives of Roquefort, and which cover only the period 1669–1789. In any case, these registers do not anywhere mention, either among the dead or among the fathers or bridegrooms, the presence of a male person following the military trade and having the forename Martial (or Marcel).

The traces of Françouneto are as hard to detect. The forename François or Françoise, the affectionate form of which, in the *langue d'oc*, is Françouneto, was widespread* in Roquefort until the end of the seventeenth century (more precisely, until the 1680s). There is a possible link here, incidentally, with the pilgrimage to Our Lady of Bon-Encontre, not far away, in which the villagers of Roquefort were assiduous participants. This rural cult was looked after in the seventeenth and eighteenth centuries by monks of the Third Order of St Francis – Saint *François* – which may explain the popularity of this particular forename in our village. Let us suppose what is quite plausible, that Françouneto lived in the seventeenth century, say, between 1620 and 1700. Had she lived in the time of Monluc, the 1560s, as Jasmin dubiously claims, all trace of her would be lost, since we have no records for sixteenth-century Roquefort. Even given the optimistic hypothesis that she lived in the seventeenth century – the most favourable assumption from the standpoint of the researcher – she would be hard to discover in the archives, for lack of information on the family names of the many Françoises with whom the parish registers of Roquefort are filled in Louis XIV's time.

A third personage remains, one who, after all, plays a very important part in our story, namely, Pascal. Here we are already on firmer ground. This cannot be a forename, that of a real person whose forename would be followed by some surname, for 'Pascal' *never* appears among the forenames, very varied though these are, of the persons baptised, married, deceased or

* This we learn from the parish registers. Jasmin was fascinated by the resemblance in sound of the name Françouneto to Magnouneto, the pet-name of his wife, whom he adored. It cannot be ruled out that Jasmin may have invented the pet-name Françouneto.

acting as witnesses which swarm in the parish registers of Roquefort and the towns and villages round about in the seventeenth and eighteenth centuries.*

There is, however, a good chance that this 'Pascal' (if a person of that name did exist) is a surname, not a forename. A pointer must be sought first of all among the local place-names. On the old cadastral plan of Roquefort[21] dated 1842, in Section A, we find a place called *Pascau*. This appears also in the land-surveys of 1820, which are preserved in the present *mairie* of the village. The place was covered with little fields, typical of the holdings of landworkers or craftsmen, and was situated on the northern edge of Roquefort, adjoining the district of Brax, between the places called *Grands-Champ*, *Toulouse* and *Hameau de Magen*.[22] The Pascal lineage might, therefore, have had their principal home, or some annexe thereto, in the place which bears that name. And the family so named might have had connexions with the communities of Roquefort, to the south, and Brax, or Sainte-Colombe, to the north, all three of which are contiguous to each other.

And, in fact, a Pascal lineage did exist in the area in which Françouneto was seen to circulate. The parish registers of the villages of Roquefort and Brax, which we have from the year 1669 onward,[23] testify to this. The first appearance of the name *Pascal* in these registers occurs on 28 March 1697, when the parish-priest, Father Dessales, records the birth (in the parish of Roquefort) of Antoine Paschal, legitimate son of Pierre Paschal and Elisabeth Gasq: he was baptised on 30 March.[24] The parents were persons who had no very deep roots in the parish, even though they had lived there, or thereabouts, for a dozen years or more. The surnames *Pascal* and *Gasq* were unknown in Roquefort from 1669 (the date when the parish registers begin) until 1697. However, we find people named Gasq living at this time in Nérac,[25] a nearby Protestant town

* On this I researched in the parish registers of Brax, Agen, Nérac, Sainte-Colombe and Roquefort.

with which the Pascal family, as will be seen, had some connexion. A year later there was another baptism linked with the Pascal lineage, when 3 March 1698 saw the birth, 'in the parish of Roquefort', of Jean Billet, legitimate son of Timothée Billet ('master-tailor in the town of Nérac') and Catherine Seguines, a dyer. This child was baptised that same day in Roquefort church. His godfather was Jean Pascal and his godmother Marie Pascal. The baptismal ceremony took place in the presence of Jean Lagraulet (bearer of an old Roquefort name) and of Pierre Pascal, neither of whom could sign their names (though Timothée Billet was literate).

This document is interesting, confirming as it does the Protestant connexions of the Pascal family (who, in the maternal line, through a marriage anterior to 1697, may have descended from Françouneto, that semi-Huguenot, the woman savouring of heresy, herself the wife of the first Pascal, whose memory was to be preserved in the oral account collected by Jasmin). Timothée Billet, whose son signs his name well and in good handwriting, was certainly of 'heretical' origin, by birth at any rate, even if later he converted to Catholicism. His home town, Nérac, was a stronghold, if ever there was one, of the Huguenots of south-western France and was linked to Roquefort by a direct road. The forename *Timothée* also distances us from classical Catholicism. Just judge by this fact: there is not a single St Timothée among all the names of French villages which begin with the word 'Saint' and which descend, through more than a thousand years, from the name-giving traditions of the Roman Church. The Huguenot reference to Timothée (Timothy) is obviously due to the close bond between the Apostle Paul and this disciple of his. Paul addressed two epistles to Timothy by name: we know the importance of the Pauline theology of justification by faith among the foundations of Protestantism. Moreover, Timothée Billet was a skilled craftsman,[26] a tailor, in the Nérac milieu of Protestant citizens, and father of a son who was literate, which makes it even more likely that he was originally a Huguenot. And I have found in the parish registers of Nérac, for the same period, this same family named Billet.[27] It contained persons whose occupation was tailoring and whose forenames were Timothée (perhaps the same person we glimpsed at Roquefort) and Isaïe – two unquestionably Huguenot forenames.

The Huguenot connexions made between the Pascal family and the Billet family of Nérac were strong. Three members of the Pascal group, named Jean, Marie and Pierre (the latter evidently illiterate), took the trouble to attend the (Catholic) baptism of young Billet, who was himself of recent Protestant ancestry. The Pascal trio thus comprised a godfather, a godmother and a witness: in other words the Pascals arrived in force for the baptism. These connexions are not absolutely in contradiction with what we learn from the oral narrative collected by Jasmin. In both cases we have a family of Catholic craftsmen (the Pascals) which keeps up consistent relations with a lineage from outside the area and is of Protestant origin (Françouneto or the Billets, as the case may be). This gives rise to a marriage (Françouneto with one of the Pascals). This union might, in the next generation, or the one after that, be preserved, maintained or refreshed, through the establishment of godparent relationships which echoed the marriage bond contracted in the past. By standing godfather to the baby Jean Billet, Jean Pascal became the *compère* (quasi-relative) of Timothée Billet, the child's father. It is well-known that men often entered into this relationship because they were already, in many cases, closely related to each other either by blood or by marriage.

This first appearance of the Pascal family, in 1697–98, is one reason why we should chronologically repatriate Françouneto into the seventeenth century. Jasmin placed her in the 1560s, in Monluc's time, because he had read Monluc's memoirs. He knew Monluc's fortress at Estillac, close to our village of Roquefort. Either Jasmin or the tradition transmitted to him by his local informants, or perhaps both, could not resist the pleasure of embellishing the tale by placing under the fictitious patronage of a warrior who distinguished himself around 1562–64 a simple story of local witchcraft that, in reality, happened later, between 1620 and 1700.[28]

For several reasons, indeed, I think that Françouneto's story, which later entered into folklore, is most probably to be situated in the period 1620–1700 (a chronology which I shall later make more precise). In that epoch of the seventeenth century, at Roquefort, the Huguenots were no longer active, dangerous, numerous and omnipresent as they may have been around 1560–80. Under Richelieu and still more under Louis XIV, Huguenots appeared in Roquefort only as remote, isolated, transient individuals, minor bogymen who were feared all the more because never actually met. Françouneto's father, for example, the only complete Huguenot in the story, appears in it only *in absentia*. This impression of the absence, or evanescence, of Protestants clearly appears in the story collected by Jasmin, even though he ante-dates his work to the years 1563–64* when the Agenais and Roquefort were indeed 'infested' with many Calvinists. The actual picture he gives of Roquefort corresponds to the situation there in the middle or second half of the seventeenth century. The people retain a memory of bloody wars of religion – those of the 1560s, certainly, but also those, much more recent and also very bloody, of the 1620s. Furthermore, on the plane of prosaic facts, which are distinct from horrified memories, the records, like the poem itself, tell us of a village that is wholly Catholic, during the reigns of Louis XIV and Louis XV, with insignificant exceptions. Altogether, over more than a century, the parish registers of Roquefort mention only two Huguenots, or ex-Huguenots, namely, the ephemeral Timothée Billet, linked by godparenthood with the Pascal family, in 1698, and a man with the characteristic forename Isaïe, father of a baby who underwen

* This pre-dating was given strong emphasis by Jasmin through mention of the massacres at Penne and Fumel. He took it from the mem of Monluc, widely published and well-known around 1835, in which massacres were described in great detail.

w
an
Pas
pari

In
succes
to the
On 2 O
senior, w
two witne
Gabriel Se
Pascal to be
was a blacks
his own funer
took place in t
Pierre Pascal se
the farrier Sento
very highly eligib
husband of Franço
collected by Jasmin
Pierre Pascal senior w
the heroine some tim
people of Roquefort
Our Lady of Bon-Encon
supra). There is no need,
with Jasmin, to Monluc a
adventure of Françouneto
place either at Roquefort o
Brax, where the church is als
find farmers at Brax whose s

another of Françouneto's suitors in our story. Thus, the parish register of Brax for 17 January 1708 records the birth of Jean Laurent, whose parents bore the same name. This same Pierre Pascal, when made a widower, may have remarried once or twice, at the end of the seventeenth century, with two successive women, born like himself out of Roquefort and named Gasq and Agès respectively. Or else, a different hypothesis, these two ladies may have married, successively or separately, one or two men named Pierre Pascal junior, sons or nephews of our Pierre Pascal senior.

Over and above the insoluble question of precise identities, what is essential is that we have here the family setting in which the episode and story of Françouneto came to birth in the seventeenth century, at Roquefort (or in some neighbouring parish, such as Brax – there are several to choose from). The people concerned are a group of craftsmen (butchers, shoemakers, dyers, tailors, blacksmiths) who, though they may have been attractive to some young girl, were poor, illiterate, semi-marginal – come from elsewhere and married elsewhere, living in the margins between districts (on the borders of Brax and Roquefort). These Pascals were suspect in the eyes of the pious peasantry owing to their former Huguenot connexions, even though they had turned Catholic.

One question remains to be answered, though. How did the story of Françouneto come to be transmitted down through more than a century, almost a century and a half, until Jasmin collected it, with all the various embellishments and distortions which it had undergone in the meantime? As it happens, we are not short of information on this point.

On 3 August 1723 Anne Pascal, born in May 1700 to Pierre Pascal and Isabeau Agès, married Bernard Lassart (or Lassort), a mason at Laplume (a small town near Roquefort). Here we find the same milieu of poor and illiterate craftsmen which is typical of the Pascals. (The Lassorts were numerous at Brax, where the Pascals had firm connexions.) Anne Pascal must have lived at Roquefort, since the *curé* calls her 'my parishioner'.

Her husband, Bernard Lassort, came to Roquefort to live with her. Six children arrived in due course, their six baptisms witnessed in every case by illiterate persons. The first baby, *Bernard* Lassort, was born on 13 August 1724 and baptised almost at once. Another Lassort (Laurent), a grown-up relation of the parents, was present at this baptism. Then number two, *Pierre* Lassort, was born on 1 July 1727. His godmother was Claire Lassort, again a relation of the parents. 12 October 1731 saw the birth of *Marie* Lassort, the couple's third child: her godmother was Marie Lestrade. A fourth baby was born on 27 March 1734, namely, *Arnaud* Lassort: the godfather was Arnaud Coveque (a name to keep in mind), and the godmother Marguerite Lestrade. *Marie* Lassort *II* was the fifth child, born on 25 April 1737. Finally, on 18 January 1740, a sixth baptism, for *Catherine* Lassort, daughter of Bernard Lassort and our fecund Anne 'Pascau' – the *langue d'oc* form *Pascau*, found also, as we have seen, in the cadastral district of Roquefort, is thus attested in the same family (Pascal) and for the same person (Anne Pascal), on equal footing with the common form, *d'oc et d'oïl*, Pascal. In short, we have here Anne Pascal *alias* Anne Pascau.* The godmother of young Catherine was named Catherine Aché or Agès, from a family which had been related to the Pascals since the beginning of the eighteenth century.

The Pascal family finally vanishes from our Roquefort and Estanquet documents after 1740, the date of birth of *Catherine*, the last child of Anne Lassort, *née* Pascal. The last adult males named Pascal had disappeared from Roquefort and Brax already in 1708, at latest. This departure of the males, observed in the documents, must have resulted either from a series of deaths, or, making a more favourable assumption, from a collective emigration by the lineage, leaving no material souvenir except the place called *Pascau*. We thus need to discover how, under these conditions, so evanescent a family managed to pass on to

* See *supra*: it is well-known that the spelling of proper names was poorly standardised at that time.

others the torch of its little family story about witchcraft, so that, at the end of the chain, it could reach Jacques Jasmin, at the beginning of the 1840s.

Fortunately, our sources are not silent on this problem of the genealogies of an oral tradition passed down through the 'long' eighteenth century. We have every reason to believe that the Pascal family lived in or around 1670–1720 in the north of the Roquefort district, where still today we find the place-name *Pascau* (=Pascal) associated with them, together with the hamlet of Estanquet, where tradition locates the tale of Françouneto.* (But, I repeat, the actual episode may have occurred in some village near to Roquefort and not necessarily in a hamlet such as Estanquet. In view of the mobility and marginality of the Pascal family, I think this possibility must be kept in mind.) The Pascals sat, moreover, astride this northern border, since they resided not only in Roquefort district but also in that of Brax, lying to the north.

It turns out that the Pascal family established close links early on with the hamlet of Estanquet, and that they probably lived there, if not at the beginning of their local career, then at least later. These links were forged with the Coveque family, inhabitants of the hamlet in question. The Coveques were, like the Pascals, marginal people from the outskirts who, in the second half of the seventeenth century (the Pascals) or at the beginning of the eighteenth (the Coveques), came and settled alongside the old-established lineages of the parish and neighbourhood. The first mention of the Coeque, or Coveque, family found in the Roquefort parish registers (which begin in 1669) is dated 13 November 1725 (marriage of Jacques Coveque with Jeanne Pavie). The Coveque lineage could therefore have been already living at Roquefort for over twenty years, if we allow the time needed for children who had recently immigrated together with their families to grow up and reach marriageable age.

* The hamlet of Estanquet is certainly old-established, as we can see from its appearance as a name borne by individuals mentioned in the earliest parish registers of Roquefort.

From 1725 onward, anyway, we find Coveques constantly turning up in the parish registers of Roquefort, right down to 1789, and thereafter in the local records of civil status from 1790 until 1855, the date at which our investigation ends. The permanent residence of the Coveque family was none other than the hamlet of Estanquet, made famous by Françouneto, whose story began there – unless, after beginning somewhere else in the neighbourhood, it soon became rooted there, as a result of the local establishment of the successive passers-on of the story. The Coveques therefore seem, in terms of the brothers, sisters and cousins engendered by the families, one after another, that bear their name, to have constituted a solidly-welded lineage, fixed around the hamlet of Estanquet where they reproduced themselves for more than a century. They often acted as godfather to each other's children. Their social level was modest, since they were almost all illiterate, from the 1720s onward. So far as we are concerned, the outstanding role among them is played by Arnaud Coveque, husband of Toinette Lespès (according to a document of 14 October 1728). Occasionally acting as godfather (for example, on 7 April 1728), Arnaud Coveque was enlisted in this role in 1734 by Anne Pascal, Lassort's wife, who was none other than the last daughter of Pierre Pascal, the man whose first wife may have been Françouneto, or who may have been a close (younger) relative of that husband. Anne Pascal chose Arnaud Coveque as godfather (28 March 1734) for the son born on 27 March of that year to her and Bernard Lassort. The boy thus godfathered was accordingly named Arnaud. Being a sensible woman, Anne Pascal-Lassort did not choose at random the godfathers and godmothers of her numerous children, but picked them among very close relatives, such as the Achés (18 January 1740), the Lassorts themselves (1 January 1727), and so on. The godfather of her fourth baby (1734), Arnaud Coveque must have been a friend of Anne Pascal's and probably a near neighbour. Now he became something more, a closely-connected *compère*. Not long afterward, the moment arrived when the Pascal/Lassort family died out, or else disappeared through emigration from Roquefort and Estanquet – at some date a little later than 1740, the last year in which this family are named in our parish registers (birth of Catherine Lassort, their last child).

Thereafter, of necessity, it was the descendants of Arnaud Coveque (*compère* and very close friend of the Pascals) who were to take charge of the Françouneto tradition at Estanquet. Arnaud Coveque, illiterate (7 April 1728) husband of Toinette Lespès, was the father of several children, including Bernard Coveque, born 14 October 1728. This Bernard Coveque, in his turn, when he reached the age of twenty-seven, married, on 1 July 1755, Anne Larroumet.* It is mentioned, on 15 May and 5 August 1762, that this man and his wife lived at Estanquet, where he worked as a carpenter (3 March 1783). Bernard Coveque and Anne Larroumet had a daughter, Anne Coveque,† born 5 May 1762. Over twenty years later (3 March 1783), she was to marry Jean Lacoste, of the parish of Estillac, near Roquefort. Lacoste came at once to take up residence at Estanquet, in his young wife's home. In other words, he came as son-in-law to Bernard Coveque, in accordance with the practice of ensuring through the women the continuity of a certain lineage on a certain landholding. On his wedding-day he was described as a 'farm-hand'. Subsequently he acquired the rank of 'farmer' at Estanquet, as we see in the registration of his death, for he died young, at thirty-two, on 5 June 1790. Be it noted that on 12 July 1788, the day of the baptism of his daughter Françoise, the godfather was Bernard Coveque, the child's maternal grandfather. This man was at that time about

* Of the three persons listed as having been present at this wedding, two were Coveques, named Jacques and Pierre. We shall have occasion to refer again to the particular closeness of this family, which was especially well equipped to pass on a precise tradition over more than a century.

† The same observation as in the previous note. The Coveque parents, father and mother, were recorded that day as inhabitants of Estanquet. The godfather was Jean Coveque, the godmother Anne Coveque. Family closeness once again.

sixty years old, and quite capable of passing on the oral tradition of Françouneto. As for the great-grandfather, Arnaud Coveque, who received the torch directly from the hands of the Pascal family, he had died on 30 December 1753, aged fifty-five: he, too, had had plenty of time to pass the story on.

Jean Lacoste, married in 1783 to Anne Coveque, and prematurely deceased in 1790, had a son from this marriage, Pierre Lacoste, who was born at Estanquet on 24 April 1784 and baptised in the presence of his grandfather, Bernard Coveque.[31] The continuity through many generations was ensured once more. We shall come upon this Pierre Lacoste again, between 1821 and 1829, and so aged between thirty-seven and forty-four. At that time, during the Restoration, he was the owner and cultivator in the district of Estanquet of pieces of land covering 2.4 hectares, and of house No. 88, depicted as a small farmyard on the cadastral plan of Roquefort, Section A, and mentioned in register no. 228 of the sectional inventory of the Roquefort land survey of 1821.[32] About fifteen years later, on 2 August 1844, this same Pierre Lacoste, now sixty, was to make a gift of this house at Estanquet to the parish church of Roquefort. I found in the communal archives of the village a document mentioning this donation.[33]

Here we encounter an essential intersection with the oral tradition that exists today (1981). This intersection suffices to justify the genealogical details set out above. The inhabitants of Estanquet remembered very well, in 1980–82, this house which, nearly a century and a half ago, was given to the church. It was the house – they are quite definite on this point – which the families living in the hamlet called and still call *Françouneto's house*. We have arrived at the crossroads.

Let us halt here for a moment. I have just passed from mentioning the archives, in which I had to carry out a tedious search, to the 'oral tradition'. I switched from being an historian to being an on-the-spot investigator (1980–82). What happened, exactly?

In the last few years I made several visits to the village of

Roquefort and the hamlet of Estanquet. There, or near there, was the scene of Françouneto's story. On a mound stand the ruins of the old château of the *seigneurs* of Roquefort, and there too, between about 1640 and 1826, stood the former parish church of St Jacques, built under Louis XIII, which was demolished, or moved from this mound to the plain of the Garonne, in the reign of Louis XVIII. This church of St Jacques had itself taken the place of the still older, mediaeval church of St Pierre, which was situated on another ridge, farther off, in the south-western part of the district. The church of St Jacques, up there on the mound, beside the château, had marked for two centuries, from Louis XIII to Louis XVIII, the dominance of the Secondat family as *seigneurs*. They had striven to take charge of everything in the village, including its church or spiritual life. During the 1820s the parishioners shook off the yoke of their masters, and brought their church down from the château to the municipal or communal *place* – a classical process in the south of France. From the beginning of the nineteenth century, or earlier, the settlement of Roquefort spread, in the usual way, down into the plain of the Garonne. The whole of it – school, *mairie*, cemetery, 'new' church dated 1826, café, post-office, presbytery and various houses – is now concentrated round the low, flat tract of land called the *place*, which has become the centre of the present-day village of Roquefort.

Let us follow the trail. From this modest centre we take a little road, now tarred, that leads to the west, or the west-south-west. We walk about 250 metres and arrive at the big stream called the Bourdasse, which is mentioned in *Françouneto*. We continue along the same road for another 250 metres, and reach the hamlet of Estanquet. In 1982 this contained only two or three old houses. The inhabitants of the place and its neighbourhood (M. Frédéric Bacqué, aged eighty, his daughter and son-in-law, Mme and M. Pouyleau, and also M. Henri Pijol and M. René Laroche, sixty) know well 'Françouneto's house' – or rather, the spot where it stood, because the house was demolished by the villagers owing to its dilapidated condition during the Second World War.

Here, then, is what is unanimously reported by the oral tradition, as scrupulously collected by me from these persons and reproduced in this book. 'Françouneto's house', I was told, was given, some time in the last century, to the church of Roquefort by a local peasant family whose son, probably the sole heir, was a seminarist and designated for the priesthood. The archives of Roquefort, which I consulted, corroborate this oral tradition and provide further details. The donation was made on 2 August 1844, the donor[34] being Pierre Lacoste, who, as we have seen, was descended in the direct line from an Estanquet family, itself joined by marriage and godparenthood to Françouneto's family. There is therefore no reason to reject the local tradition that claims this house belonged to Françouneto, or, in any case, to her immediate descendants and their closest in-laws. (Local tradition does not necessarily bother with such distinctions, which the historian, aware of the mobility and marginality of the Pascals around 1700, is obliged to recall.) The close proximity of the families, and their establishment in the hamlet of Estanquet, render such a tradition (allowing for the distinction mentioned) perfectly credible. In this case the written document comes to the aid of the oral transmission.

'Françouneto's house' had thus become, soon after Jasmin's collection of the tradition at the end of the 1830s, the property of the Church (1844). During the inventories carried out in connexion with the separation between church and state (1902–05), this house was seized from the clergy, that is, it was transferred from the parish to the local municipality, with the three plots of land attached to it. At the beginning of the 1940s the house was in a very bad state and occupied by gypsies. The *mairie* therefore demolished it, or allowed it to be demolished. Today, 'Françouneto's house' has been replaced by a small ploughed field, but the lighter colour of the soil (owing to traces of lime or débris from chalky quarry-stones) shows us clearly where the house stood, when we contrast these whitish traces with the dark furrows of the rest of the plot. This house must not be confused with another, much more substantial residence, like a small manor-house, situated in the north of the Roquefort district, on the road to Brax and on the right bank of the Bourdasse, nearly a kilometre north of Estanquet. The owner of this mini-manor was a local notable and admirer of Jasmin. Out of affectation he named his house *Françounette*, putting the name on a plaque fixed to the wall. Our informants made a point of warning against the possible confusion.

The real house of Françouneto, or of her nearest and most immediate descendant, was not a manor-house but a simple peasant dwelling situated in the hamlet of Estanquet, at the centre of a *faisande* or smallholding (see the second and third sections of the poem). The lower part of the walls consisted of masonry – hence the comparative whiteness of the soil ploughed up on the site – but the rest of it, that is, most of the house, the middle and upper parts of the walls, was made of cob (clay mixed with straw and stuffed into a framework of timber). The whole surface may have been whitened with lime (Jasmin speaks of a 'white house'). Everyone told me that the house had a roof of half-round tiles, that there were two fairly large rooms on the ground floor (perhaps a kitchen and a bedroom), while the first floor, under the tiles, was just a loft, not inhabitable. The ground was of beaten earth, except in the kitchen, which was paved. The house was almost square, about twelve or fourteen metres each side. The well was a few metres distant, west-south-west of the house, beside a road running N.N.E.–S.S.W. which connects Estanquet with Gardere. This well communicated with underground water about 20 metres down. It was walled with square bricks and topped with a round stone well-head, typical of the wells of this region. A large curved stone remains, the only vestige of this well-head beside the road and, indeed, was all that remained visible, in 1981, of 'Françouneto's house'. A garden separated this house from the road which runs from Estanquet to the Roquefort of today (this flowery garden is mentioned in the verses, themselves too flowery, of Jasmin's poem).* Finally, a barn, which is no longer there, adjoined 'Françouneto's house', standing at right angles to it: this would be the one that the lynch-mob were going to set on fire, according to the oral account collected by Jasmin. The more recent houses in Roquefort, built in the eighteenth and nineteenth centuries, are of stone. Here and there, and notably at Estanquet, one can still find a farmhouse (such as that of M. Frédéric Bacqué, near the site of Françouneto's house) or a barn made of cob which tradition (according to M. Bacqué and itself dating from 1910 or 1920) assigns to 'three centuries ago', that is, to the seventeenth century, more or less. These are the old buildings of the village which have survived from before the time when, under Louis XV or under Louis-Philippe, houses had to be built almost entirely of stone.

The cob 'house called Françouneto's' thus probably dated from the seventeenth century. In any case, it cannot be much older, since peasant dwellings made of cob which go back to the Middle Ages are rare. The relative fragility of their construction meant that they could not last more than four hundred years. Let us take it that Françouneto's little farm was contemporary with the seventeenth century, or a little earlier. This was the actual period when that oral account became crystallised which Jasmin was subsequently to collect and edit after a delay of five or six generations.

It is clear that 'Françouneto's house', as this is known today to the old inhabitants of Estanquet, is none other than the house which Pierre Lacoste gave to the church in 1844. The identity of the cadastral sites, together with the small size of the hamlet, which in the 1840s, when its population was greatest, numbered only four resident families, or no more than four houses,[35] prove that the donation of 'the house called Françouneto's' (attested by oral tradition as having been made long before 1905) and the donation by Pierre Lacoste in 1844 (well attested by the archives) are one and the same incident.

* *Françouneto*, section three.

We thus now hold a very strong thread. It descends to us from the Pascals (who became, owing to the family events that happened to them around 1660–1700, the first authors and transmitters of the oral story) and ends with Pierre Lacoste, owner of 'Françouneto's house' and also, as I shall show, the informant of the poet Jasmin in 1842. From the Pascals to the Lacostes, it passes through the Coveque family, who form, at Estanquet, the intermediate link. The whole chain can be depicted as follows:

1. The marriage of Françouneto to a (Pierre?) Pascal took place in the seventeenth century between about 1660 and 1700 in a house at Estanquet or some other place near Roquefort.
2. The lineage of the Pascals includes a *Pierre* Pascal, active around 1700, who died at sixty in 1708.
3. *Anne* Pascal, daughter of a Pierre Pascal, was active around 1710–40.

    3a. This same *Anne* Pascal was *commère* of Arnaud Coveque, active about 1730–53, whose family lived permanently at Estanquet.

4. Bernard Coveque, son of Arnaud, was active about 1750–85.
5. *Anne* Coveque, daughter of Bernard Coveque, who married Jean Lacoste, was active about 1780 and subsequent decades.
6. Their son, Pierre Lacoste, was active about 1800–44 and owner, thanks to his ancestors, of the house called Françouneto's, which he donated to the clergy in 1844.
7. Collection of the oral account by Jasmin in the house called Françouneto's.
8. Oral traditions still alive at Estanquet (1982) concerning this house, which was demolished between 1941 and 1945.

ESTANQUET

By direct filiation (the Pascals) and then by relations of godparenthood (Pascal→Coveque), and finally by direct filiation through both male and female lines (the Coveques and the

Lacostes), the story of the little witch of Estanquet thus traversed about five generations, reaching at last Jasmin the collector. He perhaps weakened the story by trying to embellish it, but, nevertheless, he respected its structure and gave it to us in all or almost all its original freshness.

Moreover, this process of handing-down until the story was ultimately collected may have been strengthened by the fact that other Estanquet families (the Pandelés and other branches of the Coveques) also told this story to their children, who in turn passed it on to *their* children.[36] On this point, however, we can only conjecture. What is essential is that we have found the main beam, that which, through the Coveques, runs from the Pascals to the Lacostes and to Jasmin, on the site of 'Françouneto's house'.

We now have to confront this reconstruction of the transmission process which I have accomplished with the collection that Jasmin actually performed on the spot. Let us look at the very brief account given by the poet* of his arrival at Estanquet, which took place probably in or about 1840.

Estanquet, a pretty hamlet, situated near Roquefort and not far from Agen. Here the memory of Françouneto still lingers. It was here, in the very house where she lived,[37] and which belongs today to *M. Bernès*, deputy-clerk for the levying of direct taxes, that the author (Jasmin) himself collected, from the mouth *of a peasant* the chief elements of her story (i.e., Françouneto's).[38]

'The house called Françouneto's', in about 1820–40, to judge by the land-survey of that period, actually consisted of two buildings (one of them doubtless a barn), at right angles to each other and contiguous, with a yard in the corner of this set-square, the whole being divided into a dwelling (quite a modest one) for the master, occupied by Bernès, a petty-bourgeois from Agen whose name appears as owner in the land-survey of 1820, and a peasant's dwelling, or barn, belonging to Pierre Lacoste (who was himself probably Jasmin's

* In *Françouneto*, 1842 edition, in the notes at the end of the poem.

informant, and may have been Bernès's tenant-farmer).[39] This Lacoste was probably a pious man, since his son became a seminarist. This piety of the final transmitter of the oral account is reflected in certain edifying details, sometimes marked by affectation, which emerge in the written account eventually produced by Jasmin.

'Françouneto's house' was thus, in 1820–40, a twofold structure. We obtain a series of binomials:

dwelling/barn
owner/farmer
minor notable/peasant
Bernès/Lacoste

My informants in 1980–81 were not concerned with this splitting-in-two which had existed in former times. They thought, essentially, of Françouneto's as being the small peasant farm house of Pierre Lacoste, the descendant, through many generations (in 1840) of the lineage which had handed down the original story throughout the eighteenth century and even longer.

Jasmin was chronologically closer than we are to the original sources of the story. He was well aware of its dual rooting in its home, the hamlet of Estanquet. The poet passed from one dwelling to another, and from one social level to the next one down. He experienced a real social descent when he moved from Bernès's dining-room to Lacoste's kitchen, but by doing so was all the better able to interview the peasant whom he was to present in his publication as having been his informant. This genuine countryman must have been Pierre Lacoste himself, or else one of his cronies in the rural society of Estanquet.

Bernès's house did indeed exist. It was inscribed in the land-survey of 1820–40 and formed part of a complex whole which was still double in 1840 and was called 'Françouneto's house', the name that would be retained by the single maisonnette which was to survive from this former pair of dwellings.

According to Jasmin himself, it was Jean-Vincent Bernès,

tax official, who introduced our poet to his peasant informant. The register of civil status for Roquefort gives us, under the date 17 April 1828, full information concerning this Bernès.[40] His name was Jean-Vincent Bernès and he was thirty-three in 1828, and so about forty-five when, around 1840, he met Jasmin. According to this register he was employed in the tax office, so Jasmin is quite accurate on that point, as on others. Bernès had a fine signature, as was proper for an official who, even though low in rank, had to be literate. He was the son of an Agen couple, Charles Bernès (died 1811) and Marie Lachassagne (died 1827). Jean-Vincent's father, though a citizen of a nearby town, may perhaps, in his distant origins, have come of Roquefort peasant stock. We do find some villagers named Bernès in that parish* when we look through the registers of baptisms, marriages and deaths between 1670 and 1780. In any case, on 17 April 1828, Jean-Vincent Bernès, son of Charles, married Louise Roux, daughter of M. Roux,† landowner, and Françoise Raynal. The bride lived with her parents until she was married, her home being at Estanquet. It was thus through these in-laws that Jean-Vincent Bernès became the owner of the house at Estanquet which came to him through his young wife Louise Roux – the house which Jasmin presents to us in 1842, in accordance with unanimous local tradition (still alive in 1982) as the house where Françouneto had lived. It was in this house, or in an annexe thereto, that the poet heard the story of the young witch, 'told by a peasant', this peasant being most likely someone close to Pierre Lacoste or even Pierre Lacoste himself, neighbour and perhaps tenant of Bernès. This Pierre Lacoste was also the occupier of a plot of land on which stood one of the parts of 'the house called Françouneto's', a dwelling presented to us as an ordinary *faisande*, typical of the locality, with a yard and at least two buildings, only one of which, transferred to the church in 1844, was to survive until the 1940s

* For example, a Jean Bernès, aged 60, was buried on 7 July 1748 at the church of St Pierre-de-Roquefort.

† The register of civil status does not give the forename of this Roux.

in its original cob. And this enabled M. Bacqué and other inhabitants of the hamlet to pass on, in their turn, what of the local tradition remained solidly established concerning 'the house called Françouneto's', to the investigator-historian who came modestly among them in 1980–82.[41]

Let us now sum up what we can claim to know about the chronology of the origins of the oral account. This amounts to three points:

1. The Monluc dating (1563–64) is most improbable.

2. The period 1618–1700 is marked locally by constant contacts between the Virgin of Bon-Encontre and witchcraft cases in the Roquefort area, and marked also by a resounding defeat for the Virgin in 1618, in connexion with a serious case of diabolical possession involving the Comtesse de Laugnac. The years 1618–1700 might well constitute, therefore, the period in which the actual troubles of Françouneto were crystallised – incorporating quite naturally the mythical schemas which previously-existing local traditions made available to credulous villagers.

3. A family named Pascal were established at Roquefort and Brax in the second half of the seventeenth century. Although Catholic, they had Huguenot connexions. These facts reinforce the preceding chronological hypotheses. A certain Pierre Pascal, probably a blacksmith, almost alone around 1660, and without brothers or sisters,* makes a highly presentable candidate, being the direct ancestor of the various Pascals who emerge from 1697 onward in the registers of the two parishes, these registers having been inaugurated in 1669. Furthermore, the lineage, both biological and spiritual (through godparenthood), which was to descend from this Pascal family is perfectly well established for the period between 1697 and 1842, at Estanquet and in relation to 'the house called Françouneto's', right down to Jasmin's collection of the story and to the oral traditions of 1980. This we know from the records, later reinforced from oral sources.

* This emerges also from a reading of the actual text of *Françouneto*.

3. *Closing up a chronological bracket*

Do other chronological reference-points exist that might strengthen still further these datings, which already fit together very well?

In this regard, we possess an interesting piece of information which has not yet been made use of here. For a long time there were two churches at Roquefort – St Jacques and St Pierre. The first-named was the parish church, while the second was the *former* parish church, which had subsequently become a mere local chapel; though, even after this demotion, it long retained some importance. This co-existence of St Pierre and St Jacques was regarded as quite normal in Françouneto's time, as we learn from the tradition collected by Jasmin. The church of St Jacques functioned, as we shall see, from about 1650 to 1825 as the 'new' parish church of the district. It was situated on the top of the hill and within the enclosure of the château of Roquefort, an area dominated for generations by the Secondat family, barons and *seigneurs* of the village. In 1826 the parishioners decided at last to shake off the tutelage of their *seigneur*, and also wished to have a larger church. Accordingly, they rebuilt their church lower down, within the *bourg* of Roquefort, in the plain, at the spot known as the *place*, or *placié*. For this purpose they demolished the church of St Jacques on the hill and used the materials so obtained:[42] the old church's life was thus quite short, from about 1650 to 1826.

Disregarding these final developments, we have to focus our attention on Françouneto's time, which was certainly a lot earlier than 1826. In those days the only two churches in existence, so far as we are concerned, were the chapel of St Pierre and the parish church of St Jacques, on the hill, which was the spiritual centre of the community throughout the reigns of Louis XIV, Louis XV and Louis XVI. This coexistence of two churches appears clearly in the narrative from which Jasmin worked. During an early period, contemporary with Françouneto, the young people of the village danced on St Jacques's day in an uncultivated, un-built-on field at the foot of a hill on which stood the château and the church of St Jacques. On other occasions in the annual cycle, both the young and the not so young, out of long-established habit, used to visit the other church of their community, which had once been the parish church but had been dethroned by the primacy given to St Jacques. This was the church of St Pierre, or St Pé, which, before the Secondats imposed St Jacques, had been the spiritual centre of the parish. It was situated on a ridge in the south-west of the district. It should be recalled, too, that the village of Brax (which may have been, rather than Roquefort, the original home of Françouneto and Pascal) also possesses a church dedicated to St Pierre. The Easter festival during which Françouneto was ostentatiously shunned by the other young people of the village was held in a church called St Pierre de Roquefort. A few weeks later came the hailstorm which was unleashed by unlucky Françouneto when she kissed the statue of the Virgin at Bon-Encontre.

A terrible storm ravaged all Roquefort. *A thunderbolt demolished the bell-tower of St Pierre's church*, and a hail . . . left the countryside only its eyes to weep with.[43]

Jasmin, at the end of the 1830s, either rightly or wrongly,[44] associated the first moves toward the abandonment of St Pierre (which took place to the advantage of the new church of St Jacques, the remains of St Pierre disappearing altogether in the course of the nineteenth century) with the dramatic circumstances – destructive thunderbolt, devastating storm – which accompanied the Françouneto affair. It is quite possible, too, that the persons who passed the narrative on down through the eighteenth century may have made this same connexion. After all, they could see the poor state that the old church of St-Pierre-de-Roquefort was in (already half-secularised), and it would have been tempting for them, whether rightly or wrongly, to include this process of decay among the temporal landmarks of their folklore-memory. However that may be, the oral narrative of *Françouneto* took for granted the co-existence of two churches, the new and the old, St Pierre and St Jacques, in the district of Roquefort at the time of the Françouneto affair. There is no special reason why we should doubt that this was so.*

In dating the legend in the time of Monluc, and more precisely in 1563–64, Jasmin thereby assigned this co-existence of the two churches to the 1560s. If it should turn out, however, that this co-existence – contemporary with a gradual transference of parochial functions from St Pierre to St Jacques – began later (in the seventeenth century, let us say), it would once more be apparent that the chronological association with Monluc is not to be taken seriously, even if Jasmin, out of concern, perhaps, to brighten up his story, thought fit to adopt or invent it. This would confirm what is indicated by other cross-checkings, namely, that Françouneto and Pascal lived, loved and suffered at least a century after the date mistakenly given them by Jasmin.

Let us consider the facts. The site of the church of St Pierre, which has today completely vanished and been replaced by ploughland, was in the south-west of the district.† This location is clear from the records and even known to the villagers of today whom I consulted on the point. In 1516, in the days of its modest splendour, this church of St Pierre was the only spiritual centre of Roquefort parish. It was 'the tax-farmer of St-Pierre-de-Roquefort' who paid the local share of the taxes levied by 'the department of the tithes of the clergy in the year 1516'[45]

* M. Bacqué remembers very clearly that, when he was young, the village *curé* went on Rogation Days to sing a *libera* on the former sites of St Jacques, on the hill where the château of Roquefort stood, and of St Pierre, near the present farm of St-Pé, in the north of the district.

† As the tractors draw the plough over the fields they still turn up well-cut stones on the former site of this church, now completely levelled. The lady who now farms at St-Pé, about a hundred metres from the former church, showed me exactly where it used to be, and this location was well known also to M. Bacqué.

for the diocese of Condom, to which the parish of Roquefort belonged. Almost a century later, in 1604, the situation had still not changed. On 1 January of that year, at Condom, Guillaume de la Capère, hereditary keeper of the register of ecclesiastical records (he bought this office on 6 July 1603), drew up a 'list and order of the benefices, offices and dignities which are in the diocese of Condom, with the holders thereof'.[46] In the rural deanery of Bruilhois, forming part of the said diocese, he mentions the existence of 'the living of St Pierre d'Aurignac, at Roquefort, which belongs to the priors of St Caprais, in Agen'. There is no mention of the church of St Jacques, which did not yet exist. This document is important for our enquiry. The move from St Pierre to St Jacques, which Jasmin presents as already under way in 1563–64, had not occurred before the end of the sixteenth century. For the whole period between 1516 and 1604 St Pierre was the only church in the parish of Roquefort. Once again the association with Monluc is rendered dubious: indeed, it has to be ruled out, since in Monluc's time the church of St Jacques did not exist.

About fifty years later, in the middle of the seventeenth century, the situation changed. We possess a register, or terrier, of the Bruilhois section of the diocese of Condom.[47] Judging by a number of dates given in the margins and in the text, this document is to be dated not long before 1656. It makes express mention of the presence of both churches, recording that at Roquefort there are two churches, St Pierre and St Jacques, under the patronage of the priors of St Caprais, in Agen. St Jacques has at last made its appearance. The parish registers of Roquefort, which begin in 1669 and continue without a break into the nineteenth century, henceforth distinguish carefully[48] between the church of *St Jacques*, up on the hill beside the Secondat château, which has become the spiritual centre of the parish, and the church of *St Pierre*, where a few masses, weddings and funerals still take place but which, out there on its remote ridge, now performs only marginal functions in the life of the district (see *infra*, Sources and Bibliography).

We have seen that *Françouneto* shows, as well as the co-existence in time of the two churches, that there was a dichotomy between them. St. Jacques, through the dominance of the *seigneurs*, determined the occasion and location of the parish festival or *bôto*, while St Pierre remained the scene of marginal ceremonies.* Therefore, the story told by Jasmin must have happened (given the other factors for its dating which I have mentioned) *after the foundation of the church of St Jacques*, an event of which, for the moment, we know only that it took place between 1604 and 1656, that is, long after Monluc's time.

Can we make our dating still more precise? To do this, we can inquire further into the matter of the two churches, St Pierre and St Jacques. This leads us to think about the local *seigneurs*, the Secondat family. We shall see that the new facts brought to light in that connexion are not without bearing on the chronology of Françouneto.

The move from St Pierre to St Jacques was associated with an initiative, not only *de facto* but also *de jure*, on the part of the great local lineage of Secondat.

It was in 1560, or, at any rate, between 1560 and 1562, that Jeanne d'Albret sold or granted to the Secondat family the *seigneurie* or barony of Roquefort. According to the Abbé J. Dubois, author of a manuscript account of the 'Châteaux and noble houses of the Agenais', which is in the library of the record office of the *département* of Lot-et-Garonne,[49] 'Jeanne d'Albret sold in 1560, on a hundred-year lease', the *seigneurie* of Roquefort to the Secondats, for 10,000 *livres tournois*. G. Tholin, another Lot-et-Garonne scholar, gives the relevant date as 1562.[50] This slight disparity of two years I have not been able

* The taking-over by the Secondats of the parish church of St Jacques and the parish festival, a relatively recent event which became *ipso facto* correlative with this new church, is clearly indicated in *Françouneto* (end of first section) by the arrival of the *seigneur* de Secondat on the scene of the quarrel which has just disturbed the normal progress of the festival. This can only have been either Gaston de Secondat, who was *seigneur* in the 1660s, or his son.

to overcome, since neither writer indicates the original source containing the text of this grant by Jeanne d'Albret. It appears, though, that 1560 is the right date. When Pierre de Secondat II, *seigneur* of Clermont-Dessous and other places, died in 1560, he already bore the title (which must have been quite recently acquired, and due to the transaction with Jeanne d'Albret) of *Seigneur de Roquefort*.[51] He was the first of his family in history to be *baron de Roquefort*.[52]

Continuously for more than three hundred years the Secondats were to reign over what became Françouneto's village. Here we find, from father to son, in order and for the period which interests us, the following noblemen, descended from an originally bourgeois lineage in fifteenth-century Berry:

(1) Pierre de Secondat II, King's councillor, treasurer-general of the finances of France in Guyenne, first *baron de Roquefort* born about 1490, died 1560.

(2) Jean de Secondat II, esquire, knight, King's councillor, *seigneur* of Montesquieu, major-domo to the King and Queen of Navarre (1515 or 1516 to 1599). He was the first member of his family to marry into royalty, through his wife, Eleanore de Brenieu, lady-in-waiting to Jeanne d'Albret, Queen of Navarre, and great-granddaughter of a princess of the royal family of England.

(3) Pierre de Secondat III, esquire, King's councillor, born at Agen (1571–1638).

(4) Finally, Gaston de Secondat, born at Bordeaux, gentleman, *baron de Roquefort* (1625–93). His descendants resided at Roquefort until the nineteenth century.[53]

It is noteworthy, at the heart of our problem, that this Gaston de Secondat, fourth *baron de Roquefort*, soon after his birth at Bordeaux on 12 April 1625, had as godfather Gaston d'Orléans, brother of Louis XIII, which confirms the high social level to which the Secondats had raised themselves. We have already met little Gaston's godmother – Serène de Durfort de Bajamont, Comtesse de Laugnac, wife of Honoré de Monpezat. This Comtesse de Laugnac, formerly bewitched, was also, as we know, the obstacle over which the Virgin of Bon-Encontre stumbled, before she failed a second time, even if only temporarily, in Françouneto's case. This first disaster suffered by the good Virgin of the district probably served as model for the second.

During the sixteenth century, and, especially, in the early seventeenth, the Secondats were literally to rearrange the district of Roquefort. They were undoubtedly responsible, in the last analysis, for the shifting of the parish centre from the old church of St Pierre to the new church of St Jacques. This holds true even if the storm mentioned in *Françouneto*, which was said to have destroyed the tower of St Pierre, and which, after all, may actually have happened, did help the Secondats a great deal in this undertaking. If so, though, the storm must have occurred a lot later than Jasmin supposed. The earlier church (St Pierre) was a long way away from the feudal mound on which the mediaeval castle was situated which became, around 1560, the property of the Secondat family. This château was also the centre of the local *seigneurie*. As far-seeing and persistent jurists, the Secondats made every effort to instal the village's new church, which was to bear the name of St Jacques, on the hill which they had thus acquired around 1560. We know that this installation of a new church took place at a date which is for the moment, undetermined, but certainly fell between 1604 and 1656 (see *supra*). The Secondats hastened to confer the name of St Jacques upon this new church which was to arise beside their fortress, although *Jacques* was not at all common (quite the contrary) among the dedications of churches in the Agenais and the Condomois. It is to be observed that the Secondats frequently gave this forename to their sons, both the first-born and the rest. Finally, this great family also rearranged to suit its convenience the cycle of festivals held in the village of which they were *seigneurs*. The parish festival was held henceforth at the foot of their château (see the beginning of the first section of *Françouneto*). It was held on St James's day in July, and no longer on St Peter's day, which is usually celebrated in

June. These two features, in space and time, are to be found in the first section of Françouneto, which is correctly placed, despite the chronological mistakes at the beginning, under the sign of the Secondats. This means that the oral narrative concerning Françouneto belongs to the exact period when this family were dominant and strongly consolidating their position, in the time of the first Bourbons, by moving the local church to a site adjoining their château.

The seventeenth century is thus the crucial epoch for the transfer of the parish church, for the re-emphasis of the authority of the Secondats over the village, and for the occurrence of Françouneto. In terms of the dynasty of the *seigneurs* of Roquefort, the epoch in question runs from 1599 to 1693. It includes the 'reign' of Pierre de Secondat III (*seigneur* from 1599 to 1638); that of his wife Anne de Pontac, who was *seigneuresse* 1600–38 and then dowager 1638–73; and, finally, that of their son Gaston de Secondat, baron and *seigneur* of Roquefort from 1638 to 1693. In the transfer, or duplication, of the village church the role played by Pierre III and, especially, his wife seems to have been vital.

According to M. O'Gilvy, author of *Nobiliaire de Guyenne et de Gascogne* (p. 263), Pierre de Secondat III, esquire, baron of Roquefort, King's councillor, patron of the Collège de Secondat in Toulouse, was born at Agen on 5 May 1571. He was baptised according to the Protestant rite by a minister named Courrac. The year 1601 saw the birth of his son *Jacques*, who became gentleman-in-waiting to King Louis XIII in 1619, at the age of 18 and died in 1634, aged 33. In 1614 another son, named Louis, had as godfather Louis XIII himself (though *in absentia* and by proxy). In 1622 the same King wrote to Pierre de Secondat III peremptorily requiring him to become a magistrate 'of the first order' in Bordeaux. Pierre died in or about February 1638. In his will (12 November 1637) he assigned the interest on a capital of 1,500 *livres*, already bequeathed by his father, to serve as dowry, every other year, for one of the girls from the foundling hospital in Agen. This tradition according to which the local *seigneur*, named Secondat, provided dowries for poor girls of the community or elsewhere, is found in *Françouneto*, where we learn that the heroine's mother was given her dowry by the *seigneuresse*: in other words, probably by Anne de Pontac herself. Finally, in the same will, Pierre asks 'to be buried in the monastery of the Augustinians in Agen, where his ancestors lie: he bequeaths to this establishment 500 *livres* for masses to be said for his soul'.[54]

The marriage of Pierre III also includes a number of elements of interest to us. His wife, Anne de Pontac, daughter of a treasurer of France in Limousin, gave him nine children, of whom the eldest was Jacques, the godson *in partibus* of Louis XIII, who died at 33, and the third was Gaston, godson of the all-too-well-known Comtesse de Laugnac, whose ex-diabolical celebrity thus extended to Roquefort, at the same time as she notoriously occasioned the first defeat of the Virgin of Bon-Encontre. Among these nine children there were also six girls, of whom two became Ursulines and one a nun having a special devotion to Our Lady.

Anne de Pontac also displayed sentiments of the loftiest piety. She died either in 1652 or in 1673.[55] On 5 November 1643 she made her will:

By this deed she bequeaths to the Capuchins of Agen an annual payment of twelve pounds of wax, to be used [evidently in the form of candles] for the celebration of the annual mass of the Purification of the Virgin, or Candlemas: a payment of five *livres* to the Blue Penitents [of Agen], on condition that they say four annual masses for the repose of the soul of Jacques de Secondat, her eldest son, deceased . . .

These various facts enable us to understand the lives of Pierre de Secondat III and Anne de Pontac, and the bearing they have on our subject.

Pierre III was born a Protestant, but, at a date unknown, either before or after his marriage, he became a Catholic. His wife was a cradle Catholic, and devout. She was an enthusiast for the cult of Mary (with candles to the fore). She was particularly attached to the Virgin of Bon-Encontre. She revered the

Capuchins, who were Franciscans like the monks at Bon-Encontre. This couple, by family tradition, provided dowries for poor girls. Furthermore, Pierre and Anne were, in 1625, friends with the Comtesse de Laugnac, whose importance for our subject we already know. It is thus perfectly comprehensible that, in the period when Pierre III and Anne ruled over Roquefort, and their surviving son succeeded them, the communal church of St Pierre should have been replaced by the seigneurial-communal church of St Jacques. It was indeed proper for a Catholic *seigneur* and *seigneuresse* (after being definitively cleansed of all Protestant stain by Pierre's conversion) to ensure the success of such an operation. It was even their duty to undertake the transfer of the church. For them it would have been an act of piety that was at the same time to their advantage, and it did indeed take place under their aegis. Between 1604 and 1656, during the rule of Pierre III and of his widow, the church of St Pierre was replaced by that of St Jacques.

We can date this transfer more precisely still. St Jacques was not popular as a patron among the parishes, livings and priories of the diocese of Condom to which belonged the parish of St Pierre-de-Roquefort. In 1604, out of 156 parishes in the diocese of Condom, only one, in the extreme south of the Condomois, bore the name of St Jacques (de Taillac).[56] A large number of village churches, however, were dedicated to the Virgin or to St Pierre.

Nevertheless, the *seigneur* and, still more, the *seigneuresse* of Roquefort, who survived her husband, had excellent reason for giving the name Jacques to the church they built on their feudal castle-mound, replacing the old church of St Pierre. In 1634 Pierre and Anne had lost their eldest son Jacques de Secondat, at the age of thirty-three. His death was certainly a disaster, both emotionally and from the standpoint of the lineage. At eighteen he had become a gentleman-in-waiting to King Louis XIII, and seemed destined to succeed, as heir to a fine fortune and also as a figure in the high society of the

Agenais and the Bordelais. In any case, the Secondats ascribed great importance to primogeniture: their domain at Roquefort was passed down through three centuries from surviving eldest son to surviving eldest son. A policy of transferring inheritance to the surviving earliest-born confirms this tendency, which, in any case, was normal for a great noble family. Marie de Secondat, for example, Pierre III's sixth child, who received a dowry of 20,000 *livres* at her marriage, was obliged, doubtless for lack of surviving children, to leave her property (in 1674) to her brother Gaston, Pierre III's third son, who had become the eldest survivor through the successive deaths of his two elder brothers. In any case, Jacques's death in 1634 must naturally have left an emotional vacuum in the heart of his mother, Anne de Pontac. Nine years after his death, this woman, whose thoughts were doubtless filled with the memory of the dear departed, bequeathed a sum of money to the Blue Penitents of Agen for the saying of four annual masses for the repose of the young man's soul. (It is not at all certain that Anne de Pontac, who was already Pierre III's widow at this time, took the trouble to provide a similar bequest on behalf of her late husband or of Louis, her second son, although he, too, died prematurely.)

There is thus a perfect explanation why the new church of Roquefort, situated on the castle-mound of the Secondats, should have been given the name of St Jacques, even though this dedication had previously been unfamiliar in the diocese of Condom. The Secondats were in this way paying a last and significant homage to their eldest son, dead so young, at the same time as they were asserting more than before their intangible domination of the new church of the Roquefort community, which had been directly created by them. This information greatly helps us in trying to determine the date of the move from St Pierre to St Jacques, which is so important for completing the chronology of Françouneto. So far, we have established, from terriers and other diocesan documents, that the move took place between 1604 and 1656. Now this bracket closes up, for it seems reasonable to suppose that the move was made between 1634, when Jacques de Secondat died, and 1656. During that interval, Anne de Pontac, helped first by her husband and then by his son and successor Gaston, completed the building of the church of St Jacques. Allowing for the time needed for decisions to be taken, and then for the actual construction of the new church, the latter cannot have been ready for use, and have 'entered into custom', especially where festivals were concerned, before the 1640s, at the earliest.

We can now provide Françouneto with a date that is reasonably certain. Our heroine belongs to the years 1611–1700, when rural witchcraft was one of the favourite targets of the Virgin of Bon-Encontre. She is later than 1618, the date of a resounding defeat suffered by that Virgin in a case of diabolical possession, which served as a tragic model for our witch. Françouneto is later than the years 1634–1650, during which the new parish church of St Jacques and the festival named in its honour were becoming established (these elements being featured in the story). She is necessarily earlier than 1708, the date when the last males of the Pascal family disappeared from Roquefort with Pierre Pascal, aged sixty, who had perhaps been, in his youth, the suitor and then the husband of Françouneto. She may have lived in the 1690s, which is when the Pascals appear for the first time in the parish register of Brax, and, more importantly, in that of Roquefort. Or else she is earlier by no more than a generation, co-existing (for example) with the youth of Pierre Pascal, around the 1660s.[57]

Here the last element for determining her date comes into play. Jasmin places the conclusion of his poem explicitly in a period which sees, if not the ending then at least the initial weakening, of belief in witches.* From this standpoint the Monluc dating of 1563–64 is totally improbable. The great waves of witch-persecution in south-western France, including the Condomois and the Agenais, came much later than 1560,

* See *Françouneto*, end of the last section.

in the first half of the seventeenth century. But if, as everything seems to suggest, the Françouneto affair took place around the 1660s, or between 1660 and 1700, these final statements by Jasmin, derived from his notes of the villager's narrative and corresponding to an important element in the local collective memory, become highly pertinent. The last epidemic of witch-hunting in Béarn and the Condomois occurred in 1670–71, and was followed immediately by the ending of prosecutions for witchcraft and the beginning of a de-criminalisation, or even a folklorising of the phenomenon, with a reversal of roles. 'Witches' henceforth were to prosecute those who defamed them, turning upside down the dangerous pattern of earlier times. If the chronology I have patiently worked out is correct, we see that, in conformity with the traditions recorded by Jasmin, the happy ending enjoyed by Françouneto corresponds to a general relaxation on the front of repression, or at least the beginning thereof – with witchcraft in Gascony, after 1671, while not wholly uprooted, yet effectively de-criminalised.[58]

At all events, the story of Françouneto is certainly later than the 1640s, when the church of St Jacques was being built; later than 1660, the first plausible date for the establishment at Roquefort of a marriageable Pascal; earlier than 1700 (the last period when there was a Pascal household at Roquefort); earlier, too, than 1702, when the tower of St Pierre was re-built.[59] She is thus much more recent than Jasmin supposed, and more recent also than was supposed by his informants, who innocently telescoped their village chronologies. She loved, suffered and married a century or more after Monluc, in whose time Jasmin or his informants had mistakenly placed her. She was contemporary not with Charles IX but with Louis XIV, in the days of the Sun-King's youth or of his maturity – in the days, too, of the last official witch-hunts, expressly so defined by Jacques Jasmin (*Françouneto*, last section, at the end). That is not all.[60] Written or edited late in the day, around 1839–40, after fifteen or eighteen decades of oral trans-mission, *Françouneto* shows, in addition to her own origins, the marks of a dual stratification. One stratum is due to Jasmin himself. The other was contributed by the peasant generations of the period in between,* which we know as 'the long eighteenth century'. Their successive accretions to or subtractions from the authentic tradition of our heroine were entrusted for completion to the wigmaker-poet of the July Monarchy. Françouneto is a real historical personage: but she also reveals to us important elements in Gascon culture which did not disappear under Louis XV and had not spoken their last word even in the epoch of the Revolution.

* At the same time, the prolonged survival of the Françouneto story, passed down from generation to generation through more than a century, supplies us with the key to the cultural reproduction of the witch phenomenon itself. In a particular region, what is witchcraft if not the totality of concrete stories about witchcraft, such as Françouneto, which are passed on down from father to son and from mother to daughter, and make available the indispensable narrative outlines for the myth? At a certain moment, these notions get applied, as canonical criteria, to a particular individual, who is then proclaimed to be a sorcerer or sorceress, and subsequently, to be the father or mother of such, and so on.

Postscript

[Written in response to a review by Pierre Eickell of the French edition of this book in *Les Nouvelles Littéraires* of 1 June 1983]

Pierre Eickell has criticised my interpretation of *Françouneto* and the historical restoration I provide for it in the third part of this book. Replying to him, I would say that I have in no way denied the important element of literary creation embodied in Jasmin's poem. On the contrary, I emphasise it more than once. It remains the fact that Jasmin, far from relying purely and simply upon his imagination, proceeded in this case, as in all his other writings, from oral traditions which he collected on the spot – regarding the *charivari*, the story about a blind man in the village of Castel-Culier, his own recollections, and so on. There is no reason to reject his own formal acknowledgement of this fact, nor to deny *a priori* that, as he tells us himself, he drew the 'principal features'[1] of the story of *Françouneto* from a folk-memory passed on to him by a peasant of Estanquet.

I point out above that Jasmin's work is placed within the setting of witchcraft cases in Gascony (abundant and well-defined in the seventeenth and eighteenth centuries) and also in the broader setting of European witchcraft cases in the same period, information about both of which has been made available to us by the work of scholars and historians, and through records and documents which I too have consulted.

What Jasmin tells us is quite clear.[2] He collected the factual nucleus, or 'principal features', of the Françouneto story in the tiny hamlet of Estanquet (in the commune of Roquefort, a few miles from Agen), in the house of one Jean-Vincent Bernès, an official in the revenue department at Agen. As I have shown above, this J.-V. Bernès was indeed living in that place at the end of the 1830s. Since his works were widely read in Agen and thereabouts, Jasmin could hardly have risked incurring a repudiation by this person. The poet had, of course, plenty of time to embroider the story of Françouneto, and certainly did not fail to do that. But he could not have created it out of nothing. The hamlet of Estanquet still exists. 'Françouneto's house' was demolished forty years ago, during the Second World War, but the old inhabitants of the hamlet know it and knew it then as such and under that name. They described it to me precisely, giving its dimensions, the materials of which it was built, and so on. What is more, one of the traditions imparted to me by an elderly resident of Estanquet, M. Frédéric Bacqué (concerning the transfer of this house to the commune) is confirmed by a deed of 1844 which I found in the records of the commune of Roquefort.

I did not base myself solely, as M. Eickell alleges, on the mere occurrence of a particular Pascal, whose name appears in the *Françouneto* poem, in the parish register covering the hamlet, the district and the village. Actually, by means of a thorough examination of the archives of the parish of Roquefort, I demonstrated the existence, within a well-defined bracket of dates (1697–1708), of a *group* of Pascals in Françouneto's village. This group, as revealed in the parish register of the locality, has exactly the same features as it has in the poem. What we see is a little group of craftsmen, situated in a marginal area and connected with Protestantism. Such a connexion, in a village that was 99.9 per cent Catholic, was no ordinary matter. The sole marriage contracted by a member of this group during the period in question recalls precisely, as I shall show, the marriage of Françouneto.

I did not merely mention a vague relation between some godfather and some grandmother. I established a highly exact and axial genealogy, extending from the Pascal family, towards the end of the seventeenth century, to the person who supplied Jasmin with his information in Françouneto's own house at Estanquet.

I mentioned also some other indices shared by the poem with the history of the village or the district: the distinctive historical features of the pilgrimage to Bon-Encontre at this time, and the coexistence of the two churches Saint-Pierre and Saint-Jacques, in the poem and on the ground, in the period in question. These indices make it possible to establish further confirmation of the chronological bracket, placing the story of Françouneto firmly in the second half of the seventeenth century and very probably at its end.

I simply proposed a change in chronology. Jasmin dated his *Françouneto* in the 1560s, in the days of Monluc. I showed that this dating is wrong, and was probably fastened by the writer upon the oral tradition he collected, or perhaps belatedly added by the bearers of that tradition. I showed that the story used in *Françouneto* is actually set in the reign of Louis XIV, not in that of Charles IX. Furthermore, I left full freedom to literary critics, whose trade and special skills are different from mine, to examine the strictly 'creative' aspects of the poem, which lie outside its nucleus of fact and chronology.

M. Eickell proceeds implicitly from the notion that *Françouneto* has nothing to do with any reality that can be subjected to analysis. But my approach respects both Jasmin's text and the facts. I explore the many convergent indications provided by the at least partly factual character of the traditions reported by Jasmin. Thereafter, the documents suggest a number of paths to be followed. In the end, these paths *all* intersect so as to designate a certain period and a certain family, the Pascals, craftsmen close to the Huguenots, as the actual foundations of the original story which Jasmin subsequently expanded into his poem.

This reaction to an opponent has led me to carry my research further, so as to establish a more exact identification of Françouneto with a real person. So far I have confined myself to determining the chronological bracket within which she lived; i.e. between the *terminus a quo* years 1650–71 (beginning of the coexistence of the two churches, St Pierre and St Jacques, at Roquefort, and the last wave of witch-hunting in 1671) and the *terminus ad quem* years 1702–08 (the year 1708 marks the end of the presence of male Pascals at Roquefort, while the year 1702 corresponds to the repairing of the bell-tower of St Pierre after its possible destruction by lightning, mentioned in *Françouneto*). In this postscript I intend to proceed further: I am going to undertake a re-examination of the materials so as to identify Françouneto, or at least the particular woman of flesh and blood who originally played her role as a witch in the hamlet of Estanquet.

Let us begin at the most elementary level. The poem *Françouneto* is, to some extent, grafted upon an actual past episode which took place between 1671 and 1702. It tells us of a marriage celebrated at Roquefort between a girl accused of witchcraft and a certain Pascal. The name Pascal, as I have shown, is not, despite first deceptive appearances, a forename but a surname, which was borne at Roquefort by three male persons, two of whom were adults and the other a 'post-adolescent': namely, Pierre Pascal, Pierre Pascal II, and Jean Pascal, in 1697–1700. It is in the period of those four years that the three men named appear in the parish register of the village, as witnesses to a baptism, fathers of new-born babies, or bridegrooms, and later, as persons deceased (the parish register of the adjoining village of Brax confirms the chronological bracket relevant to this trio).

The simplest procedure to follow therefore consists in looking in the parish register of Roquefort for the marriages which joined a girl who was resident locally with a boy, also resident locally, bearing the surname Pascal. The list is soon complete. I find only *one* such marriage between the critical dates 1671 and 1702. Indeed, I can add that this is the *only* marriage, celebrated locally, in which the bridegroom's name is Pascal, between 1669, when the parish register begins, and 1790, when the present-day system of civil registration takes its place. Nor are any more Pascals to be found in this village after 1790 or throughout the nineteenth century.

The marriage in question was celebrated by the *curé* Dessales, at Roquefort, between Jean Pascal and Marie Sordès, on 6 May 1700. The celebrant calls both parties 'my parishioners'.[3] This expression means that both of them were resident in the parish, but does not necessarily imply that they were born there. In fact, Marie Sordès was born in 1674 in the neighbouring village of Brax, while Jean Pascal and the other members of his family must have come to Roquefort, at some date earlier than 1697, from another community, probably not far from Roquefort, but which we do not know.

A little more can be said about the uniqueness of this Pascal marriage at Roquefort. There are, to be sure, in this village, other couples where the husband's surname is Pascal, and I have even mentioned two of them: Pierre Pascal and Elisabeth Gascq (known to us through the birth of Antoine Pascal on 28 March 1697), and Pierre Pascal II and Isabeau Agès (known to us through the birth of Anne Pascal[4] on 14 May 1700). As the Roquefort register does not record the death of an Elisabeth Gascq between 1697 and 1700 we may reasonably suppose that these were two distinct couples and, consequently, that there were two different men named Pierre Pascal. One of these, whom I shall call Pierre Pascal senior, was to die at the age of sixty in October 1708.

The weddings of these two couples, if they were celebrated at Roquefort, must have taken place before 1669, since they do not appear in the parish register, which is complete between that date and 1697–1700: or, a much more probable supposition, these weddings were celebrated elsewhere than at Roquefort, between 1669 and the 1690s. In any case, the dates of the two births respectively registered by these two couples in 1697 and 1700 makes it highly improbable that we are dealing with marriages that took place at Roquefort thirty or more years before, that is, earlier than 1669. However long the period of several decades during which women named Elisabeth Gascq and Isabeau Agès may have been fertile, it would indeed be a lot to ask of the documents (or of the absence of documents) to put those two weddings so far back. It is more likely that they took place elsewhere, before the Pascals moved to Roquefort. In our search for Françouneto as a person we are thus thrown back on the one and only marriage recorded at Roquefort between 1669 and 1700 (or even 1790) that involves another Pascal. This is the marriage of Jean Pascal and Marie Sordès, on 6 May 1700. Consequently, a very reasonable question arises: is Marie Sordès Françouneto?

The objection based on the difference of forenames – Marie instead of Françoise, Marianneto instead of Françouneto – is not, in fact, invalidating. The name 'Françouneto' may be an invention of Jasmin's, inspired by its resemblance to the pet-name of his wife, whom he loved dearly: 'Magnouneto'. However, this supposition conflicts with the fact that the peasant traditions of Estanquet and Roquefort preserved the name Françouneto ('Françouneto's house'), right down to 1981. But we only need to remember how important *nicknames* were in the onomastics of olden times, an importance which Abbé Mateu, a distinguished scholar of the Agenais, has confirmed for us further after his own researches in the old parish registers of the Agenais or Lot-et-Garonne. A girl might well be named Marie and yet be nicknamed Françoise, or Françouneto, at Estanquet-Roquefort in 1700. Or she could have been named Marie-Françoise, so that she is recorded as Marie in the written register when her marriage is entered therein, even though she is still Marianneto or Françouneto to her relatives and friends when they speak to or about her. Besides, the name Marie, or Marianneto, is mentioned in Jasmin's poem (second section) when he describes the Buscou party. It refers to another girl, to a friend or a possible doublet of Françouneto, during the festivities of that evening. There is therefore no problem here.

In any case, the fact that the marriage took place, in both instances, in May or June – 6 May 1700 according to the parish register, and *three weeks after the Feast of the Virgin in May* according to the poem – is not at all incompatible with the identification I am offering.

Moreover, the placing of a new bell in the bell-tower of the church of St Pierre on 1 August 1702 (according to the register), or two years after the likely date of the lightning stroke which destroyed that bell-tower (according to the poem, in its fourth section), gives us another chronological reference-point. In the short run it validates the identification of the Françouneto-Pascal couple with Marie Sordès and Jean Pascal, who were married in 1700. In relation both to the short season for marriages (May–June) and to the years in which the young family was formed (1700–02), the coincidence is striking. Certainly, there is nothing that tells against it.

If we put aside the objection concerning forenames, we are then struck by the similarities to be observed between the Marie Sordès-Jean Pascal couple and the Françouneto-Pascal pair.

Let us take another look at what we have discovered by comparing Jasmin's poem with the parish register. First, a point concerning the place where the two persons live. In the poem Françouneto and Pascal are both resident in the village of Roquefort, and have been since childhood or youth. This does not necessarily mean that they were both *born* in Roquefort. Similarly, in the register, when the *curé* Dessales married Jean Pascal and Marie Sordès, he addressed them as 'my parishioners'. They are both resident in Roquefort, then, and have been for some time (a dozen years or a little more), even if (to judge by the list of baptisms in the parish register of Roquefort for the years 1669–90) these two parishioners were not actually born in the village. (In the case of Marie Sordès we are fully informed. The parish register of Brax, the parish adjoining Roquefort to the north,[5] shows this girl as having been born, on 20 February 1674, as the legitimate child of Jean Sordès and Guiraude Tartas. This father and mother then disappear completely from the parish registers of the villages where Marie Sordès was to live: from the register of Brax – which, to be sure, has many gaps in 1675 and the two or three following years but is complete thereafter – and from that of Roquefort, which, on the other hand, is continuous from 1669. There is thus no reason to reject the picture given by the poem, wherein Françouneto's parents disappear soon after her birth, the father by emigrating and the mother by early death. We can even say that the Huguenot connexions of Françouneto's father would have made him emigrate some time during the years 1674–86, which was the period of the great dispersion of Huguenots from south-western France, before, during and immediately after the Revocation of the Edict of Nantes.)

As for the family situations of the young man and the young woman (Pascal and his bride), they differ from each other in a way that is absolutely parallel in the two cases – the register and the poem.

According to the oral tradition collected by Jasmin, which he turned into the poem, at the time of the events described Pascal is not an orphan: his father and mother are both living. A very young man, he takes part in the local dances and festivities. He belongs, in the village, to the band of *guyatets*, Occitan* for 'little lads', who are perhaps not long out of adolescence. Although his father is a blacksmith (*Françouneto*, second section), young Pascal has not yet decided on a trade at the time when he falls in love with Françouneto. True, he is able to wield a hammer: but he does this clumsily, and we can well understand his unfitness for the work, since at that moment he has already been bewitched (*Françouneto*, second section). His parents' house serves the needs of more than one trade. It includes, as the main feature, the typical small forge of a farrier. But it corresponds also to a modest agricultural holding, where, after the family's ruin, only a single scythe is to be found. Finally, in the first section of the poem, Pascal is engaged in agriculture and animal husbandry as well as working in his father's forge: he is described as a blacksmith (*Françouneto*, second section) but also as a *shepherd* and a *peasant* (*Françouneto*, first section). Let us take it that, many-sided like all the young men of humble origin in this rural area, he is still at the beginning of his working life, and is very far from having definitely chosen his trade. As an adolescent he shares in the work in his

* Translated in the French version of the poem simply as *garçons* – *Trans.*

father's forge: when married, but still young, he will be able to decide on a different craft. (In the *register*, Pascal is described, indeed, as a butcher, at the time of his death in 1706 at the age of twenty-two.) As regards Pascal's parents, both living, we note that, in the *poem*, his mother has all her faculties, but his father is old and ill. (Let us remember that in those days, if one's body had become weak for one reason or another, one was liable to be called 'old' at fifty.)

The family situation of the girl Françouneto, in the poem, is quite different from that of her suitor and husband-to-be, Pascal. She no longer has either father or mother. Her father, a Huguenot suspected of dealings with the Devil, has fled the country. Her mother has died of 'sorrow', or perhaps simply of some psycho-somatic illness resulting from the dramas caused by the heretical and sorcerer-like activity of her spouse. Her death occurred soon after the birth of her daughter. Françouneto still has her grandmother, with whom apparently she lives. In any case, whether or not Françouneto was born in a neighbouring village, the two women in the poem, the old one and the young, both live in the commune of Roquefort. Françouneto actually lives at Estanquet. Is her grandmother related to her on her father's side or on her mother's? From the poem this is not clear. In any case, this slight uncertainty does not affect the fact that, married long before to the heroine's grandfather (paternal or maternal), the relative in question bears *ipso facto* a maiden name (the only name recorded in the parish register) which differs from her married surname – in other words, *which is not the same as Françouneto's maiden name*. This grandmother, hidden somewhere in the parish register, is thus impossible to find, even with the aid of her granddaughter's name.

Finally, Françouneto, a coquette and even rather cool, is in no hurry to get married. It is not out of the question that this beautiful girl has already been for a long time the idol of the countryside; that she will soon be twenty-five and have to resign herself to spinsterhood; and that, in any case, she is older than the *guyatet* Pascal who is courting her. We observe, also in Jasmin's work, that there is another marriageable girl in the circle round Françouneto, namely, Marianneto. And we must keep in mind the special links, mentioned in the poem, that associate Françouneto with the village of Brax, which adjoins Roquefort and Estanquet: this village is the home of a boy named Laurent, the son of rich peasants, who is courting our heroine (*Françouneto*, second section).

Let us now compare these family data (concerning the two central characters in the oral tradition collected by Jasmin and in his poem) with what the parish register of Roquefort actually tells us. First of all, as regards Pascal. The Jean Pascal who is introduced to us by the register in 1700 corresponds well to the description given in Jasmin's poem. He is very young. When he dies, on 31 October 1706, six years after his wedding, the *curé* of Brax, who buries him, gives his age as twenty-two. Even if this age is an underestimate, we can say that the boy was married, on 6 May 1700, when he was still very young – at sixteen (according to the registers I have compared), or perhaps (if the Brax register is inaccurate), at seventeen or eighteen. All this fits very well, alike with the picture of a *guyatet* given to us in the poem and with the somewhat strange nature (also according to the poem) of Pascal's marriage with Françouneto. This is, indeed, not the wedding of a young man already settled in life, aged twenty-four or twenty-five, but of a boy who is marrying a girl more mature than himself, as the result of a sudden decision, such as that taken by our hero in the last section of Jasmin's poem. According to the register, the boy and his young wife moved subsequently to Brax, a few kilometres to the north, which was his spouse's birthplace. There he took up the trade of butcher, which is ascribed to him by the parish register of Brax at the time of his death in 1706.

Who, according to the parish register, were Jean Pascal's actual parents? This document does not name them (the *curé* of Roquefort at that time, in the notes which accompany his mentions of baptisms, weddings and burials, has little to say about the fathers and mothers of the persons married or buried). But the register nevertheless shows clearly the existence of two generations of Pascals. The younger is that of Jean Pascal himself: he is aged seventeen, at least, perhaps about eighteen, at the time of his marriage in 1700. The older generation, which gives birth to the younger, is that of Pierre Pascal: he dies, aged sixty, in 1708, and so is already fifty-two in 1700, when his son marries. It is perfectly plausible to assume that this Pierre Pascal is Jean's father, that young man having been engendered by Pierre when the latter was at the quite normal age for fatherhood, thirty or a little over. Here we even have a choice. The register for the years 1697–1700 shows us that there were *two* men named Pierre Pascal, one the husband of Elisabeth Gascq and father of a baby born on 28 March 1697, the other the husband of Isabeau Agès and father of a baby born on 14 May 1700. One of these two is very probably the father of Jean Pascal, allowing for the logic of differences in age. In other words, Jean Pascal, at the time of the episodes around 1700 which Jasmin describes, still has his father Pierre, who is indeed old for that period (fifty-two) and possibly ill. This 'aged' person dies a few years later (in 1708). Jean Pascal also has his mother, Elisabeth Gascq, or maybe Isabeau Agès. It will be seen that the situation of Jean Pascal, in relation to both his parents, as given in the register, is exactly the same as the poem describes for 'Pascal' himself.

The poem shows us a girl who has lost both parents and has only a grandmother who, *a priori*, bears a maiden name different from hers, and, on the other side, a boy who still has both parents living. The couple Jean Pascal and Marie Sordès, as we know them from the parish register, thus seemingly correspond – even in such details as the age and state of health of Jean Pascal's parents – to what we are told in the poem. Furthermore, the general chronological bracket; the month when the wedding takes place (May); the occurrence immediately after this (in the register) of the repairing or replacement of a bell in

1702 (this reference being logically subsequent to the destruction of the bell-tower by lightning in the poem, a few weeks before the wedding, which the register places in 1700); the fact that the wedding celebrated at Roquefort between a Pascal who is a craftsman with Protestant connexions and the witch can correspond *only* to the sole marriage of a Pascal who is a craftsman with Protestant connexions which is recorded by the parish register at Roquefort, within the chronological bracket mentioned and during the entire duration of the register under the *ancien régime* (1669–1790); all this points strongly to Marie Sordès as the most probable prototype of Françouneto. Moreover, Marie Sordès is without father or mother, in the register; she has a grandmother, but the register records only names, practically never kinships, telling us nothing about the latter apart from what can be deduced from identity of names; this grandmother bears, by definition, a surname – or, more precisely, a maiden name, the only name recorded by the registers in the case of women – which differs from that of her granddaughter. Again, Marie Sordès is linked with the village of Brax, like Françouneto in the poem, wherein we read that she is being courted by one Laurent, from a family of well-to-do peasants of that parish. According to the register, Marie was born at Brax in 1674, of parents who were perhaps married at Brax or at Roquefort before 1669, the date when the parish registers of these two villages begin. She left Brax to make her home, while still young, at Roquefort, and to marry there. Then, with Jean Pascal, who had become her husband, she was to return and settle down at Brax. The orientation towards Brax is thus clear both in the poem and in the real world of the register. We should add that Jean Pascal died only six years after his wedding. This death can certainly not have detracted from the reputation or suspicion of possessing the evil eye that attached to the former 'witch' who had become his wife. The disparity of age, in the register, between the two young people at the time of their wedding (she twenty-six, he eighteen or even younger) corresponds well to the rather strange atmosphere that prevails in the poem. What we read there is the tale of a relationship between a *guyatet* and a girl who has already been courted over a long period, and who has been able during all that time to keep a cool heart and a cool head.

Therefore, until better information comes to hand, I consider that the best candidates for the roles of Françouneto and Pascal are, in 1700, none other than Marie Sordès (probably nicknamed or sub-named Françouneto) and Jean Pascal. Which, of course, does not mean that Jasmin, exercising the sovereign powers of a writer of fiction, has not substantially enriched or even greatly altered his characters.

In conclusion, returning to the central theme of Part Three of this book, let us note Jasmin's use of terms that are quite out of place for the sixteenth century: the *jerkin* (*justaucorps*) worn by the churchwarden uncle of the soldier Marcel, and the *sabre* and *cockade* worn by the soldier himself. Self-educated but highly cultivated, Jasmin knew very well that these terms did not fit with the age of Monluc. This is therefore yet another argument (insufficient in itself, but, added to dozens of others, creating a snowball effect) for dating the *factual* nucleus of the story in the seventeenth century and the *transmission* of the oral text in the eighteenth. The bearers of this tradition imparted to Jasmin in 1840 not only the outline of the plot but, also, perhaps, certain concrete details (jerkin, sabre, cockade) which had been repeated and passed on by the peasants themselves. Their memories would still have been familiar with the styles of clothing and weaponry prevalent around the year 1700, which were to continue in use throughout the long period of the end of the *ancien régime* that followed it. There was nothing in all that which evoked the age of Monluc.

Sources and Bibliography
References
Index

Sources and Bibliography

[Note the following abbreviations: ADLG – Archives départementales, Lot-et-Garonne; AC – Archives communales.]

1. *Books and articles*

Jean Angely (canon), *Notre Dame de Bon-Encontre*, Editions Bon-Encontre, 1949, especially p. 23 (archaeological or stylistic data and finds of money, showing that the Virgin of Bon-Encontre and her cult go back to the fourteenth century, at least).

Abbé Barrère, *Histoire religieuse et monumentale du diocèse d'Agen*, Agen, 1856, Vol. II, pp. 380–90 and *passim* (the case of the Comtesse de Laugnac, at Bon-Encontre and elsewhere). See also, *ibid.*, p. 214 *et seq.*, a (somewhat uncritical) account of the legendary origins of Bon-Encontre.

François Bavoux, *Hantises et Diableries dans la terre abbatiale de Luxeuil*, Monaco, 1967, p. 77 *et seq.* Anne Vissot dries up the udders of the cows in the neighbouring village, where her husband lived as a boy. She takes away their milk and gives it to her own cows, and so is able to sell a lot of butter. We recognise the type of activity imputed to Françouneto in the seventeenth century, to the Mimalés around 1786 and to the sorcerers of the Bocage Normand in 1970: they improve their own well-being or add to their possessions at the same rate at which they diminish those of their opponents.

François Bayle and Henri Grangeron (Toulouse physicians), *Relation de l'état de quelques personnes prétendues possédées* . . ., Toulouse, 1682. The two authors describe an epidemic of hysteria in a village of the south-west. 'The possessed vomit or spit out pins, which are the demon's "charm". When closely watched, and their mouths inspected before the exorcism sessions begin, none of the girls spits out any

Conjurations faites à un démon possédant le corps d'une grande Dame. Ensemble des estranges responses par luy faites aux saincts Exorcismes en la chapelle de nostre Dame de la Guarison, au diocèse d'Auch, le 19 novembre 1618 et jours suivants, suivant l'attestation de plusieurs personnes dignes de foi, Paris, 1619, 16 pages. (Bibliothèque Nationale, microfiche. Repulsive smells emitted by the demon possessing the body of the Comtesse de Laugnac, originally bewitched by means of a flower.)

Pierre Deffontaines, *Les Hommes et leurs Travaux dans les Pays de la Nouvelle-Garonne*, Lille, 1932 (reprinted by Quesseveur, Agen, 1978), p. 399, confirms the absence of bridges (mentioned by Jasmin) over the Garonne at Agen in the seventeenth and eighteenth centuries. See also, in this connexion, G. Tholin, 'Ponts sur la Garonne', *Revue de l'Agenais*, Vol. 5, 1878, p. 439 *et seq.*, and Jules Andrieu, *Histoire de l'Agenais*, Paris–Agen, 1893, p. 144 *et seq.*

Jeanne Demers et Lise Gauvin, '. . . Loups-garous québécois', *Littérature*, 45, February 1982, pp. 79–113.

Abbé J. Dubois, *Châteaux et Maisons nobles de l'Agenais*, MS in the library of the Archives Départementales, Lot-et-Garonne, 1930, Vol. 5, pp. 126–7. Data on Roquefort and the Secondats in the seventeenth century. According to this researcher, Anne de Pontac, *seigneuresse* of Roquefort, died on 29 August 1652, and not in 1673, as another source indicates. Her son Gaston de Secondat, *seigneur* of Roquefort, the Comtesse de Laugnac's godson, married in 1647 Gabrielle de Gardes. (The Abbé Dubois obtained this information from the Archives Départementales, Gironde, B.763, and from the parish registers of St Etienne d'Agen. It was certainly around these dates, 1647–52, that the church of St Jacques de Roquefort made its appearance – the event constituting the *terminus a quo* of Françouneto, whose *terminus ad quem* is situated around 1700.

Abbé Durengues, *Pouillé historique du diocèse d'Agen*, Agen, 1894. (Inclusion of the parish of Roquefort in the diocese of Condom under the *ancien regime*.)

Jean Duvernoy, *Le Registre d'inquisition de Jacques Fournier, évêque de Pamiers*, Toulouse, 1965. This work, which served as the basis for my *Montaillou* (1975), also provided Carlo Ginzburg with many pointers for his investigation of the popular myths* about magical flights by the souls of sorcerers (in some cases in animal form) which enable them to enter a Beyond that is often identified with the country of the dead. This supernatural place sometimes contains a variety of riches, powers and information which are subsequently placed by the owner of the travelling soul, when the latter has returned to its body, at the disposal of his community, or else of himself and his family. These 'night journeys' belong to an old European, and even Siberian, tradition (shamanism). We meet them too in the *pays d'oc*, which is no exception and, indeed, provides some original examples. In the seventeenth and eighteenth centuries the werewolves and their like in this region (Marie de Sansarric in the form of a goat, and the Mimalés as wolves, if not Françouneto) were accused of the worst of crimes. Their good sides no longer showed up except in tiny doses. Thus, the Mimalés still dispensed some prosperity, but only to their own family, and the Sansarric woman acted on occasion as healer, but only in relation to persons she herself had previously harmed.

In the *pays d'oc* in the Middle Ages treatment of this sort of person (capable of changing into animal form and taking magical flight by night) as being diabolical was less certain than it became later on. The shamans of this region, or those who played their role, might be absolutely beneficent. This was the case (in Jacques Fournier's register) of Arnaud Gelis, messenger of souls at Pamiers in the county of Foix in about 1310–20. He brought back from his trips to the country of the dead – trips for which he duly prepared with copious intakes of wine – information and benefits for the living. According to Ginzburg the same details (heavy drinking before setting off on magical journeys, sometimes accompanied by change into animal form) are found among the sorcerers of the Valais (1428) and the *Benandanti* of Friuli (1575). As for Gelis's trip to the country

* Ginzburg is, of course, absolutely sceptical regarding the *actual* performance of the rites of the *sabbat*, so dear to the inquisitors. However, he thinks that in the conceptual construction of this *sabbat*, after 1350 (roughly), some elements taken from popular culture were first juxtaposed, then merged with those that the clerics drew from the ideological arsenal of their learned culture. What took place was both suppression of popular culture by learned culture *and* contamination of the latter by the former. These processes were neither simple nor unidirectional.

of the dead, Ginzburg compares this with similar journeys undertaken for utilitarian purposes by the *Benandanti*, by the *Kerstniki* in the Balkans, the *Kallikantzaroi* in Greece, the *Taltos* in Hungary, the *Burkudzauta* in Ossetia and the Shamans of Lapland and Siberia.

Other phenomena are reported in Jacques Fournier's register concerning the magical flight of a soul, changed into an animal, into the country of the dead, in order to bring back various good things – all this happening while the body to which this soul belongs is sunk in a propitious sleep. For example, in the same period, *circa* 1320, we have the myth of the lizard, as related by Philippe d'Alayric, native of a village in the county of Foix.[1]

Once upon a time, two believers [in Catharism] found themselves close to a river. One of them fell asleep. The other stayed awake, and from the mouth of the sleeper he saw emerge a creature like a lizard. Suddenly the lizard, using a plank [or was it a straw?] which stretched from one bank to the other, crossed over the river. On the other bank there was the fleshless skull of an ass. And the lizard ran in and out of the opening in the skull. Then it came back over the plank and re-entered the sleeper's mouth. It did that once or twice. Seeing which, the man who was awake thought of a trick: he waited until the lizard was on the other side of the river and approaching the ass's skull. And then he took away the plank. The lizard left the ass's head and returned to the bank. But he could not get across. The plank was gone. Then the body of the sleeper began to thrash about, but it was unable to wake, despite the efforts of the watcher to arouse it from its sleep. Finally, the watcher put the plank back across the river. Then the lizard was able to get back and re-enter the body of the sleeper through the mouth. The sleeper immediately awoke; and he told his friend the dream he had just had.

'I dreamed,' he said, 'that I was crossing the river on a plank; then I went into a great palace with many towers and rooms, and when I wanted to come back to the place from which I had set out, there was no plank! I could not get across: I would have been drowned in the river. That was why I thrashed about (in my sleep). Until the plank was put back again and I could return.'

The two believers wondered greatly at this adventure, and went and told it to a *Parfait*, who gave them the key to the mystery: the soul, he told them, remains in a man's body all the time; but a man's spirit or mind goes in and out, just like the lizard which went from the sleeper's mouth to the ass's head and vice versa.

The passage could not be more explicit. The sleep of the subject of the experience cannot be interrupted; it is almost supernatural, during the whole period that the spirit-lizard is absent. The change into animal (in this case, reptile) form is clearly described. Departure into a different country is emphasised by the existence of a barrier (a river or stream) and of a moveable bridge which marks the crossing into a strange *Beyond-the-river* or *Beyond-the-bridge*. That this Beyond is connected with death, and even with the country of the dead, is shown well enough by the donkey's skull which serves as the final scene of the lizard's journey. To be sure, the lizard-hero does not bring back a treasure from his trip, as happens in other versions of the myth, early-mediaeval or modern, but that it is indeed possibly a journey to a place of fabulous riches is shown by the presence in that Beyond of a wonderful palace, the ultimate aim of the journey. Finally, a precise distinction is made by a scholar (one of the 'Perfect' of Catharism) between the *soul*, as depicted in the learned religions (Catharism and Christianity, though enemies, are enemy brothers), which would never risk such adventures, and the *spirit*, as known to a humbler, more popular and traditional culture, which is independent of the dogmas of scholars. Significantly, this spirit belongs to a mere rank-and-file Cathar and not to one of the 'good men' or 'Perfect', belonging to the intellectual aristocracy at the head of the Albigensian heretics. Such a rather low-class spirit may therefore yield to the animal and magical metamorphoses dear to the old popular and peasant culture which is neither particularly Christian nor, of course, Cathar.

This fourteenth-century myth from Ariège survived without much change in Occitanian and Gascon folklore. Arnaudin collected it – simplified by the wear and tear of time, but perfectly recognisable – in the Landes, where it was attested by tradition so late as the end of the nineteenth century.

Needless to say, neither Arnaudin nor his informants knew anything of Jacques Fournier's register, which had not been published in their time.

One day, two men were journeying together. When they halted *en route*, to wait for the heat of the day to pass, one of them fell asleep in the shade.

While this man was asleep, the other one saw a fly come out of his companion's mouth and enter the skeleton of a horse's head which lay nearby. And this fly flew around inside the horse's skull, visiting all its nooks and crannies. Then it returned into the sleeper's mouth. When the sleeper awoke, he said: 'If you only knew what a fine dream I have just had! I dreamt that I was in a château where there were many, many rooms, each more beautiful than the last. You would never believe it. And under this château a great treasure was buried.'

Then the other said to him: 'Do you want me to tell you where you went? You went into this horse's head . . . I saw your soul come out of your mouth in the form of a fly and move around and about inside that skull, and then return into your mouth.'

So, then, these two men lifted up the horse's skull and dug the ground beneath it, and they discovered the treasure.[2]

This myth is not peculiar to the Occitanian culture, for we find it also in Irish folklore (Maurice O'Sullivan, *Twenty Years A-growing*, London, 1936, pp. 14–16).

That the myth (well attested in the county of Foix in the fourteenth century, and become folklore in the Landes in modern times) haunted Occitanian and Franco-Provençal culture from a very remote period is shown, for the early Middle Ages, by the dream of King Gontran of Maurienne, in Savoy. This Frankish monarch, whose adventure occurred around 565–585 AD, and who has the reputation of being good and just, despite his deplorable taste for whores (*meretrices*), wished to go hunting in the forest. He was accompanied by one of his henchmen. When tired, he went to sleep, leaning in a friendly way against the body of this henchman, or on his knees. Then, out of the sleeping King's mouth came a reptile, which tried to cross the stream that flowed hard by. To help it, the henchman laid his unsheathed sword across the stream. The creature was thus able to cross the stream without difficulty. It went as far as the foot of a mountain, then returned, along the sword, and re-entered the sleeper's mouth. The King woke up and told his dream: 'I crossed a river by an iron bridge. I went into a grotto at the foot of the mountain, and found there treasures beyond counting.' They went and searched in the grotto, and found there a huge quantity of gold and silver. With this precious metal Gontran endowed the local church and relieved the poor. There is no need to dwell on the resemblance of this story, of which we possess three versions, to the little myth that was related in Ariège around 1320. The transformation of the sleeper's soul into an animal, with magical departure and access to a wonderful wealth-bringing Beyond, is fully present in our text. The two earlier ones (mediaeval Savoy and Ariège) stand aloof from an official religion which is not hostile but remains external to them (the whore-fancying king endows churches, but has nothing clerical about him!). The third one (modern Landes) emerges in an autumnal state of folklorisation. The Occitanian or Franco-Provençal culture thus produces, in different circumstances and periods, out of a propitious bodily sleep, either spirit-lizards which reveal palaces or treasures, or werewolves which also possess supernatural capacities, but have to be kept clear of. This twofold production is found in many other European cultures, but it needs to be examined locally, so as the better to place our sorcerers, who are often endowed with capacities of this sort, in a wider cultural and mythical context, which also contributes to their creation.

Sources: For King Gontran, see the chronicle of Sigebert de Gembloux for the year 585, in Migne's *Patrologie latine*, Vol. 160, 1880, p. 110. See also the *Histoire des Francs*, Book III, Chapter 3, by Aymon, monk of Fleury (*Patrologie latine*, Vol. 139, 1880, p. 694), and the *Chronique* of the Region of Prüm (*Patrologie latine*, Vol. 132, 1880, pp. 31–2). These three passages in the Abbé Migne's work all deal with the story of Gontran of Maurienne. I am grateful to Mme M.-J. Tits who helped me greatly in my search for sources. The late René Nelli and Charles Joisten had previously suggested these remarkable references, in private letters. This affords me the opportunity to pay homage to two great researchers, who were also poets, and men of great spirit and great heart. See, in this connexion, R. Nelli, in *Folklore*, the review of ethnography in southern France, No. 122, Summer 1966, p. 20. According to Van Gennep, the basilica at Maurienne was founded in 565 AD (see A. Van Gennep, 'Légendes et chansons de geste en Savoie', in *Religions, Moeurs et Légendes*, Paris 1908–14, Vol. 4, pp. 186–7).

Géraud Duzil, *Notre-Dame-de-Bon-Encontre*, Agen, 1842.

E. E. Evans-Pritchard, *Witchcraft, Oracles and Magic among the Azande*, Oxford, Clarendon Press, 1937.

J.-M. Eyraud, *Les Secondat de Montesquieu*, Bordeaux, Féret et Fils, n.d. (Detailed genealogy of the Secondats of Roquefort.)

Jeanne Favret-Saada, *Les Mots, la Mort, les Sorts*, Paris, 1977 (essential). (Eng. trans., *Deadly Words: Witchcraft in the Bocage*, Cambridge, C.U.P. 1980.)

Jeanne Favret-Saada, *Corps pour corps, Enquêtes sur la Sorcellerie dans le Bocage*, Paris, 1981.

V. Foix, 'Glossaire de la sorcellerie landaise' (in the eighteenth and nineteenth centuries), *Revue de Gascogne*, 1903 and 1904. (*Adroumilhoun*, or shamanic sleep. *Bichère* or *béchèrre* ['were-goat': see Part One of this book, towards the end]. *Dame blanque*. Soothsayers and counter-sorcerers. Werewolves. *Mandago* or mandragora and 'were-goat'. *Mau dat*. Evil eye. *Sedas* or sieve for turning, etc. Many of these definitions were derived from oral questioning, but records from the *ancien régime* were also used).

J. Gardère, 'Un visiteur de sorciers en Condomois en 1671', *Revue de Gascogne*, Vol. I, 1901, pp. 408–13. (Last large-scale epidemic of witch-hunting in the Condomois.)

J. de Gassion, *Remonstrances et Arrêts faits aux ouvertures des plaidoiries*, Paris, 1630, especially pp. 480–561. (The Ramonet case in Béarn, after 1609.)

Carlo Ginzburg, 'The witches' sabbat', unpublished communication at the colloquium on popular culture held at Cornell University in April 1976 (on the *sabbat* and peasant shamanism). See also the communication at the same colloquium by Mary O'Neil, *Sacerdote ovvero strione* (a study of sorcery in sixteenth-century Italy which discusses the canonical formula *qui scit sanare scit damnare* – 'he who can heal can also harm').

Christian Guyonvarc'h, *La Mort de Muirchertach, fils d'Erc*: translation of a mediaeval Irish document, with commentary, not yet published. Sin, a mythical witch, amorous, breaker of arms, breaker-up of marriages, maker of bad weather and of agricultural riches, producer of goat-headed monsters, killer – is she the grandmother, or great-aunt, of our half-real, half-mythical witches of modern times, through continuity or the superposition of narrative schemas? In any case, my thanks to C. Guyonvarc'h, who introduced me to this intriguing Irishwoman.

G. Hanlon, *Culture et Comportements des élites urbaines en Agenais condomois au XVIIe siècle*, unpublished third-cycle thesis presented at Bordeaux University in February 1983. I learnt of this fine work after completing the present book. See, especially, p. 526 (the pilgrimage to Bon-Encontre): pp. 543–4 (the blasting of the church-tower at Marmande in 1672, a possible model for the blasting of that of St Pierre about 1700): pp. 551–2 (Marie Barast, a witch of Agen, paralysing arms and killing babies).

(Hélie). The *Chronique* (of Agen) attributed to Brother Hélie, text edited and introduced by the Abbé André Mateu, Agen, Quesseveur, 1977 (an essential first-hand document for the Laugnac case of 1618). This publication by M. Mateu, a great improvement on previous transcriptions, enables us (together with the documents by Sylvius and Malebaysse) to establish the three main stages in the diabolical possession of the Comtesse de Laugnac: (1) In 1617 a magician of Lyons, Brother Eusèbe, who later disappears from the story, bewitches the future countess, then a virgin, by means of flowers: (2) this possession becomes manifest for the first time on the new countess's wedding night, when she cannot consummate her marriage (in 1618): (3) the possession becomes worse during a pilgrimage which the countess makes to Bon-Encontre, where the diabolical intervention of Brother Natal (who gets burnt for it) aggravates her condition.

G. Henningsen, *The Witches' Advocate*, Reno, Nevada, University of Nevada Press, 1980. (A fundamental work on the dream aspect of sorcery and counter-sorcery in the Basque country at the beginning of the seventeenth century.)

Inventaire imprimé des Archives communales de Lot-et-Garonne, p. 114, Archives de Roquefort, E sup 614 GG1, 1669–99; parish of St-Jacques-de-Roquefort, with its annexes, including St Pierre.

P. Lamouazade, 'Deux procès de sorcellerie . . .', *Revue de Gascogne*, Vol. 1, 1901, pp. 402–8. (A sorcerer causes some illnesses and cures others, in people and animals, in 1672, in the area of St Gemme and Montfort.)

P. Lamouazade, 'La sorcellerie à Corneillan, etc.', *Bulletin de la Société archéologique du Gers*, second quarter, 1909, pp. 145–9.Continuity of witchcraft in (present-day) Gers through the seventeenth, eighteenth and nineteenth centuries.

P. de Lancre, *L'Incrédulité et Mécréance du sortilège* . . ., Paris, 1622. (Data, scattered through this large work, on witchcraft at Clairac, in the Agenais, and on the miracle with ghosts at Bon-Encontre, etc.)

J.-F. Le Nail, 'Procédure contre des sorcières de Seix en 1562', *Société ariégeoise: sciences, lettres et arts*, Vol. 31, 1976, pp. 155–232. The witches of Seix (in present-day Ariège) in 1562 have much in common with Françouneto. All, like her, are minor figures. They belong to a lineage of witches that includes some young spell-binders of her sort. They poison people, they attack both babies and grown-ups; they act by means of fire, poison and personal contact; they go for their victim's arm and paralyse it; they do evil to their neighbours and very close relatives (husbands, etc.); though they can harm, they can also act positively as healers; they live alone; they are accused by the community, through its gossip; they have a link with the Devil (but this does not include the stupid story about the *sabbat*); they are not werewolves, or, if they are, only implicitly so (by their harmful action at a distance). They deserve to take their places alongside Gérarde Mimalé, Marie de Sansarric (and Stedelen!), among the counterparts of Françouneto in the south of France: hundreds of others have remained unknown or little known. See Part One of this book.

Alan Macfarlane, *Witchcraft in Tudor and Stuart England*, London, 1970.

R. Mandrou, *Magistrats et Sorciers en France au XVIIe siècle*, Paris, 1968.

Sébastien Michaelis, *Histoire admirable de la conversion d'une pénitente séduite par un magicien . . . exoricsée l'an 1610*, Paris, 1613. This classic account of the Gaufridy case at Aix was doubtless not unknown to the ecclesiastics and laymen who investigated or dealt with the Laugnac case at Agen in 1618.

H. C. Erik Midelfort, *Witch-Hunting in South-Western Germany, 1562–1684*, Stanford, Stanford University Press, 1972. (Importance of hail, treated by Catholics as sent by the Devil and by Protestants as sent by Providence. On pp. 101–4 I note a kind of Swabian Françouneto, but she is treated only in outline.)

E. William Monter, *Witchcraft in France and Switzerland; the Borderlands during the Reformation*, Ithaca, Cornell University Press, 1976. (Were-wolves and hail-makers in the sixteenth century on the north-eastern borders of the Franco-Provençal region.)

Pierre Montresse, *Nouvelle Histoire d'une fille du diocèse d'Agen . . . laquelle a vomi plusieurs horrible. animaux*, Bibliothèque Nationale, 8°Tb 73196 (Toulouse, 1695). 'A Cartesian physician of Toulouse tries to prove that the girl in question was not bewitched. The account of the case includes, however, a fine story about someone being bewitched by a kiss from the sorceress, and the writer's attempt to exorcise the victim. The case occurred to the north of Villeneuve-sur-Lot, at the edge of the Périgord forest. The girl vomited insects, and possibly large toads as well, during a fairly long period (over six months). The physician tries to convince us that the girl had previously swallowed them . . . A scene occurs during mass after the symptoms had disappeared for a few months' (analysis by G. Hanlon).

R. Muchembled, in the symposium *Prophètes et Sorciers dans les Pays-Bas, XVIe–XVIIIe siècle*, Paris, 1978.

R. Muchembled, *Cultures populaires et Culture des élites*, Paris, 1978.

R. Muchembled, *Les Derniers Bûchers*, Paris, 1981.

R. Nelli, *Le Languedoc et le Comté de Foix, le Roussillon*, Paris, Gallimard, 1958.

M. O'Gilvy, *Nobiliaire de Guyenne et de Gascogne*, Paris, 1858, Vol. II, pp. 251–66. (On the Secondats de Montesquieu – see, particularly, pp. 263–5 for the Roquefort Secondats.)

Jean-Pierre Piniès, *La Trilogie sorcellaire en Bas-Languedoc; Breish, endevinaire, armier*. Duplicated copy in the municipal library of Carcassonne of a third-cycle thesis of Toulouse University. An excellent ethnographical study (especially p. 90 *et seq.*, on the present-day powers of local sorcerers). It should be observed that in the twentieth century the werewolf almost vanished from southern French sorcery, probably as a result of the physical extinction of wolves. Animal disguise and magic flight through the air from a sleeping body is still found, right down to a period close to our own, but animals other than the wolf are involved. Also, in 1960–80, there is no longer talk of the anti-sexual variety of witchcraft (*aiguillette*) which was important in the seventeenth century. It may have been a victim, even into our own time, of the triumphant Victorianism of 1880–1950.

A. Plieux, 'L'ancienne paroisse de Vicnau', *Revue de Gascogne*, 1883, Vol. 24, p. 126. (The werewolf in the Condomois.)

Daniel Poirion, *Le Merveilleux dans la littérature française du Moyen Age*, Paris, P.U.F., Collection 'Que sais-je?', 1982, p. 30. The mandrake, that wondrous forest plant, in mediaeval romances. It was to survive into the witchcraft practised in Gascony under the *ancien régime* (see the case of the Mimalés).

Claude Proust, a Celestine monk, *Le Guide des pèlerins de Notre-Dame de Verdelais*, Bordeaux, 1700, pp. 3–5. The re-launching of this pilgrimage, in south-western France, at the beginning of the seventeenth century, in ways rather similar to those (Italianate?) described at Bon-Encontre, a century earlier. See also, in the same connexion, Michel Lurton, 'N.-D. de Verdelais, 1492–1953', in *Revue française d'histoire du livre*, 1979, pp. 341–58, and Archives départementales, Gironde, series G 669 (exorcism of a girl at Verdelais). (Reported by G. Hanlon.)

L. W. Ravenez, *Histoire du Cardinal François de Sourdis*, Bordeaux-Paris, 1867. Especially pp. 380–3, on the Laugnac case.

W. Recroix, *Les Peintures . . . de la Chapelle de Garaison*, Pau, 1981. Data on this chapel and on the way in which the Virgin there succeeded in curing the Comtesse de Laugnac, whereas Bon-Encontre had failed.

Georges Rocal, *Vieilles Coutumes magiques et dévotieuses du Périgord*, 1922, republished Périgueux, 1971. Studies survivals of the world of magic in Dordogne at the beginning of the twentieth century, including witches and those who cast the evil eye – p. 36.

R. P. Vincent de Rouen, *L'Heureuse Rencontre du ciel et de la terre ou l'invention miraculeuse de l'image de la mère de Dieu, honorée sous le titre de N. D. de Bon-Encontre en l'église du Tiers Ordre de Saint François*, Toulouse, 1642. (Archives Départementales, Lot-et-Garonne, 4 Mi 59 [R1].) A garrulous and useful work. It reproduces most of the successful cures mentioned in the MS in the Archives Départementales, Lot-et-Garonne, *fonds* Marboutin 12 J 14, but says nothing of the Laugnac scandal (1618) and provides, deliberately, an edifying counterpoint to this silence.

S. Seligman, *Das böse Blick*, Berlin, 1910.

Alfred Soman, 'La sorcellerie vue du Parlement de Paris, au début du XVIIe siècle', *Actes du 104e Congrès des Sociétés Savantes*, Bordeaux, 1979, section on modern and contemporary history, Vol. 2, pp. 393–405, Paris, Bibliothèque Nationale, 1981. On a remarkable model of sorcerers as bringers of riches to themselves or to others, etc. See also a fine article by the same writer in *Annales ESC*, Vol. 32, 1977, pp. 790–814.

J.-C. Sournia, *Monluc*, Paris, 1981. (Shows the belatedness of the black legend of Monluc – which was, as we have seen, grafted artificially onto the chronology of Françouneto.)

Isaac Sylvius (Protestant polemicist), *Miracles des diables chassés a Bon-Encontre*, Montauban, 1620. A rare book: there is a copy in the municipal library of Bordeaux, shelf-mark T 8684/1–3.

G. Tholin, *Études sur l'architecture religieuse dans l'Agenais*, Agen-Paris, especially p. 319. In the general list of churches in the diocese of Agen, sixty-eight are dedicated to the Virgin, forty-eight to St Pierre, and many others to SS. Jean, Martin, Caprais, Foy, etc., but St Jacques is practically unrepresented. (See Part Three of this book.)

G. Tholin, *Le Livre de raison des Daurée d'Agen*, Agen, 1880.

G. Tholin, *Abrégé de l'histoire des communes du Lot-et-Garonne* (*arrondissement* of Agen), Auch, Cocharaux, 1900. (p. 12 *et seq.*, the Laugnac case, and, pp. 29, 60, the Secondats of Roquefort, including the grant to them of this village at the beginning of the Wars of Religion).

G. Tholin, *Histoire de Montpezat*, Auch, 1898, pp. 262–8. (Genealogical data on the Comtesse de Laugnac and her family.)

M. Tierny, 'Les sorciers du Bas-Armagnac', *Revue de Gascogne*, 1896, Vol. 37, pp. 71–4. See also J. Brana, 'Sorcellerie à Eauze (1643–44)', *Revue de Gascogne*, 1884, Vol. 25, pp. 358–60. (Soothsayers, surgeons and 'visitors' against sorcerers, during a year of dearth.)

(Jacques de Vitry), *The Exempla of Jacques de Vitry*, edited by Thomas Frederick Crane, Kraus Reprint, 1967.

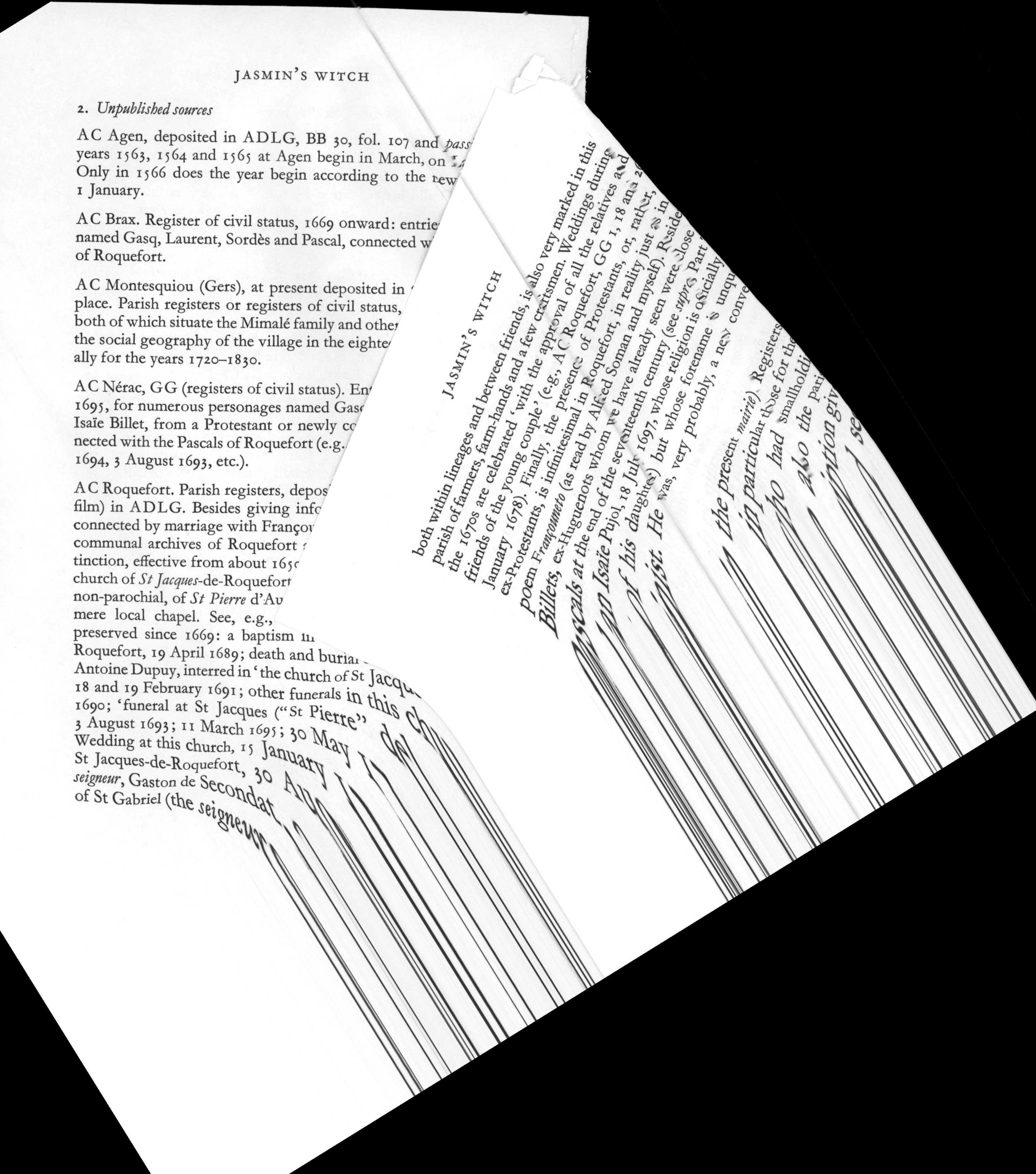

2. *Unpublished sources*

AC Agen, deposited in ADLG, BB 30, fol. 107 and *pass*
years 1563, 1564 and 1565 at Agen begin in March, on
Only in 1566 does the year begin according to the new
1 January.

AC Brax. Register of civil status, 1669 onward: entrie
named Gasq, Laurent, Sordès and Pascal, connected w
of Roquefort.

AC Montesquiou (Gers), at present deposited in
place. Parish registers or registers of civil status,
both of which situate the Mimalé family and other
the social geography of the village in the eighte
ally for the years 1720–1830.

AC Nérac, GG (registers of civil status). En
1695, for numerous personages named Gas
Isaïe Billet, from a Protestant or newly co
nected with the Pascals of Roquefort (e.g.
1694, 3 August 1693, etc.).

AC Roquefort. Parish registers, depos
film) in ADLG. Besides giving info
connected by marriage with Françou
communal archives of Roquefort
tinction, effective from about 165
church of *St Jacques*-de-Roquefort
non-parochial, of *St Pierre* d'Au
mere local chapel. See, e.g.,
preserved since 1669: a baptism in
Roquefort, 19 April 1689; death and burial
Antoine Dupuy, interred in 'the church of St Jacque
18 and 19 February 1691; other funerals in this ch
1690; 'funeral at St Jacques ("St Pierre" de
3 August 1693; 11 March 1695; 30 May 17
Wedding at this church, 15 January 17
St Jacques-de-Roquefort, 30 Au
seigneur, Gaston de Secondat
of St Gabriel (the *seigneur*

S. Seligman, *Das böse Blick*, Berlin, 1910.

Alfred Soman, 'La sorcellerie vue du Parlement de Paris, au début du XVIIe siècle', *Actes du 104e Congrès des Sociétés Savantes*, Bordeaux, 1979, section on modern and contemporary history, Vol. 2, pp. 393–405, Paris, Bibliothèque Nationale, 1981. On a remarkable model of sorcerers as bringers of riches to themselves or to others, etc. See also a fine article by the same writer in *Annales ESC*, Vol. 32, 1977, pp. 790–814.

J.-C. Sournia, *Monluc*, Paris, 1981. (Shows the belatedness of the black legend of Monluc – which was, as we have seen, grafted artificially onto the chronology of Françouneto.)

Isaac Sylvius (Protestant polemicist), *Miracles des diables chassés a Bon-Encontre*, Montauban, 1620. A rare book: there is a copy in the municipal library of Bordeaux, shelf-mark T 8684/1–3.

G. Tholin, *Études sur l'architecture religieuse dans l'Agenais*, Agen-Paris, especially p. 319. In the general list of churches in the diocese of Agen, sixty-eight are dedicated to the Virgin, forty-eight to St Pierre, and many others to SS. Jean, Martin, Caprais, Foy, etc., but St Jacques is practically unrepresented. (See Part Three of this book.)

G. Tholin, *Le Livre de raison des Daurée d'Agen*, Agen, 1880.

G. Tholin, *Abrégé de l'histoire des communes du Lot-et-Garonne* (*arrondissement* of Agen), Auch, Cocharaux, 1900. (p. 12 *et seq.*, the Laugnac case, and, pp. 29, 60, the Secondats of Roquefort, including the grant to them of this village at the beginning of the Wars of Religion).

G. Tholin, *Histoire de Montpezat*, Auch, 1898, pp. 262–8. (Genealogical data on the Comtesse de Laugnac and her family.)

M. Tierny, 'Les sorciers du Bas-Armagnac', *Revue de Gascogne*, 1896, Vol. 37, pp. 71–4. See also J. Brana, 'Sorcellerie à Eauze (1643–44)', *Revue de Gascogne*, 1884, Vol. 25, pp. 358–60. (Soothsayers, surgeons and 'visitors' against sorcerers, during a year of dearth.)

(Jacques de Vitry), *The Exempla of Jacques de Vitry*, edited by Thomas Frederick Crane, Kraus Reprint, 1967.

2. *Unpublished sources*

AC Agen, deposited in ADLG, BB 30, fol. 107 and *passim*. The years 1563, 1564 and 1565 at Agen begin in March, on Lady Day. Only in 1566 does the year begin according to the new style, on 1 January.

AC Brax. Register of civil status, 1669 onward: entries for persons named Gasq, Laurent, Sordès and Pascal, connected with the Pascals of Roquefort.

AC Montesquiou (Gers), at present deposited in the *mairie* of this place. Parish registers or registers of civil status, and land-surveys, both of which situate the Mimalé family and others in the history and the social geography of the village in the eighteenth century, especially for the years 1720–1830.

AC Nérac, GG (registers of civil status). Entries, between 1680 and 1695, for numerous personages named Gasq, or Timothée Billet, or Isaïe Billet, from a Protestant or newly converted milieu, and connected with the Pascals of Roquefort (e.g., 7 July 1687, 27 September 1694, 3 August 1693, etc.).

AC Roquefort. Parish registers, deposited (originals, and on microfilm) in ADLG. Besides giving information on the Pascal family, connected by marriage with Françouneto (see Part Three *supra*), the communal archives of Roquefort also clearly demonstrate the distinction, effective from about 1650 onward, between the new parish church of *St Jacques*-de-Roquefort and the former church, henceforth non-parochial, of *St Pierre* d'Aurignac, which increasingly became a mere local chapel. See, e.g., the parish registers of Roquefort, preserved since 1669: a baptism in the church of St Jacques-de-Roquefort, 19 April 1689; death and burial of the *curé* of Roquefort, Antoine Dupuy, interred in 'the church of St Jacques-de-Roquefort', 18 and 19 February 1691; other funerals in this church, 11 October 1690; 'funeral at St Jacques ("St Pierre" deleted)-de-Roquefort', 3 August 1693; 11 March 1695; 30 May 1715; 15 January 1757, etc. Wedding at this church, 15 January 1757; christening of the bell of St Jacques-de-Roquefort, 30 August 1693, in the presence of the *seigneur*, Gaston de Secondat, and his wife Gabrielle, with invocation of St Gabriel (the *seigneuresse's* patron saint), St Jacques (the name of the parish church for which the bell was being blessed), and St Pierre (the name of the former parish church, a fraction of a league to the south). In contrast* to this christening of the bell of St Jacques-de-Roquefort, funerals in the former parish church of St Pierre d'Aurignac on 13 September 1681, 27 and 28 February and 11 March 1695, wedding at St Pierre d'Aurignac on 25 November 1681, etc.; burials in the cemetery of this church on 9 November 1671, 26 September 1675, 14 May 1676, 10 September 1677, and 18 August 1681. All these records concerning St Pierre d'Aurignac are counterposed in the 1670s to the funerals and weddings 'in the church of Roquefort', meaning the official church of St Jacques-de-Roquefort (cf. *supra*).

In short, apart from some express allusions to a chapel at Sourdignac, a third, but minor, place of worship, in the north of the district, the parish register of Roquefort from its beginning in 1669 contrasts 'the church and cemetery of St Pierre d'Aurignac' (16 September 1675, 30 December 1675) with 'the church of Roquefort', giving no further details (21 September 1671, 7 May 1680, etc.). In these circumstances, the latter church cannot be other than St Jacques-de-Roquefort – expressly mentioned in 1656 in the terrier of the diocese of Condom and often referred to as such in the parish registers of 1669–99. Note also that the parish register of the 1670s lists about eighty per cent of the parishioners as illiterate, which gives an overwhelming impression of ignorance in a parish which at that time was receptive to witchcraft. The family and religious structures were, in their own ways, very strong here. The first natural child, or bastard, a baby girl, appears on 31 August 1683, whereas the register of baptisms (perfectly kept) in the young parish of Roquefort, continuous since 1669, has recorded in the previous fourteen years none but legitimate children. (True, some bastards may have been baptised and/or abandoned in the neighbouring big town of Agen: the temptation to do this would have been strong.) Village cohesion,

* That this christening of a bell does indeed relate to the church of St Jacques-de-Roquefort, honoured in this way by the precedence given to the saint it was named after, Jacques (which name, nevertheless, out of respect for feudal hierarchy, came after that of the patron saint of the *seigneuresse*, Gabriel) is proved, *a contrario*, by the christening of the bell of the other church, St Pierre d'Aurignac, on 1 August 1702 (parish register for that date) with the single name of St Pierre.

both within lineages and between friends, is also very marked in this parish of farmers, farm-hands and a few craftsmen. Weddings during the 1670s are celebrated 'with the approval of all the relatives and friends of the young couple' (e.g., AC Roquefort, GG 1, 18 and 26 January 1678). Finally, the presence of Protestants, or, rather, of ex-Protestants, is infinitesimal in Roquefort, in reality just as in the poem *Françouneto* (as read by Alfred Soman and myself). Besides the Billets, ex-Huguenots whom we have already seen were close to the Pascals at the end of the seventeenth century (see *supra*, Part Three), I find an Isaïe Pujol, 18 July 1697, whose religion is officially Catholic (baptism of his daughter) but whose forename is unquestionably Biblico-Calvinist. He was, very probably, a new convert, like the Billets.

AC Roquefort (kept in the present *mairie*). Registers of civil status for the nineteenth century, in particular those for the 1830s. Numerous *faisandiers* (farm-hands who had smallholdings), notably at Estanquet (31 August 1830). See also the parish register for 18 January 1787 (same dating). The description given by Jasmin of this hamlet of Estanquet (*Françouneto*, second section, Françouneto's *faisande*) is confirmed.

AC Roquefort, set of files recently deposited in ADLG. Files marked 'communal property', 'various deeds', etc. The 'suit by the *maire* against the Baron de Roquefort (=Secondat)' contains interesting documents on the churches of *St-Jacques-du-haut* and *St-Pierre*.

AC Roquefort, unclassified documents, deposited in ADLG. A nominal roll of the census of 1851, showing four families or households at Estanquet, the heads of two of these being farm-hands, one a share-cropper, and one a landowning farmer. They include the Castex, Pandelé and Coveque families, lineages established long before in this hamlet or village, and originally contemporaries of the Pascals.

ADLG, archives of communes deposited in the record office of the *département*: E Sup 323 and E Sup 500. A few data (for 1605, 1610, and 1721) on the pilgrimage to Bon-Encontre.

ADLG, Series G, ecclesiastical files: records of the Bishopric of Agen, register shelf-marked C1 in the old classification, particularly fol. 19, concerning the pilgrimage to Bon-Encontre in the sixteenth century.

ADLG, series G, records of the Bishopric; pastoral visits by Bishop Nicolas de Villars (1594–1608), *fonds* C2, – p. 523. A Virgin in an oak-tree at the church of Notre-Dame-de-*Bonnes-Nouvelles*, near the château of Biron and the forest of the Sarladais; just as at *Bon-Encontre*, at Notre-Dame-de-Verdelais, and at Nostra Signora della Quercia (=oak-tree), near Viterbo. This reference to the ADLG was kindly given me by G. Hanlon.

ADLG, 2 J 52, diary of Malebaysse (of Agen); essential, especially for the year 1618 and the Laugnac case.

ADLG, 2 J 57, year 1520: notes on the origins of Protestantism in the Agenais, and especially in Nérac, in the 1520s.

ADLG, 2 J 59, year 1790: second-hand notes by Labrunie, not very original. They relate to the Laugnac case (1618) and are recorded in the superior spirit of the Enlightenment ('I have reported this fact in order to acquaint the reader with the attitude of those days').

ADLG, 2 J 60, Argenton collection (eighteenth century), with a quite unjustified correction of '1617' to '1618' for the Hélie document concerning the Laugnac case (which did in fact begin in 1617).

ADLG, Series G, *fonds* of the former Bishopric of Agen, register F2. This is a detailed report of the exorcism of the Comtesse de Laugnac's servants (1618), when the Devil proved to be too much for the Virgin of Bon-Encontre – a document which presages the Loudun reports of 1632 and could be subjected to analyses such as those carried out by M. de Certeau on Urbain Grandier and his circle.* From this docu-

* For example, an extract from the beginning of this document: 'Folio 1: The said Sieur de Lescases (the priest) began the mass at six o'clock. Guilhaumette (one of the servant-girls) heard the mass piously and received the Holy Sacrament without becoming agitated. She remained calm after the mass, until the recitation of the Litanies began, when she started to throw herself about. Immediately after the Litanies were over she grew calm again. Then the exorcism started. She listened without stirring. Anbec was commanded *ut accederet ad linguam et recitaret juramenta solita et apponeret ambas manus supra pedes crucifixe in formam crucis et levaret supra dextram*. She obeyed promptly. At the first word, *Ego*, she resisted more than normally, and afterwards too, at the same words . . .'.

ment we see, too, how traditional, canonical and well-attested are the pious actions performed by Françouneto at Bon-Encontre (offering a candle, kissing a holy image, etc.).

ADLG, 12 J 14, *fonds* Marboutin. Register of the miracles and cures recorded at Bon-Encontre from 1584 to the end of the seventeenth century. Many phenomena that we should nowadays describe as hysterical appear to have found a happy solution at Bon-Encontre. The same observation applies to the similar miracles recorded in the book by Father Vincent de Rouen. Noticeable also in this manuscript is the hiatus of five years, 1618–23, during which the local Virgin abstained from performing any miracles – a gap evidently due to the frightful Laugnac scandal and the condemnation to the stake, in the same connexion, of one of the religious in charge of the shrine.

References

Jasmin, Hairdresser–Poet

1. See George Sand's *La Petite Fadette*, based upon Jasmin's *Les Frays Bessous (Les Deux Frères Jumeaux)*.
2. On the errors in Michelet's *The Sorceress*, see Norman Cohn, *Europe's Inner Demons* (1975), pp. 105–7.
3. On Jasmin there are essays or biographies by Léon Rabain (1866), Raoul Vèze (1901), Jacques Augarde (1933), Gaston Guillaumié (1941) and Charles Pujos (1965). The poet's works (*Papillotos*) were published between 1835 and 1863, and republished in 1889 and 1898.

Part One

1. R. Muchembled, *Culture populaire et culture des élites . . . (XVe–XVIIIe siècles)*, Paris, Flammarion, 1978, p. 289. See also J.-F. Le Nail, 'Procédures contre les sorcières de Seix [in present-day Ariège] en 1562,' *Société ariégeoise, Sciences, lettres et arts*, Vol. 31, 1976, pp. 156–60.
2. R. Muchembled, *La Sorcière au village (XVe–XVIIIe siècles)*, Paris, Plon, 1979, p. 124.
3. *Ibid.*, p. 124.
4. *La Sorcière*, 1862 (English translation, *The Sorceress*, 1905).
5. *The Witch-Cult in Western Europe*, Oxford, 1921.
6. *I Benandanti*, Turin, Einaudi, 1966 (English translation, *The Night Battles*, London, 1983).
7. E. E. Evans-Pritchard, *Witchcraft, Oracles and Magic among the Azande*, Oxford, 1937.
8. Yves Castan, *Magie et Sorcellerie a l'époque moderne*, Paris, Albin Michel, 1979.
9. Jeanne Favret-Saada, *Les Mots, la Mort, les Sorts*, Paris, Gallimard, 1977; (English translation, *Deadly Words*, Cambridge, 1980), and *Corps pour Corps*, Paris, Gallimard, 1981.
10. Alan Macfarlane, *Witchcraft in Tudor and Stuart England*, London, 1970; R. Muchembled, works already cited, and see also his *Prophètes et Sorciers dans les Pays-Bas, XVe–XVIIIe siècles*, Paris, Hachette, Collection

'Temps et Hommes', 1978, and, especially, *Les Derniers Bûchers*, Paris, Ramsay, 1981. I have benefited (the responsibility for the ultimate result being mine alone) from the invaluable advice of Robert Muchembled and Alfred Soman, who kindly gave me their comments on the text of *Françouneto*, which I sent them.

11. Castan, *op. cit.*, p. 239.

12. R. Mandrou, *Magistrats et Sorciers en France au XVIIe siècle*, Paris, Plon, 1968.

13. Castan, *op. cit.*, pp. 184–5.

14. *Les Dernier Bûchers* . . ., pp. 42–3 and *passim*.

15. *Las Papillotos de Jasmin coiffur, tomo segoun*, in French and Gascon, Agen, 1842. The poem *Françouneto*, in a bilingual version, French and Occitan, with facing texts, both being written by Jasmin and dated 1840, begins on p. 163 of this second volume of his works.

16. Note that, according to *Françouneto*, section four, the soldier Marcel unscrupulously *paid* the sorcerer from the Black Wood to accuse Françouneto of devilish doings and at the same time, by means of his curse, to deprive her of her vital energy. On the payment given to counter-sorcerers, soothsayers and healers, see the documents of 1598 and 1600 quoted by A. Soman, 'La sorcellerie vue du Parlement de Paris au début du XVIIe siècle' (Ministry of Universities, Commission on Historical and Scientific work, transactions of the 104th Congress of Learned Societies (*Sociétés savantes*), Bordeaux, 1979, Vol. 2, p. 403, Paris, Imprimerie Nationale, 1981). See also the analogous case of Jean Bedu (Berry, 1815) in Marc Baroli, *La Vie quotidienne en Berry*, Paris, Hachette, 1982, p. 227.

17. See my two studies on the *aiguillette*, in *The Peasants of Languedoc*, Urbana, Illinois, 1974, pp. 204–5 and *The Mind and Method of the Historian*, Hassocks and Chicago, 1981, pp. 84–96: also Le Nail, *art. cit.*, p. 165.

18. Compare Muchembled, *Les Derniers Bûchers* . . ., p. 50.

19. George M. Foster, articles in *Journal of American Folklore*, LXXVII, 1964, pp. 39–44, and *American Anthropologist*, LXVII, no. 2, 1965, pp. 293–315.

20. Soman in *Sociétés savantes*, 1981 (see note 16), and Favret, *Deadly Words*, p. 66.

21. Muchembled, *Les Derniers Bûchers*, pp. 61–2: Favret, *Deadly Words*, p. 24: M. Augé, 'Sorciers . . .', *Annales*, January 1979, p. 79; and, especially, Soman, *Sociétés savantes*, 1981 (see note 16), p. 396.

22. Muchembled, *Les Derniers Bûchers*, and Augé, *op. cit.*

23. This point was strongly made by the participants in the colloquium held at Cornell University, in April 1982, on popular culture, especially by scholars working on witchcraft in Italy in the sixteenth century.

24. Philippe Joutard has pointed out, in his thesis on the Camisards, similar chronological 'telescopings' in oral traditions, handed down

through the centuries, which show a greater or lesser degree of fidelity to their specific origins.

25. The Mimalé file was discovered by Yves Castan when he was preparing his doctoral thesis, published in Paris in 1974 as *Honnêteté et Relations sociales en Languedoc*, and he gives on pp. 584–6 an extract from it. The reference to the Archives Départementales, Haute-Garonne, *fonds* of the *Parlement*, is: 'Liasse du sénéchal d'Auch: Montesquiou, juge de la baronnie, plainte du 10 mai 1786: *in depositum* Parlement de Toulouse, 15.1.1787: sentence du 23.7.1789(?).' Unfortunately, this file is unavailable, owing to the upheaval suffered by the records of the *Parlement* through the cataloguing process still under way. I had to be content with the notes (fortunately, very detailed) taken by Yves Castan when he had access to the file, and which this remarkable historian passed on to me. In addition, the records of the commune of Montesquiou (Gers), kept in the town-hall, provided me with numerous facts about Mimalé, from the parish registers and registers of civil status from 1600 to 1840 and from the land-survey (plan and original) carried out under the Restoration.

26. I obtained the references to these two writers from Littré's dictionary.

27. See Eugène Le Roy, *Le Moulin du Frau*, Paris, Fasquelle, 1905.

28. *Revue de Gascogne*, 1903, p. 453 *et seq.*

29. F. Mistral, *Trésor du félibrige* . . ., under the word 'mandragore'.

30. All these data come from the parish registers and the land-survey of the 1820s, kept in the present *mairie* of Montesquiou.

31. The Castan file: see also Castan, *Honnêteté* . . . p. 584.

32. Memorandum by an advocate (Castan file). The expression *mau dat*, or 'given evil', is classical, in Gascon, for defining harm due to spells (see the thesis by M. Bordes).

33. Le Nail, *art. cit.*, pp. 174, 219, 220. The case of the witch Arnaude de Barrau, in 1562, for action against Jehanne Barbes: 'On the day that the said deponent Jehanne Barbes met the said de Barrau on the road and right of way through the field of the said Cap de Loys, as she passed, the said de Barrau touched the said deponent with one of her arms on the muscle of the left arm, and straightway the said deponent felt a great coldness in the said arm, which remained greatly troubled, and she could do nothing about it. And when the Thursday after Easter came, when it was midnight, the deponent felt a sudden blow which greatly troubled the said arm, and she could not do anything to put it right. So it remained for a long time, and she could not use the said arm for any purpose.'

See also the corroborative testimony of Guillalme, sister of Jehanne Barbes: 'On Good Friday last, the deponent left the house of Jehan Bernard Barbes, her father, together with Jehanne Barbes, her sister, to go to the town of Saint-Girons, to hear the sermon in the church of Saint-Valhé. As she was walking along the road and right of way through a field belonging to Cap de Loys, of Saint-Girons, the deponent, together with her sister Jehanne Barbes, encountered Arnaulde de Barrau, who is reputed to be a poisoner. The latter greeted the deponent and her sister with these or similar words: "God be with you, lovely girls!" and said that she was going to the farm and house of their said father. To which the deponent and her sister replied that she might well go there, and would find their mother there. Upon which the said de Barrau told the deponent and her sister that, if anyone should ask about her, they should say that they had not seen her. She turned back three times as she walked away, to threaten the deponent and her sister that, if they said otherwise, they would pay for it with their bodies. And as she passed the sister, the said de Barrau touched the muscle of her left arm, and soon the sister felt this muscle greatly troubled. And on Thursday after Easter, about midnight, as she lay in bed, she became very sick in this arm, and for a long time could do nothing about this. If she could not find any remedy, she was in danger of death and of never using that arm again. And she could not dress herself unaided. And this she knows because she was present and saw it all.'

34. We shall find in a case in Béarn, connected with Marie de Sansarric (end of this chapter), the idea that witchcraft attacks the shoulders, arms and hands of the victim, sometimes passing through his head. See exactly the same belief on the part of a Gascon of Condom in the 1750s; in his case, however, the hands went black, not yellow as in that of Joseph Bénac (*supra*). See the excellent *Journal de ma vie* by J. L. Ménétra, edited by D. Roche, Paris, Montalba, 1982, p. 47.

35. See on this subject the communication on witchcraft in sixteenth-century Italy presented in April 1982 to the colloquium on popular culture organised by Cornell University (text by M. O'Neil).

36. Littré, *Dictionnaire*, article 'train', in Vol. 4, p. 2298, column 2: also Mistral, *Trésor* . . ., article 'trin'.

37. Le Nail, *art. cit.*, *passim*, especially p. 204 (murder of husband) and p. 179 (hail). On hail-making sorcerers still active in 1783, in the Landes, see the case of Jean Vignau of Poyartin, healer and (as an act of retaliation) hail-maker, who was condemned for his hail-making to the galleys (V. Foix, in *Revue de Gascogne*, Vol. 4, 1904, pp. 127–8).

38. See note 17, *supra*.

39. Le Nail, *art. cit.*, pp. 170–1, 184 and 201–4, and B. Amilha, *Tableu . . . del parfet crestia*, Toulouse, 1673, p. 234 (reprinted, Foix, 1899, pp. 238 and 248).

40. *Françouneto*, third section.

41. Communication on witchcraft in sixteenth-century Italy, Cornell colloquium, *art. cit.* In Gascony and the Landes the Gospel, in 1671, also protects small children against witchcraft (V. Foix in *Revue de Gascogne*, 1904, p. 65).

42. The Castan file and Castan, *Honnêteté . . .*, p. 585.
43. To be mentioned also is the role in combating witchcraft more or less effectively played by *relics* placed on the body of the possible victim (*Françouneto*, second section, the intervention by Pascal's mother).
44. *Françouneto*, second section: see, too, the ruining of the flowers – roses and daffodils – in the young witch's garden when she is 'unmasked' (*Françouneto*, section three).
45. *Françouneto, ibid.*
46. *History of Agen in the sixteenth and seventeenth centuries*: the chronicle of Brother Hélie, text edited and introduced by André Mateu, Librairie Quesseveur, 1977.
47. See, in this connexion, the remarkable work by Michel de Certeau, *La Possession de Loudun*, Paris, Gallimard, Collection 'Archives', 1970, pp. 28 and 49–53. In the sixteenth century notable doctors like Paul Zacchias emphasised the importance of the sense of smell as the way of entry for sorcerers' poisons (*ibid.*).
48. See above, p. 8. It is interesting that fennel, used against witches in Friuli, according to Ginzburg's *Benandanti*, serves the same purpose, under the name of *herbe de St Jean*, in south-western France (V. Foix, in *Revue de Gascogne*, 1903, p. 379).
49. G. Henningsen, *The Witches' Advocate*, University of Nevada, 1980, p. 390 and *passim*.
50. This victory of theirs is a boon to the historian, for, thanks to it, we are again spared the prefabricated charges regarding the *sabbat*, dictated to the pseudo-guilty by witch-burning magistrates. With the help of the Mimalés, we are plunged straight into rustic veracity.
51. This etymology has been challenged. For François Bordes, in his thesis, the Occitan word *fatchilhès* comes from a Latin word which is also the origin of the French word *facture*.
52. On the local traditions of the Condomois and Gers regarding the inauspiciousness of the twelve-day cycle, see the old but still valid work by Bladé, in *Littératures populaires de toutes les nations*, Vol. 20, Paris, 1886, p. 237 *et seq.*
53. A. Van Gennep, *Manuel de folklore français contemporain: Tome Premier, VII, première partie: Cycle des Douze Journ*, Paris, Picard, 1958.
54. F. Mistral, *Trésor du félibrige*, Aix, reprinted 1979, article 'fado'.
55. Van Gennep, *Manuel . . ., op. cit.*, pp. 3029–30: see also *Revue de Gascogne*, 1892, p. 116, and 1903, pp. 261 and 363.
56. On the witch as cause of destruction of crops by hail or in other ways, see a fine passage on hail induced by witchcraft, in 1568 at Neuchâtel, in Muchembled, *La Sorcière au village . . .*, p. 133 and also his *Les Derniers Bûchers*, p. 50. The *curé* (regarded as a magician) can also divert hail on to another district so as to preserve his own village (Montaillou tradition,

collected in 1975 by the author from Mme Durand, a farmer in her seventies).

In the Pyrenees, a witch who caused hail to fall in 1562, in Le Nail, *art. cit.*, quoted by Y. Castan in *Magie et Sorcellerie* . . ., p. 67: also, in the canton of Lucerne about 1600, *ibid.* p. 88. We have here, as in Françouneto's case, a charge of hail-making witchcraft, without learned intrusions – no sign of the *sabbat* or other inventions (?) by inquisitors or magistrates. See also the example of the hail-making sorcerers of Berry in Marc Baroli, *Vie quotidienne en Berry au temps de George Sand*, Paris, Hachette, 1982, p. 227. There is a very good discussion of the problems of hail-making witchcraft in Switzerland and the Franco-Provençal or Jurassian part of France in E. William Monter, *Witchcraft in France and Switzerland: The Borderlands during the Reformation*, Cornell University Press, 1976, Chapter 6, pp. 151–9. It appears that, in the sixteenth century, the Catholic courts punished hail-makers, whereas the Protestant magistrates, who believed that bad weather was the work of Providence, declined to engage in this type of repression. Our hail-makers in south-western France, Françouneto included, came under the authority of magistracies and municipalities that were Catholic.

57. The best work on the werewolf which has appeared recently is that of Monter, *op. cit.*, p. 144 *et seq.* (an extensive review of the subject) and Ginzburg's *Night Battles*, pp. 28–32 and *passim* – a penetrating analysis which brings out the positive functions of the werewolves, their power to promote fecundity, which has too often been overlooked, leaving only a mere harsh negativity, as result of the belated persecution of these creatures by the Church.

58. According to Castan (photocopy of the advocate's memorandum) and also, for a few lines only of the documents, extensively quoted in this paragraph, Castan, *Honnêteté* . . ., p. 585.

59. The seventeenth-century Livonian werewolf seeks to preserve or increase the wealth and well-being of his village community. The Gascon werewolf – who, never having disappeared, enjoyed a full revival in the eighteenth century: see F. Bordes's thesis – seeks to increase his own wealth or power, or that of his farm (*à la* Mimalé), and does this sometimes at the expense of others. He may be a healer (of the ills he has himself induced) – see the case in Béarn mentioned at the end of this chapter. As between the two the difference is therefore not total, and the beneficial effects have not vanished. There is merely a movement from concern for the community to concern for the individual or family holdings, or, if you like, a movement (in terms, however, of historical facts, not of polemic) from Ginzburg's thinking in terms of communities to the individualist thinking of Macfarlane, Muchembled and Favret. It is here, no doubt, that Muchembled's analyses, which I have to some extent argued against *supra* (p. 21), may be found pertinent.

60. V. Foix, 'Glossaire de la sorcellerie landaise', *Revue de Gascogne*, 1903, p. 368 and, especially, p. 450 *et seq.*; F. Bordes, *La Sorcellerie en Béarn, Landes et Labourd sous l'Ancien Régime*, Ecole des Chartes thesis, 1977 (on the revival of the werewolf in south-western France in the eighteenth century).
61. R. Mandrou, *Magistrats et sorciers en France au XVIIe siècle . . .*, p. 186 *et seq.*
62. Monter, *op. cit.*, p. 149 and *passim*.
63. Foix, *art. cit.*, p. 450.
64. J. Demers and L. Gauvin, 'Frontières du conte . . . quelques loups-garous québécois', *Littérature* (Larousse), February 1982, p. 14.
65. Ginzburg, *Night-Battles*: see also his remarkable communication to the Cornell colloquium of April 1982, on popular culture, entitled: 'The witches' sabbat: popular cult or inquisitorial stereotype?'
66. From this standpoint the woman Mimalé and Marie de Sansarric, both being werewolves, root Gascon witchcraft in those journeys to the country of the dead with which Françouneto is already less closely connected. On this link between the werewolf and death, see the peasant traditions collected by N. Rétif de la Bretonne, in *La Vie de mon père*, Paris, Garnier, 1970, pp. 231–41. The Sansarric case is taken from Gassion (1630).
67. *Monumenta Germaniae Historica. Legum sectio II, capitularia regum francorum tomus II, additamenta Hdludovci Pii capitularia*, no. 196, August 829, p. 45.
68. Text in Mgr J.-M. Vidal, *Bullaire de l'inquisition française au XIVe siècle et jusqu'à la fin du grand schisme*, Paris, Letouzey, 1913, pp. 113–15.
69. Vidal, *op. cit.*, p. 115.
70. *Ibid*, p. 115; Vidal quotes, in this connexion, Lagrèze-Fossat, *Etudes historiques sur Moissac*, Vol. II, pp. 297 and 462, Paris, 1872 – straining somewhat the meaning of the document.
71. Cohn, *op. cit.*, p. 204.
72. What follows is all taken from Joseph Hansen, *Quellen . . . sur Geschichte des Hexenwahns . . .*, Bonn, 1901, pp. 92–4.
73. In his recent lectures at the Collège de France (October 1982), Carlo Ginzburg suggested, basing himself on documents, the following chronology. In 1321 the King of France and the Bishop of Pamiers made a slanderous attack on the lepers, the Jews and some mythical Arab kings, accusing them of Devil-worshipping activity with a resemblance to the *sabbat*. After 1348, in the Alpine region (matric in this respect), these charges were directed against the Jews alone, with the accusation that they spread the plague: then, after 1360, against the Jews and the rural sorcerers, and soon after, mainly against the latter, who were alleged to have engaged in sectarian conspiracies in the form of Satanical *sabbats*. These charges, which were at first (in 1321) pure inventions, ended, after the terrible experiences (plague, etc.) of 1348–1450, by merging with the very old popular culture

of the sorcerer who does both bad and good, and formed the cultural complex of the *sabbat*, thereafter not breakable into its different constituents, from the fifteenth to the early eighteenth century.

Part Three

1. Blaise de Monluc, *Mémoires*, Pléiade edition, Paris, 1964, pp. 487–8 and 537–8.
2. I obtain this date, Friday, from various datings indicated in Monluc, *op. cit.*, pp. 554 and 1236.
3. *Françouneto*, second section: Pascal's mother and the town-crier of Roquefort both, independently, say that the New Year's Eve party was held on a Friday.
4. AC Agen, BB 30.
5. See also the Labrunie-Argenton MSS in ADLG, 2 J 67 (for the years 1560–67), and Jules Andrieu, *Histoire de l'Agenais*, Paris–Agen, 1893, Vol. I, Chapter 9. I think it is pointless, in any case, to dwell upon the 1560s, since the Monluc chronology is irrelevant to the story of Françouneto (see *infra*).
6. Jasmin writes (*Françouneto*, in *Papillotos*, 1882 edition, p. 54, n. 1): 'The cruelties inflicted by Monluc upon the Protestants at Penne, the details of which he himself gives in his curious commentaries . . .'.
7. The confusion with Monluc's time may have been made, before Jasmin, in the oral tradition which passed the story of Françouneto down through the eighteenth century. However, M. Sournia has shown that the black legend of Monluc appeared, even amongst scholars, only in the eighteenth century. It is therefore not certain that it contaminated the oral tradition so early as that. The dark aspects of Monluc seem to have entered Jasmin's thinking from his own reading rather than from what he was told by the villagers.
8. Printed works and records mention, for the seventeenth century, dozens of cases of paralysis and blindness cured at Bon-Encontre. These two afflictions are often – though not, of course, always – hysterical in origin. See Sources and Bibliography.
9. See *Histoire de Notre-Dame-de-Bon-Encontre d'après les documents authentiques* . . . by a Marist priest, Avignon, 1883, p. 96 *et seq.*
10. The case that follows is taken from ADLG, 12 J 14, *fonds* Marboutin (register of miracles accomplished at Bon-Encontre).
11. *Ibid.*
12. *Ibid.*
13. This young lady was the daughter of Hector Renaud de Durfort, *seigneur* of Bajamont, and Anne de Gontaut-Biron, his second wife (G. Tholin, *Histoire de Montpezat*, Auch, 1898, pp. 262, 263, 265). See also

G. Tholin, *Abrégé de l'histoire des communes du Lot-et-Garonne*, Auch, 1900, art. 'Bon-Encontre', p. 12.
14. See the *Histoire d'Agen aux XVIe et XVIIe siècles*, the chronicle attributed to Brother Hélie, edited and introduced by André Mateu, Agen, Librairie Quesseveur, 1977.
15. Isaac Sylvius, *Miracles des diables chassés à Bon-Encontre et Garreson, là où est traitée de la vertu des exorcismes et de la vérité des miracles de l'église romaine*, Montauban, 1620. This work, now extremely rare (there is a copy in the municipal library of Bordeaux, shelf-mark T 8684/1–3), was written by a Protestant polemicist. I thank once again M. Hanlon, the young Canadian scholar who greatly helped me on this point and many others, especially in my researches in the Archives Départementales, Lot-et-Garonne.
16. Hélie, in Mateu, *op. cit.*
17. In 1618 the Archbishop of Bordeaux, who died in 1627 and showed moderation in the Laugnac case, was named François de Sourdis (see L. W. Ravenez, *Histoire du Cardinal François de Sourdis*, Bordeaux–Paris, 1867, p. 380 *et seq.* and *passim*). In 1632 the Archbishop of Bordeaux was Henri d'Escoubleau de Sourdis, undoubtedly a kinsman of the above. To his great credit, he also strove, although in vain, to calm public opinion at the beginning of the affair of the Ursulines (M. de Certeau, *La Possession de Loudun*, Paris, Gallimard, 1970, pp. 58–9).
18. ADLG, 12 J 14, *fond* Marboutin.
19. G. Tholin, *Histoire de Montpezat*, 1898, p. 267.
20. It is certain that the Comtesse de Laugnac always retained something from her diabolical troubles of 1618. 'In the 1650s, this countess, who, though, perhaps, no longer possessed, was still given to folly, was the cause of a new lawsuit in connexion with some diamonds she had deposited as security for a sum of 1,600 *livres* she borrowed from Pierre Constans, merchant, and Raymond Fénelon. She died in 1652, after paying 1,554 *livres* of the amount due. Charles de Montpezat, her husband, paid off the outstanding debt, but Angélique de Xaintrailles, his daughter, claimed recovery, through the courts, of the gold crosses and 64 small diamonds which constituted the amount handed over to Constants, as being a gift from her mother. We do not know what the result was. What is certain is that Charles de Montpezat II, Comte de Lauganc, and his successors, made large gifts to the chapter of Agen, as we learn from the Abbé Barrère in his *Histoire religieuse et monumentale du diocèse d'Agen*' (G. Tholin, *Histoire de Montpezat*, *op. cit.* p. 166).
21. There are two copies of this plan, one in the land-survey of Agen, the other in the ADLG, in the cadastral documents of the nineteenth century.
22. See also this 'hamlet of Magen' on the excellent map of the canton of Laplume, in the *arrondissement* of Agen, drawn from the combination-plan

of the land-survey by L. de Sevin-Talive, chief road-surveyor, and kept at the ADLG, which was used in making the map included in this book.
23. ADLG, originals and microfilms of the parish registers of these two villages for the years 1669–1789. The Roquefort register is complete for all the 120 years, but the Brax register has a few gaps between 1669 and 1700.
24. Godfather Antoine Dessalles, student; godmother Catherine Daurio; witnesses Jean Daurio, born 7 January 1669, and Hugues Carnicas (?) who 'were unable to sign their names'. The Daurios were an old Roquefort family, as can be seen from the earliest of the registers (1669).
25. See, e.g., AC Nérac, GG, 11 October 1693 and 27 September 1694.
26. On the relation between Protestantism in southern France and urban craftsmen, from the sixteenth century onward, see my *Peasants of Languedoc*, Eng. trans., Urbana, 1974, p. 158 *et seq.*, and also the theses of Mme Estève and M. Sauzet.
27. AC Nérac, GG, 7 July 1787 and 13 August 1693.
28. Other instances of chronological telescoping of this sort (confusion in the memory of the people of the Agenais between the wars of 1621 and 1562, owing to the simplifications effected, one after another, by the persons who passed on the folklore) are to be found in respect of other regions and centuries, in the Cévennes and in Auvergne, which also enter into the oral culture of Occitania (see Philippe Joutard, *La Légende des Camisards: une sensibilité au passé*, Paris, Gallimard, 1977, and Pierre Charbonnier, *Une autre France. La seigneurie rurale en Basse-Auvergne du XIVe au XVIe siècle*, Clermont-Ferrand, Institut d'Etudes du Massif Central, 1980, I, pp. 463–5.
29. See, for example, AC Brax, GG, 20 February 1674.
30. This name is spelt in different ways, as Agès or Ayché (c.f. AC Brax, GG, 17 April 1702). This is the *only* marriage of a Pascal (the bride being, in this case, a Sordes) that is registered at Roquefort between the first appearance of the family in the parish register, in 1697, and their disappearance as male bearers and transmitters of the name (after 1708, which saw the last appearance of a male Pascal, 60 years old, who died in that year). We cannot therefore entirely rule out the possibility that Marie Sordes may be Françouneto. However, Jean Pascal was a butcher (see *infra*), not a blacksmith, and the bride seems not to have been from Roquefort, and therefore not from Estanquet. She was not named Françoise, and so we should have to suppose that her forename (Marie) was different from her nickname (Françouneto). This is not out of the question, but it gives rise to many difficulties and requires many suppositions. Which is why we are going to explore the possibilities that exist in earlier years, and in particular in the 1660s, in the time of the previous generation of the

Pascals, or, what comes to the same thing, during the youth of Pierre Pascal, who was in his sixties during the 1700s and could be, in the age of Colbert, a possible candidate for the role of Françouneto's husband. (That would have been his first marriage). Generally speaking, these Pascals, through the choice they made of their spouses (all from outside) and through their late appearance in the parish register, seem to have been outsiders whose installation in the village went back only a few decades, at most, and certainly not to the age of Monluc.

31. At this baptism (27 April 1784) Jean Lacoste, father of baby Pierre, was literally surrounded by Coveques, bearers of the Françouneto tradition. Besides Anne Coveque, his wife (who was doubtless still confined to bed as a result of the birth), we see listed Catherine Coveque, illiterate, godmother to the baby, along with Bernard Coveque and Pierre Coveque, also present at the ceremony. Only Pierre Lacoste, illiterate, godfather to the baby, represented the father's family, in face of these four Coveques. And at the baptism of a Coveque baby, on 20 July 1767, godfather and godmother were both Coveques.

32. Three copies exist of this land-survey and plan of 1821: one in the *mairie* of Roquefort, one in the Archives Départementales, Lot-et-Garonne, and one in the land-survey office in Agen. The last-mentioned copy will shortly also be deposited in the Archives Départementales.

33. AC Roquefort, a recent deposit in the ADLG. It is the file marked 'property of the commune, various deeds', which contains this deed, as a loose sheet.

34. Archive reference: see note 32.

35. This list of the 'hearths' of the hamlet we are particularly interested in is among the fiscal and electoral lists for Roquefort, preserved in the part of the AC of this village that was recently deposited in the ADLG (but has not yet been catalogued).

36. In the list of electors in Roquefort in 1843 (AC Roquefort, recently deposited in the ADLG, but not yet catalogued) we find in that year, in the hamlet of Estanquet, a Bernard Coveque, or Covecque, a well-to-do farmer at Estanquet who was certainly a descendant of the Coveques who lived in the hamlet for over a century and contributed to the transmission of the Françouneto tradition. His tax-assessment was for 32 francs, so that, under the property-qualification franchise of the July Monarchy, he had a vote.

37. Where she lived, or where her descendants or close kinsfolk lived not long after her: on this point I am more careful than Jasmin. The Pascals seem not to have established themselves at Estanquet, or, at least, in Roquefort, until ten or twenty years before 1697.

38. Jasmin's fame was originally (and still remains) local, in the Agenais. He did not invent Bernès, and it would have been hard for him to expose himself, in his own town, to a denial from this civil servant concerning the

oral account he had collected with the latter's help. This is a further guarantee of the reliability of Jasmin's material.

39. In the sectional inventory of Roquefort (ADLG, Roquefort land-survey, 1821, register no. 228) there is a person named Pierre Lacoste, the owner of 4.8 *arpents* (=2.4 hectares) and of house no. 88, which we find in the ADLG on the land-survey plan for the hamlet of Estanquet. This place, no. 88 on the plan, is a farm-yard and adjoins the house of M. Bernès, which is numbered 72, 82 and 81, all of these structures forming a single group of buildings.

40. This register is kept in the local *mairie*.

41. In this account I have emphasised the most important filiation, the one that runs, through the Coveque lineage, then eventually through the maternal line, through the Lacostes, directly and certainly from the tradition of Françouneto and Pascal in the seventeenth century to the house known as Françouneto's in 1840. But it was the whole Coveque lineage, with its paternal lines which are both ramified and turned back upon themselves, through intra-familial godparenthoods, that (together with the Coveques–Lacostes) could and must have propagated at Estanquet (where there were still Coveques in the middle of the nineteenth century) and in Roquefort generally, the Françouneto tradition.

42. See the deliberations of the municipality of Roquefort in the years 1822–26 (especially 22 September 1822, 27 March 1826, 30 April, 18 May and 2 November 1826). (AC Roquefort, recently deposited in ADLG). These passages mention the parish church of St Jacques 'at the top of the rock' (= on the castle-mound) and the new church to be built (completed in 1826) on the *place* or *placié*, in the plain.

43. On page 266 and in note 17, p. 401, of the 1842 edition of *Les Papillotos*, in the volume which contains *Françouneto*, Jasmin says: 'Saint Pierre, former parish church (of Roquefort). Nothing of it remains, not even ruins.' That was not true in the eighteenth century, or even at the beginning of the nineteenth, when the parish registers and municipal deliberations show the church (now no longer the parish church) or chapel of St Pierre as being in a bad state but still standing, and sometimes used for baptisms, weddings, funerals, festivals, etc. See also *infra*, note 57.

44. *Françouneto* was dated by Jasmin *1840*, even before it was published in 1842, so that it cannot have been collected on the spot before the end of the 1830s.

45. Bibliothèque Nationale, MSS, new French acquisitions, Ms 25025, p. 2685. In that year, 1516, the tax-farmer of the parish of 'St Pierre-de-Roquefort' paid three *livres*. I am grateful to M. Jean Burias, archivist of Lot-et-Garonne, who supplied me with valuable references on this point.

46. Document published by J. de Bourrousse de Lafore in *Recueil des travaux de la Société d'Agriculture, Sciences et Arts d'Agen*, Vol. VII, 1854–

1855, p. 11, right-hand column. See also H. Tholin, *Aide-mémoire pour servir à l'histoire de l'Agenais*, Auch, 1899, pp. 106 and 113.
47. AD Gers, register G59, p. 77 (terrier of the diocese of Condom).
48. *Inventaire des Archives communales du Lot-et-Garonne*, p. 114 (for Roquefort), analysis of register E.sup.614, GG1, 1669–99.
49. Manuscript dated 1930 in the ADLG: this reference is to Vol. 5.
50. G. Tholin, *Abrégé de l'histoire des communes du Lot-et-Garonne*; in the section devoted to the *arrondissement* of Agen.
51. Jules de Bourrousse de Lafore, 'Monographie de Roquefort', *Revue de l'Agenais*, Vol. 7, 1854–1855, p. 125 (copy in the library of the ADLG).
52. We must admit, however, that the matter is not entirely clear. A grant (by Jeanne d'Albret) of the estate of Montesquieu to Jean de Secondat II, in return for 10,000 *livres tournois*, and which may have included Roquefort, is dated 2 October 1561. (M. O'Gilvy, *Nobiliaire de Guyenne et de Gascogne*, Paris, 1858, p. 234). In any case, what counts, for our purpose, is that since 1560, 1561 or 1562 at the latest, the Secondats were, quite certainly, *seigneurs* of Roquefort.
53. All this is taken from Jean-Max Eylaud, *Les Secondat de Montesquieu*, Bordeaux, Féret et Fils, n.d. See also, fundamental for this matter, the 'Monographie de Roquefort' mentioned in note 49 (pp. 124–9).
54. M. O'Gilvy seems to have obtained these facts from the archives of the château of La Brède, whose present owner, a lady, apparently does not intend to make them available to researchers. According to another source, the Secondat-Montesquieu material at La Brède also includes part of the old records of Roquefort, which would have been very important for the present investigation. I have had no alternative but to bow to the refusal given me, in friendly and polite terms, by the lady who now possesses them.
55. O'Gilvy and the Abbé Dubois differ on this death-date.
56. Bourrousse de Lafore, *art. cit.*, p. 159.
57. Let me stress this. In the parish registers of Roquefort and Brax the Pascals are well represented between 1697 and 1708, but totally absent, whether as babies, bridegrooms, brides, witnesses, corpses, godfathers or godmothers, during the decades preceding 1697, that is, since 1669, when the series of registers begins. A Pascal, belonging to a poor, semi-marginal family (see *Françouneto*, section two) cannot have arrived at Roquefort, or Brax, more than a few decades, at most, before 1697. But it is unthinkable that this family could have formed an ancient lineage, rooted in one or other of these two parishes since the time of Monluc, 137 years before the official emergence of the Pascals in the local parish register.
58. Bordes, thesis, p. 129 *et seq.*
59. Françouneto (whose episode occurred some time between 1660 and 1700) was held responsible for the storm which destroyed, in that period,

the tower of St Pierre d'Aurignac at Roquefort, the former parish church which had become a mere local chapel. This damaged tower was furnished on 1 August 1702 with a new bell, christened, as was proper, 'St Pierre' (according to the parish register of Roquefort for that date, kept in the ADLG). This repairing of the old church does not in any way clash with the tradition reported by Jasmin, and in the chronology I suggest the christening of the bell constitutes a *terminus ad quem*.

60. I repeat, the years 1660–1700 lent themselves very well to the actual occurrence of an episode such as this, and to the made-up stories which accompanied it. These years saw, in the Condomois, two great waves of witch-hunting, which were followed by the definitive ending of that activity. Waves of witch-hunting were often due, in those days, to 'visitors' who took a special interest in the matter, together with children and youths in the parishes, who appointed themselves persecutors. Here, there and everywhere they detected low-level magicians, male and female, with the active complicity of the rural population. Gers, the Condomois, Chalosse, Béarn, Labourd, and Gascony in general, were the scene of these incursions or eruptions in the middle of the century, followed by a return of calm after 1670. (On all this, see Bordes, p. 121 *et seq.*). Given these conditions, it is understandable that, under Louis XIV (whether in his youth or in his majority), the Françouneto affair could have ripened without difficulty in this climate of concern with witchcraft and un-bewitching in its final phase. Our heroine herself bears witness to this calendar, since the sources present her, explicitly or symbolically, as the last of her kind in her village.

Postscript

1. See the other texts in Jasmin's *Papillotes*, editions of 1842, 1882, etc.
2. *Françouneto*, in *Papillotes*, 1842 edition, notes at the end of the poem.
3. Roquefort parish register for that day.
4. *Ibid.*
5. ADLG, IV E 40–1.

Sources and Bibliography

1. J. Duvernoy, III, 152 (see my *Montaillou*, Eng. trans., London, Scolar Press, 1978, pp. 351–2).

2. Félix Arnaudin, *Contes populaires de la Grande-Lande*, 1st series, new edition, revised and expanded (the book was first published in 1887), Groupement des Amis de Félix Arnaudin, Sabres, 1977, p. 254.

Index

172896
84 J311 CL562
Le Roy Ladurie, Emmanuel.
Jasmin's witch
ISSUED TO
172896
84 J311 CL562
Le Roy Ladurie, Emmanuel.
Jasmin's witch
DEMCO

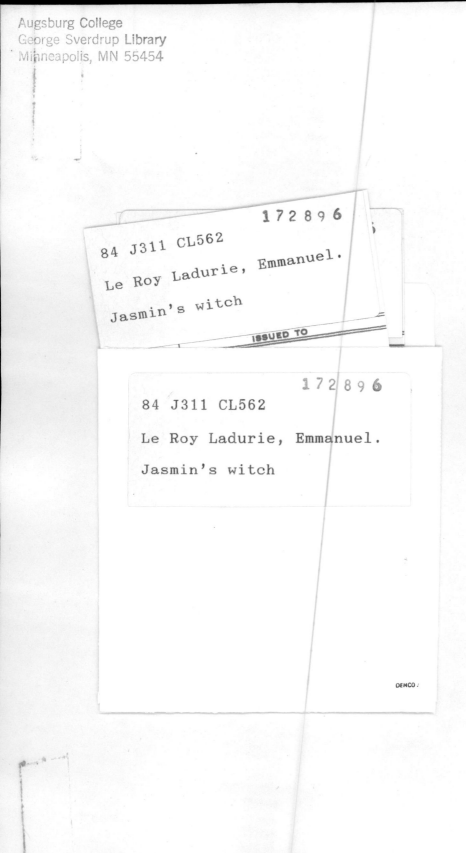